PRINCIPLES AND PRACTICE OF INFORMATION SECURITY

Protecting Computers from Hackers and Lawyers

Linda Volonino, Ph.D.

Canisius College

Stephen R. Robinson

Verity Partners, LLC

with contributions by Charles P. Volonino

PEARSON

Prentice Hall

Upper Saddle River, New Jersey 07458

Library of Congress Cataloging-in-Publication Data is available.

Executive Editor: David Alexander
Publisher: Natalie E. Anderson
Project Manager: Lori Cerreto
Editorial Assistant: Robyn Goldenberg
Media Project Manager: Joan Waxman
Senior Marketing Manager: Sharon M. Koch
Marketing Assistant: Danielle Torio
Managing Editor (Production): John Roberts
Production Editor: Maureen Wilson
Permissions Supervisor: Suzanne Grappi
Manufacturing Buyer: Michelle Klein
Cover Design: Kiwi Design
Cover Illustration/Photo: GettyImages
Composition/Full-Service Project Management: Progressive Publishing Alternatives
Printer/Binder: Phoenix

Credits and acknowledgments borrowed from other sources and reproduced, with permission, in this textbook appear on appropriate page within text.

Pearson Education LTD.
Pearson Education Singapore, Pte. Ltd
Pearson Education, Canada, Ltd
Pearson Education–Japan
Pearson Education Australia PTY, Limited
Pearson Education North Asia Ltd
Pearson Educación de Mexico, S.A. de C.V.
Pearson Education Malaysia, Pte. Ltd

10 9 8 7 6 5 4 3 2 1
ISBN 0-13-184027-4

Dedicated to all those who are learning how to make the cyber world safer and more secure. And to Charles and Rick for their support.

L.V.

To Louisa, who makes so many things possible.

S.R.R.

BRIEF CONTENTS

CONTENTS

PREFACE

PROTECTING COMPUTERS FROM HACKERS AND LAWYERS

WHY THIS EXTENDED PERSPECTIVE ON INFORMATION SECURITY?

This book helps you understand the fundamental principles and practice of information security. It introduces you to the technology and legal perspectives of cyber security that have become a part of our lives. You will learn about software and hardware technologies needed to defend against intrusions by hackers, viruses, and worms that probe the Internet looking for vulnerable networks to victimize, disgruntled employees, and other adversaries. Effective defenses require understanding the reasons why intrusions occur and the motives of the intruder.

From the legal perspective, you will learn how to protect against liability risks, lawsuits, negligence claims, and "smoking email evidence." With the emergence of Homeland Security initiatives in 2002 and the *National Strategy to Secure Cyberspace* in 2003, the demand for trained information security professionals far exceeds the supply. Securing cyberspace is an extraordinarily difficult challenge that is leading to new courses of study in colleges and universities throughout the world.

THE NEW SECURITY FOCUS

Many books on data and network security have focused almost exclusively on technology issues and defenses. Certainly, there is no security without firewalls, antivirus (AV) software, access control, and encryption. But in order for companies to build effective information security programs, they need to ask what is at risk, what needs to be protected, and what are the consequences of failure? After these questions have been answered, then the policies and technologies that safeguard data and provide evidence of "reasonable standards of care" can be selected.

ESSENTIAL BUSINESS, TECHNOLOGY, AND LEGAL CONCEPTS

Principles and Practice of Information Security provides students and professionals with the necessary managerial, technical, and legal background to allocate resources most effectively. Networks can never be 100% secure, and organizations cannot afford investment mistakes.

This book is intended to be a well-rounded reference on hacker and virus exploits; attacks against e-commerce and online operations; and the vulnerabilities of wireless technology, social engineering, and electronic fraud. It also explains the risk from violations of ethics or privacy rules, exposure from electronic discovery in civil and criminal cases, and how to comply with recent legislation. Relevant recent legislation includes the Uniting and Strengthening America by Providing Appropriate Tools Required to Intercept and Obstruct Terrorism Act, which is better known as the USA PATRIOT Act (part of which has been included as an appendix in this text).

Most companies are impacted by the Health Insurance Portability and Accountability Act (HIPAA) and the Gramm–Leach–Bliley (GLB) Act. In the introduction to the HIPAA legislation (part of which has been included as an appendix in this text), Congress stated its intent to "combat waste, fraud, and abuse in health insurance and healthcare delivery" and protect patient privacy. Regulations passed by the Security & Exchange Commission (SEC) now demand that electronic communications by publicly traded companies be retained for a period of not less than three years to help combat corporate corruption.

BENEFITS OF A CROSS-DISCIPLINARY APPROACH

As you may know, information security issues extend far beyond defending computer systems, networks, and wireless devices from external attack. Basically, if security fails, then liability risks increase.

No longer can responsibility for managing information security be delegated to technical experts. Attackers and fraudsters will always have weapons that are one step ahead of the defenders. Strong commitment, informed people, organizational policies, secure practices, and the law drive effective security. Yet there has not been a cross-disciplinary book to help students and professionals quickly become current on what has become a fundamental business issue. This book is designed to be such a resource. The scope of the information security issues that are covered are shown in Figure P.1.

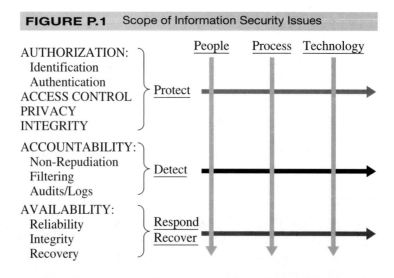

FIGURE P.1 Scope of Information Security Issues

WHO NEEDS TO READ THIS BOOK?

STUDENTS AND THOSE IN PROFESSIONAL CERTIFICATE PROGRAMS

This book is written for students and professionals in business and law schools. Computer security is important to students majoring in information systems (IS), computer science, telecommunications, human resource and industrial relations management, law, finance, and health care management. Those who are required by law to safeguard the confidentiality and privacy of information belonging to customers, clients, patients, business partners, or employees would benefit from reading this book. And it is for those who must safeguard a company's intellectual property and trade secrets and protect against financial fraud.

The roles of professionals that have a vested interest in reading this book include senior and line management, human resources, information systems, finance, accounting, compliance, house counsel, and entrepreneurs.

ATTORNEYS, LAW ENFORCEMENT PROFESSIONALS, AND CIVIL LITIGATORS

Others who need to know about security are those who must protect against unauthorized access to confidential or classified information or who need to learn about computer crimes, criminals, and methods. The topics on computer forensics and electronic discovery relate directly to the ability to carry out their responsibilities.

PRIVACY OFFICERS, HIPAA COMPLIANCE OFFICERS, AND HEALTH CARE PROVIDERS

A third audience is those who are facing federal mandates to implement information security and privacy protection procedures. HIPAA and GLB compliance regulations and implications are considered to be much broader than the security and legal issues surrounding Y2K or asbestos.

COMPUTER USERS

This book is for concerned users, including those who would be at significant professional or financial risk if someone gained control over their computers—or identities—and compromised their email, finances, or reputations. No one can afford to be ignorant of what is needed to ensure safe use of computers and networks.

COMPLETE PICTURE OF THE BUSINESS CASE

Security and digital liability protection programs must begin with a complete picture of the business case. Therefore, we provide everything that those who are responsible for information security need to know to make and justify tough security investment decisions. This is important for several simple reasons:

- Few people in positions of responsibility are fully aware of the nature and extent of cyber security risks. Nor do they know how to manage or contain them. The success of numerous hacker attacks, discovery of incriminating email evidence, and systemic underfunding of information security initiatives are proof that greater awareness is needed.

- Installation of defensive technology such as firewalls does not prevent lawsuits. Many times it does not even prevent intrusions.
- Human nature demands convenience over diligence. Employees are the front line of defense against digital calamity, yet "safe computing" is a discipline that few employees have mastered at home, on the road, or in the office. Worse, common online habits and practices that seem safe are often the most dangerous.
- The majority of successful cyber attacks are launched from *inside* the targeted organization or by former employees with insider knowledge.
- With mobile warriors and virtual offices, privileged information is frequently carried off the premises. It might be left unprotected on portable devices that might be lost or stolen.
- The paperless office has had inadvertent side effects. In the physical world, access to documents is restricted. If document destruction is necessary, it can be done if all copies can be found. But with digital documents, there are no physical limits.

NO TECHNOLOGY OR LEGAL EXPERTISE REQUIRED

Neither technical nor legal expertise is required to understand the concepts and issues. As such, this book can be required reading for everyone as part of an enterprise-wide computer security awareness program.

We deliberately introduce legal language and hacker vocabulary when needed. As a professional, familiarity with the terminology of information security and law is important and helpful to understand the material. Also, much of the terminology is becoming conventional. The media is now reporting such news as: "Spoofing and hijacking allowed an attacker to pose as a legitimate user without a third party being aware of this identity theft." Spoofing is a technique to conceal both the author's true identity and the email service provider that was used to send the message.

BASED ON FIELD EXPERIENCE

This book began as a series of cyber security and computer forensics seminars designed to teach executives and business owners about the risks of loss, liability, and litigation that they encounter when their employees or hackers misuse company computer resources—and how to implement effective defenses. Interest soon expanded to human resource managers, technology executives, compliance officers, attorneys, health care providers, and law enforcement and prosecutors. Cyber security awareness grew dramatically in 1999 with the epidemic of email-borne viruses, liability risks of the Y2K bug, and several high-profile hacker intrusions. Then in September 2001 came a heightened sense of the need to fortify critical information infrastructures against cyber terrorism. And as has been mentioned, the *National Strategy to Secure Cyberspace* and Department of Homeland Security have motivated individuals and businesses to take security more seriously. This book is intended to be such a resource.

ORGANIZATION OF THE TEXT

PART I: DIGITAL LIABILITIES AND RISK MANAGEMENT

Building an information security program starts with knowing what is at risk, what must be protected, and the consequences of security breaches. Part I begins by identifying cyber threats, first-party and third-party risks, and other compelling reasons for security concern. The first five chapters explain how the failure to protect digital assets exposes organizations to loss, liability, or lawsuits. This understanding is needed to justify expenditures for employee training, network monitoring, and many other cyber security defenses. The taxonomy of threats and vulnerabilities in Chapter 3 organizes them into categories to help readers understand the scope of cyber risks. Information security is not complete without examining the legal liabilities that companies are exposed to whenever employees or hackers misuse company networks, email, or the Internet. The importance of a four-tiered Digital Liability Management (DLM) defensive infrastructure is explained.

PART II: POLICIES, PRACTICES, AND DEFENSIVE TECHNOLOGY

Part II describes the policies, practices, and technologies that are needed to manage the business and security risks described in Part I. Acceptable-use policies (AUP) are discussed, and most importantly, a comprehensive sample AUP is provided. It also provides guidelines for deploying secure-use practices and policies. In Chapter 8, defensive and offensive hardware and software technologies are explained, such as firewalls, packet filters, routers, sniffers, port scanning, buffer overflows, biometrics, encryption, and intrusion detection systems.

PART III: COMPUTER FORENSICS, ELECTRONIC EVIDENCE, FRAUD, AND COMPUTER CRIME LAWS

In Part III, electronic documents and records, which can be used as evidence or e-evidence, are discussed. The importance of computer forensics became widely known by the Department of Justice when it prosecuted Microsoft, several Wall Street brokerage firms, Enron, Andersen, and many other companies. Broadly defined, e-evidence is any electronically stored information on any type of computer device that can be used as evidence in a legal action.

The specialty areas of computer forensics and ERM are covered because email and other electronic documents are considered official company records by the Supreme Court. They are, therefore, subject to search and discovery. Computer forensics investigations, and many high-profile cases involving e-evidence, consist of analyzing electronic devices (e.g., computers, PDAs, cell phones, iPAQs, voicemail, servers, disks, zip drives, or backup tapes) and communication media (e.g., instant messaging or chat rooms). Chapter 9 gives an overview of ERM, which becomes extremely important when e-records must be recalled as part of a legal action—either voluntarily in support of an investigation or involuntarily in the event of a subpoena.

PART IV: PRIVACY

Chapter 11 examines privacy challenges, the weakness of privacy defenses, and their controversies. The ease with which information can be collected directly from individuals or gathered in stealth mode by invasive technologies presents new challenges to protecting individual privacy.

The appendix outlines the Health Insurance Portability and Accountability Act of 1996 (HIPAA) that went into effect in April 2003. HIPAA sets medical security and privacy rules and procedures to prevent health care fraud and abuse. HIPAA compliance requirements and a glossary of key HIPAA terms are defined because managers must comply with health care privacy issues or potentially face federal felony charges.

FEATURES

- This book is written for students as well as for professionals in information systems, financial accounting, human resources, health care, legal policy, and law. It covers the entire range of best security practices—obtaining senior management commitment, defining information security goals and policies, transforming those goals into a strategy for monitoring intrusions and compliance, and understanding legal implications. Topics also include computer crime, electronic evidence, and cyber terrorism. Readers will learn about computer forensics and the 3 C's of evidence—care, control, and chain of custody. This book also covers the critical need for electronic records management to defend against "smoking email" messages that could damage an organization. Lastly, the fundamentals of civil rights, privacy protection, and identity theft are examined.
- The chapters address the three properties of information security—technical, managerial, and legal. They provide a thorough examination of the technologies, managerial issues, and legal risks associated with safeguarding information and privacy.
- Reference materials include an extensive glossary of technological and legal terms, an index of abbreviations and acronyms, online and traditional references, and the objectives of legal statutes such as the USA PATRIOT Act, Computer Fraud and Abuse Act, and HIPAA.
- *Cases on Point* at the beginning of each chapter provide real-world context for the chapter. They cover real-life cases involving information security theft, hacking, viruses, and more.
- *CyberBriefs and LegalBriefs* throughout the chapters highlight information security issues, happenings, and laws. These mini-updates help students focus on what is happening in information security today.
- *@lerts* scattered throughout the chapters provide brief tips, facts, and warnings in an easy-to-recall format.
- *Discussion Questions* at the end of each chapter provide content-specific review and reinforcement to help students test their knowledge of the chapter.

MYCOMPANION WEBSITE
www.prenhall.com/volonino

The secure MyCompanion Website includes password-protected resources for instructors: Instructor's Manual, Test Item File, and Image Library (text art). The student area features PowerPoint slides, Destinations Links (Online Resource list), Glossary of Terms, and Glossary of Acronyms.

ACKNOWLEDGMENTS

We gratefully recognize the expertise of the Prentice Hall team—our senior executive editor David Alexander, our project manager Lori Cerreto, our development editor Theresa O'Dell, and Beth Wood for encouraging our partnership with Prentice Hall. Thank you for making textbook authorship a rewarding experience. And special thanks to Charles Volonino for his research and organization of the end materials.

   The authors and Prentice Hall would like to thank the following people for their feedback and contribution to the text. Your efforts are appreciated, though, we know, never fully compensated.

J. Michael Cummins, Georgia Institute of Technology
Subhankar Dhar, San Jose State University
M. Barry Dumas, Baruch College CUNY
Joseph E. Dvorak, Community College of Allegheny County-Boyce Campus
Ming Fan, University of Washington
Virginia Franke Kleist, West Virginia University
Gerard Klonarides, Florida International University

We also want to recognize the support of Michael L. Battle, U.S. Attorney, and Martin L. Littlefield, Assistant U.S. Attorney, U.S. Department of Justice, Western District of New York; Paul McCarthy, New York Assistant Attorney General; and Richard P. Salgado, senior counsel with the Computer Crime Intellectual Property Section (CCIPS) of the Criminal Division of the U.S. Department of Justice. They provided invaluable information about white-collar crime, federal statutes, handling of electronic evidence, and civil and criminal investigations of computer crimes. And a special thank you to Howard L. Meyer, Esq., for his invaluable insights into the impacts of computers and email on the legal process and profession.

Linda Volonino
Stephen R. Robinson

CHAPTER 1
SECURITY IN A GLOBALLY CONNECTED ECONOMY

Learning Objectives

◆ The scope and principles of information security.

◆ Legislation and liability issues.

◆ Computer crimes.

◆ Hackers and exploits.

◆ New ethic of responsibility.

INTRODUCTION

Today there is no question that information security is a complex and critical issue affecting organizations and users throughout the world. This chapter outlines the principles of information security in a global economy that is dependent on network communications and electronic data. It explains why a defensive infrastructure requires senior management support, strict policies, secure practices, and updated technology. The chapter introduces legislative, legal, and ethical issues that have become inseparable from information security management.

WHAT IS INFORMATION SECURITY?

DEFINITION

Defining the scope of **security** in the context of information technology and electronic commerce is not a trivial task. Security is defined as the policies, practices, and technology that must be in place for an organization to transact business electronically via networks with a reasonable assurance of safety. This assurance applies to all online activities, transmissions, and storage. It also applies to business partners, customers, regulators, insurers, or others who might be at risk in the event of a breach of that company's security. Ultimately, it may be the court that is called on to decide whether reasonable security existed at the time of the breach.

SECURITY GOALS

In a world of unlimited resources and no concern for **privacy** or efficiency, nearly perfect security would be easy to achieve. Privacy, the state of being left alone and free

⟨ **CASE ON POINT** ⟩

COMPUTER "NERD" JAILED FOR GLOBAL VIRUS ATTACK

Simon Vallor, a 22-year-old Welsh Web designer and hacker, was tracked down by the FBI and Scotland Yard after creating one of the world's most widespread viruses. He pleaded guilty under the Computer Misuse Act and was sentenced in January 2003 to two years in jail, which is one of the heaviest sentences yet for spreading computer viruses. Vallor was caught because he boasted in an Internet chat room under the name "Gobo" that "at last there's a Welsh virus."[1] Vallor showed no reaction to the sentence, but comments on his Website, www.devilwithin.com, indicate that he had not expected a jail sentence.

Vallor admitted releasing three virus programs called Resedi B, Admirer, and Gokar. All were in the form of email attachments that, when opened, would send themselves to addresses in the user's email directory. In some cases, the viruses also deleted all the data on the hard drive on November 11. Gokar was the third most prevalent virus, at one point infecting hundreds of thousands of computers in at least 46 countries. It clogged up networks and caused computers to crash. Some estimates have put the cost of cleaning infected computers at millions of pounds.

The viruses included lines of Wiccan poetry, false terrorist warnings, messages of love, and in one case a picture of Winnie-the-Pooh. These techniques intrigued recipients into activating and spreading it further.

Graham Cluley, senior technical consultant at the antivirus company Sophos, said, "Unlike hacking, writing viruses is completely pointless. It seems that a lot of Simon Vallor's viruses just included text to show off to his mates. Maybe he was trying to increase his social standing."[2] Hacking is unauthorized access, or access in excess of authority, to a computer network or information system for profit, criminal activity, or other personal gain.

from surveillance, is a fundamental right protected by the U.S. Constitution. Since the mid-1960s, the federal government has passed several Constitutional amendments and privacy laws, including the Privacy Act of 1974 and Data Privacy Act of 1997. In the real world, however, security goals must be balanced against the investment they require and the economic drag they create.

This is a balance we are all familiar with in the world of conventional business and our daily lives. We invest in physical security for our businesses and homes, buy insurance to mitigate the risk of financial loss to ourselves and liability claims for losses to others, comply with applicable laws or regulations, and discipline ourselves to avoid behavior that we know to be unduly risky. We also adjust our methods and investments according to changes in the nature of threats, the availability of superior technology, and the value of the assets at risk.

@LERT
There are no small security or policy breaches—only large ones that are caught early.

APPLYING CONVENTIONAL PRINCIPLES TO THE CYBER WORLD

All of these principles apply directly to the cyber world. Putting *cyber* in front of a threat or breach does not make it something new. On the contrary, it often makes companies and individuals vulnerable to old crimes in a new medium.

Why then is it so difficult to apply those conventional principles to the cyber world? Mainly because we have had hundreds of years to refine our understanding of risk, as well as our laws as they relate to conventional business. The accelerated adoption of network computing and surrounding technologies, such as wireless and the World Wide Web (WWW), has far outpaced our ability to fully identify the threats, quantify the risks, understand the technology, and develop our defensive strategies. Globally, however, the ability to communicate and transact business electronically provides nearly limitless opportunities for economic development and prosperity.

Often we first connect our businesses to the Internet or supply-chain partners, and later worry about the consequences. Even those who choose to be proactive about security tend to overemphasize technological approaches to what they perceive to be a technological problem. Recent experience has shown that this can be a very expensive and potentially disastrous mistake.

THE DIGITAL LIABILITY MANAGEMENT (DLM) MODEL

There is, however, a rapidly evolving body of knowledge around the principles and practice of cyber security that gives proper weight to the organizational and process dimensions along with the appropriate technology. We use what we call the **Digital Liability Management (DLM)** model to explain how people, process, and technology all play a key role and must work in concert in order to implement an effective cyber security program. The four tiers of the DLM model are shown in Figure 1.1 and will be discussed in detail in Chapter 4.

Armed with this knowledge, one can construct and implement policy and technology plans to exploit the potential of the Internet while managing the security risks. In reality, a security budget that is not based on such plans is really just a slush fund, and most likely an inadequate one.

FIGURE 1.1   DLM Defense Infrastructure Model

Tier 1	Senior management commitment and support
Tier 2	Acceptable-use policies and other statements of practice
Tier 3	Secure-use procedures
Tier 4	Hardware, software, and network security tools

THE PRINCIPLES OF SECURITY

SECURITY IS COMPLEX

The issues surrounding information security and efficient risk management are neither clear nor easy to resolve. Nor is security convenient or cheap. There are numerous valuable corporate assets to protect: cash, intellectual property, customer data, reputation, etc. Their protection involves diligent policy enforcement and technological acumen. The three bases of security principles can be seen in Figure 1.2.

What's more, protecting assets includes guarding against both *hackers* and *lawyers*. We use this phrase to highlight that security entails protection against the risk of loss, liability, or litigation from two distinct sources.

Hackers

As stated earlier, hackers are those who engage in intrusive or malicious actions against a business by way of its computing infrastructure. The U.S. federal statute 18 USC § 1030(e) broadly defines a **hacker** as an "outsider" who breaks in and uses a computer for any purpose, or anyone who accesses a computer with authorization and uses such access to obtain or alter information in the computer that the *accesser is not entitled to obtain or alter.* This category includes expert hackers, who write **exploits,** and novice hackers, called **script kiddies.** An exploit is a tool or technique to take advantage of vulnerability in a computer system to exceed the users' authorized level of access. Script kiddies are those who use existing hacker tools and virus-building code that are widely available on the Internet. They may not know enough to develop new viruses, but they can be just as disruptive and destructive as expert hackers. In this hacker category are also identity thieves, those involved in espionage, vandals, employees who exceed authorized access, disgruntled employees, or social/political activists.

@LERT
PricewaterhouseCoopers reported that hacker (those who engage in intrusive or malicious actions against a business by way of its computing infrastructure) attacks alone had cost the world economy a staggering $1.6 trillion in 2001.

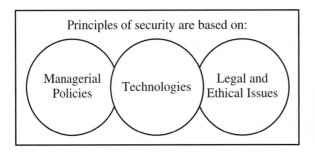

Principles of security are based on:

Managerial Policies

Technologies

Legal and Ethical Issues

FIGURE 1.2
The Three Bases of Security Principles

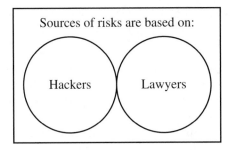

FIGURE 1.3
The Two Sources of Risk

Lawyers

Lawyers are those who take legal action against an individual or organization. That action may be on behalf of employees, customers, business partners, shareholders, the government, or others. These actions may be the result of a **tort,** which simply stated is "a wrong." Torts are civil (as opposed to criminal) wrongs resulting from a breach of a legal **right** or **duty.** A right is a legal claim that others not interfere with a protected interest, such as property (computers or proprietary data) or privacy. A duty is a legal obligation not to interfere with a protected interest. Negligence **(negligent torts)** involves conduct that creates, or fails to protect against, an *unreasonable risk* of harm. Figure 1.3 shows the two sources of risk. Negligence claims can stem from the failure to protect customer data or the illegal, irresponsible, ignorant, or unethical behavior of employees.

While the potential for damage from hackers is more evident, it is important to recognize that *hackers do not file lawsuits* for harassment, privacy invasion, disclosure of confidential information, copyright infringement, or investment fraud. Lawyers do that.

SECURITY IS DIFFICULT TO COST-JUSTIFY, BUT NOT IMPOSSIBLE

Repeatedly, references are made in the media that security investments cannot be cost-justified because they do not add to the bottom line. This is a fallacy on several levels.

First, security policies and technology can help avoid economic loss well in excess of the required investment. For example, the **Code Red** and **Nimda viruses** caused extensive damage to businesses worldwide. In 2001, Nimda and Code Red both attacked security vulnerabilities in Microsoft's IIS (Internet Information Services) Web server product.[3] According to the FBI, Code Red infected more than 250,000 U.S. computer systems in just nine hours in July 2001. The virus clogged the Internet to such an extent that it decreased traffic flow by 40%. The **denial of service (DOS)** attacks that they caused, lost productivity, and direct expenses to repair, clean, and restore stricken computer systems cost over $3 billion, according to research firm Computer Economics.[4] DOS refers to an attack on a network or server that is caused when it receives more **hits** (requests for service) than it can respond to—so the overwhelmed server "denies service." These infections were avoidable through the use of basic procedures to keep the installed software up-to-date. Additional investment in security was not required.

Second, while quantification of risk exposure and liability is challenging, several useful risk assessment metrics and projections do exist. These are discussed at length in Chapter 5.

Finally, in an interconnected economy, only those businesses perceived as "safe" will be allowed to connect or access business partners' networks. A reputation for inadequate security will severely limit the ability to conduct business or generate revenue.

@LERT
Typically, by the time an intrusion or infection is detected, the damage is already done.

SECURITY IN THE INFORMATION ECONOMY

GLOBAL ECONOMY IN TRANSITION

It is well documented and accepted that the global economy is in a period of transition from the industrial age to the information age. We are quick to embrace the technology and reap the economic benefits of enhanced productivity and global reach. We are reluctant, however, to acknowledge the dark side of this revolution; i.e., the potential for criminals and even terrorists to enhance their productivity and their reach using the same technology.

We are even slower to recognize that those who may attempt to do harm often come from *inside* the organization and work behind the front line of defensive technology. Little wonder, then, that the perception of security is driven by tangible threats that require intruders to physically enter a business to steal. What is needed are adjustments to our perceptions and priorities in recognition that key business assets are digital, portable, and vulnerable to anyone globally when businesses are connected to an external network.

LEGAL LIABILITY ISSUES

A similar revolution is occurring with regard to the legal liability that is generated in the course of doing business. Interconnected businesses must be stewards not only of their own information assets but those of their employees, partners, and customers as well. Failure to uphold that trust will result in expensive and embarrassing litigation. This dimension of risk assures that the viability of the entire enterprise rides on the ability to secure information. Yet managers tend to treat investments in information security as a discretionary technical exercise. Nothing could be further from the truth, and this book sets out to meet the challenge of getting that message out to those who most need to hear it.

GUIDE TO THE RISKS INHERENT TO CONDUCTING BUSINESS IN A NETWORKED ECONOMY

We undertook this challenge because there is no existing guide to the technical and legal aspects of digital liability that also offers an in-depth discussion of the *people* and *process* dimensions of an information security management program. The business and professional world is at a critical juncture—brought about by heightened fear and publicity about computer crime, efraud, privacy invasion, identity theft, and liability exposure.

This juncture has created the need for a guide to understanding *all* of the risks that are inherent to conducting business in a networked economy. We have quickly reached the point where even the smallest and most traditional of businesses engage in some form of ecommerce, and most have taken the plunge without understanding, or preparing for, the potential consequences.

MISTAKES, MALICE, AND MISCHIEF INCREASE LIABILITY—AND LEGISLATION

Although most investments in information security to date have been directed at thwarting potential cyber intruders bent on relatively simple acts of theft or vandalism, a less obvious threat has emerged with far more serious economic consequences.

ELECTRONIC EVIDENCE

The recent wave of corporate scandals has taught us that **electronic evidence** (e-evidence), in the form of archived emails and transaction histories, has become a primary point of attack for both prosecutors and civil litigators targeting a specific business. These attacks can extract a price far greater then any hacker. They threaten a company's very existence via civil and criminal penalties, regulatory action, or damage to a victim's reputation. Both hackers and lawyers have useful allies: Company insiders who will compromise any defensive strategy out of malice, ignorance, or sheer lack of discipline. Figure 1.4 shows the rise in cyber attacks in the late 1990s.

THREATS TO INFORMATION SECURITY

Employees
Across many job functions, employees routinely create, access, or distribute confidential or valuable information to customers, partners, and other employees. In doing so, they all pose a threat to information security. A lost laptop, a divulged password, or a bribed systems administrator can defeat some of the most sophisticated and expensive IT security and create a multi-million-dollar liability.

Lawsuits and Insurance Premiums
Victims of security breaches will seek reimbursement for losses due to data exposure or theft. Increasingly they will be filing lawsuits against other organizations whose systems had been compromised by digital attacks. Experts predict that this will open up litigation floodgates in a manner that will make the recent tobacco or asbestos litigations seem limited by comparison. Insurance companies will extract heavy premiums for assistance in managing the risk and hold their customers to a very high standard for preventive measures to be taken before policies can be written.

Regulators
Regulators will try to deal with the political mandate to assure a safe and reliable marketplace. They are hampered by jurisdictional ambiguity inherent in a globally interconnected economy where buyers in one country transact business with sellers in a second country via brokers and computers located on other continents. The result will be a steady stream of regulation that is consistent only in that it will be at least one step behind the current state of the technology.

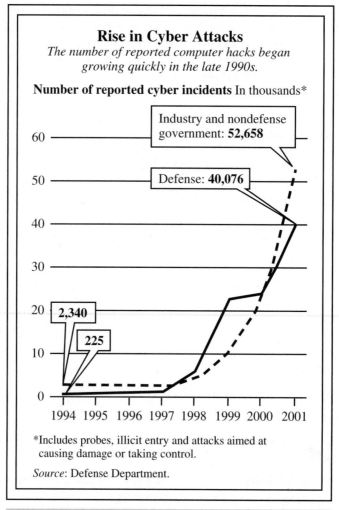

FIGURE 1.4 Rise in Cyber Attacks

@LERT
Those with network access must have responsibility and accountability for its use.

EXTENDED LEGISLATION AND RESPONSIBILITIES

LIABILITY ISSUES AND REGULATORY OBLIGATIONS

For any organization that maintains customer data, security breaches may result in liability for loss of confidential information, data corruption, or breach of privacy obligations. Liability of this sort may be imposed as a result of a contractual obligation to maintain data securely. In addition, there may be a regulatory obligation imposed by legislation. Examples include the **Health Insurance Portability and Accountability Act (HIPAA)** of 1996, the **Gramm–Leach–Bliley Act (GLB)** of 1999, or the **Children's Online Privacy Protection Act (COPPA),** which require the safeguarding of customer personal data.[5] The privacy and security provisions of the GLB Act and security provisions of HIPAA have extended the legal issues.

Gramm–Leach–Bliley Act

GLB regulations pertaining to the financial services industry require board and management involvement in the development and implementation of an information security program. The board must approve an institution's written information security program and then oversee the program's development, implementation, and maintenance.

Health Insurance Portability and Accountability Act

HIPAA specifies the privacy, security, and electronic transaction standards with regard to patient information for all health care providers. Providers need to reassess computer systems and internal procedures for compliance. Breaches of medical privacy, for example, disclosure of patient records via emails or unauthorized network access, will have mandatory penalties. Regulatory bodies are, in effect, forcing managers to take security seriously by mandating the protection of informational assets from abuse, exposure, or unauthorized access.

In addition, an insecure system not only jeopardizes its owner, it can potentially be used to launch attacks on other external facilities, thereby raising issues of potential liability to third parties and their customers for exposure of private information or denial of service.

ELECTRONIC RECORDS RETENTION

Technological advances also pose new legal obligations for counsel and corporate clients regarding **electronic records management (ERM)** and document retention. ERM relies on policies for managing the retention, destruction, and storage of electronic records. An effective document retention policy ensures that electronic documents are efficiently handled and neither retained too long nor destroyed too soon.

Electronic records issues and the consequences of noncompliance became widely known as a result of the publicity surrounding the demise of Enron and Arthur Andersen LLC. Also relevant is **computer forensics,** or discovery of electronic evidence, that imposes unique risks on companies and impacts litigation strategies.[6]

The United States **Department of Justice (DOJ),** which is responsible for the prosecution of federal crimes, filed numerous lawsuits that relied on e-evidence. Most notably, those filed against Microsoft by the DOJ and leading Wall Street brokerage houses by New York Attorney General Eliot Spitzer are proof of the risk posed by unmanaged email content and retention. They have illustrated that illegal or unethical activities are discoverable because they leave behind evidence or a record of their occurrence. Many companies have learned that offensive jokes sent via the company's email system can become damning evidence in an employee's harassment lawsuit, even if those jokes are unrelated to the case.

⟨ **CYBERBRIEF** ⟩

THE LOVEBUG VIRUS INFECTS THE WORLD

The LoveBug, or ILoveYou virus, appeared in Hong Kong on May 11, 2000 and spread rapidly via email throughout the world. LoveBug arrived looking like a safe email message with a file attachment called *love letter for you.txt.vbs*. But the attachment appeared as *love letter for you.txt* because the .vbs did not appear. In this way, the virus was disguised as a safe plain-text file when in fact it was destructive computer code.

At the Hamburg offices of the German newspaper *Abendblatt*, system administrators watched as the virus destroyed 2,000 digital photographs. Belgians could not withdraw cash from ATMs that the virus had disabled. In Paris, L'Oreal shut down its email servers, as did other businesses throughout Europe. Up to 70% of the computers in Germany, the Netherlands, and Sweden were impaired. Ford, Siemens, Silicon Graphics, Fidelity Investments, and Microsoft were adversely affected.

In London, Parliament had to shut down its servers. On Capitol Hill, dysfunctional email systems forced a rare silence in Congress. Over 80% of federal agencies, including the Defense and State departments, were temporarily out of email contact.

The virus corrupted at least four classified, internal Defense Department email systems; affected NASA and the CIA; and ultimately affected over 45 million users in over 20 countries.

Source: Goodman, Marc D., and Susan W. Brenner. "The Emerging Consensus on Criminal Conduct in Cyberspace." *UCLA Journal of Law Technology*, (3) 2002.

INTERNATIONAL ORGANIZATIONS

On a global basis, nations throughout the world are concerned about cyber crime, as are many international organizations, including the United Nations, the G-8, the European Union, and the Council of Europe. The CyberBrief on page 11 illustrates the global reach of security risks.

DOJ DEFINES COMPUTER CRIME

The U.S. DOJ broadly defines **computer crime** as "any violation of criminal law that involves a knowledge of computer technology for their perpetration, investigation, or prosecution."[7] Simply stated, computer crimes are crimes that require knowledge of computers to commit. Increasingly, employees need to know how to use computers to perform their jobs. Criminal activity from both malicious hackers and malcontent insiders is on the rise. As such, networked organizations not only need to defend against heightened risk of crime, they must further ensure that employees with access to corporate computer systems do not violate codes of ethics, privacy rights, or federal or state laws.

CONGRESS EXPANDS COMPUTER CRIME LEGISLATION AND AUTHORITY

Since 1984, Congress has followed a dual approach to fighting computer crime. The **Counterfeit Access Device and Computer Fraud and Abuse Law** of 1984 and subsequent

<CYBERBRIEF>

BUSH ADMINISTRATION'S NATIONAL STRATEGY TO SECURE CYBERSPACE

President Bush's Critical Infrastructure Protection Board released the report, "The National Strategy to Secure Cyberspace" in 2003. It is a component of the effort to increase national security after the September 11 attacks. Its purpose is to create public and private cooperation to regulate and defend the national computer networks from hazards like viruses and terrorist attacks. Ultimately it will provide an Internet strategy for the Department of Homeland Security. Securing cyberspace is a difficult strategic challenge that requires coordinated and focused effort from our entire society, the federal government, state and local governments, and the private sector.

Source: The White House. http://www.whitehouse.gov/pcipb

amendments address computer crimes in which the computer is the subject of the crime. In these computer crimes, there is no analogous traditional crime so special legislation was needed. This line of statutes culminated in the **National Information Infrastructure Protection Act** of 1996 (NIIPA). The government also updated existing statutes so that they could be used to prosecute traditional crimes that had been committed with the use of a computer, particularly fraud and embezzlement.[8]

Recognizing cyber crime (computer crime) as a matter of national security, Congress included provisions in the **USA PATRIOT Act,** which stands for *Uniting and Strengthening America by Providing Appropriate Tools Required to Intercept and Obstruct Terrorism Act.* It was enacted on October 26, 2001 and significantly changed computer crime laws. It expanded the authority of law enforcement to intercept electronic communications. The fundamental techniques of terrorism, espionage, fraud, and other traditional crimes have not changed—only the medium has changed.

NEW ETHIC OF RESPONSIBILITY

In July 2002, President George W. Bush called for a "new ethic of responsibility" in corporate America. He emphasized that preventing fraud and other abuse was a corporate responsibility for which senior executives and directors would be held accountable. The **Sarbanes–Oxley Act** has legislated that responsibility.

This directive imposes enormous responsibility on companies, their management, and employees to safeguard the integrity of the information that is used internally and released externally. This has significant implications with regard to controlling access to financial data. More than ever, boards of directors and audit committees are being required to perform stringent due diligence and demand assurance that corporate data achieves the highest possible integrity.

Chapter Summary

Information security is not a technology problem, and no single security measure will protect computer systems or networks. It is a global problem confronting every business because of its reliance on telecommunications. Crimes committed with computers often do not respect national boundaries.

In this chapter, we discussed the types of external and internal security breaches and legal liabilities that need to be protected against. Effective security requires the commitment of senior management and a plan that incorporates policies, secure use practices, and updated technology. Not only

are companies vulnerable to viruses, hackers, and computer crimes, they are open to lawsuits if, through their negligence, other companies are victimized. To liability exposure from negligence claims, companies must proactively protect employees and data from illegal, irresponsible, ignorant, or unethical behavior.

We provided a broad overview of the dramatic increase in specialized legislation, executive (presidential) initiatives, and judicial (DOJ) review to combat computer crime, protect the critical national infrastructures, and ensure that the U.S. economy is not disrupted.

Key Terms

- security
- privacy
- Digital Liability Management (DLM)
- hacker
- exploits
- script kiddies
- tort
- right
- duty
- negligent torts
- Code Red and Nimda viruses

- denial of service (DOS)
- hits
- electronic evidence (e-evidence)
- Health Insurance Portability and Accountability Act (HIPAA)
- Gramm–Leach–Bliley Act (GLB)
- Children's Online Privacy Protection Act (COPPA)
- electronic records management (ERM)

- computer forensics
- Department of Justice (DOJ)
- LoveBug virus
- Computer crime
- Counterfeit Access Device and Computer Fraud and Abuse Law
- National Information Infrastructure Protection Act (NIIPA)
- USA PATRIOT Act
- Sarbanes–Oxley Act

Discussion Questions

1. Why or how might creating destructive viruses increase the "social standing" of Simon Vallor or those similar to him? Are there effective deterrents against their activities? Explain.
2. How can a company deter employees from opening potentially destructive email attachments? What are other methods to prevent virus infections that are spread by email attachments?
3. Explain what this statement means: "There are no small security or policy breaches—only large ones that were caught early." What are the implications for organizations that are making information security investment decisions?
4. Which are potentially more dangerous to a company: hackers or script kiddies? How do their attack methods differ? How might their motives differ?
5. What is the difference between a tort, a right, and a duty?

6. What electronic records would most likely be of interest to the DOJ or Attorney General when investigating a company suspected of fraud or negligence? What computer devices contain electronic evidence? Can that evidence be permanently and irretrievably destroyed?

7. What are some of the problems underlying the President's plan to monitor the Internet and do surveillance on users? What is your position on this "national security" issue?

8. Section 1029 of Title 18 of the U.S. Code (USC §1029) makes it an offense to engage in certain activities involving *access devices*, which it defines as "any card, plate, code, account number, electronic serial number, mobile identification number, personal identification number, or other telecommunications service, equipment, or instrument identifier, or other means of account access that can be used . . . to obtain money, goods, services, or any other thing of value." The statute also prohibits activities involving *counterfeit access devices*, which it defines as "any access device that is counterfeit, fictitious, altered, or forged, or an identifiable component of an access device or a counterfeit access device." What types of crimes are punishable under USC §1029? Why was this law necessary?

Endnotes

1. Arthur, Charles. "Web Designer Who Created Computer Virus Is Jailed." *The Independent (London)*. January 22, 2003. P. 7.

2. Rozenberg, Gabriel. "Computer 'Nerd' Jailed for Global Virus Attack." *The Times (London)*. January 22, 2003. P. 9.

3. Costello, Sam. "'Nimda,' 'Code Red' Still Alive and Crawling." *CNN.com*. May 8, 2002. http://www.cnn.com/2002/TECH/internet/05/08/nimda.code.red.idg/index.html

4. Hulme, George V. "One Step Ahead. Security Managers Are Trying to Be Prepared for the Next Blended Threat Attack." *InformationWeek*. May 20, 2002.

5. Raysman, Richard, and Brown, Peter. "Computer Security Breaches—Who May Be Held Responsible?" *New York Law Journal*. Vol. 227. May 14, 2002. P. 3.

6. See, for example, http://www.law.com/special/supplement/e_discovery/

7. National Institute of Justice, U.S. Department of Justice. *Computer Crime: Criminal Justice Resource Manual* 2 (1989).

8. Jacobson, Heather, and Green, Rebecca. "Computer Crimes." P. 39 *American Criminal Law Review*, P. 273. Spring 2002.

CHAPTER 2
SOURCES OF DIGITAL LIABILITY

Learning Objectives

◆ How to assess and protect against digital liability exposure.

◆ Business and legal reasons for concern about cyber risks.

◆ Common sources of risk and liability.

◆ Standards of reasonableness and tests of negligence.

INTRODUCTION

Chapter 2 outlines compelling business and legal reasons why organizations can no longer ignore cyber risks, or their consequences. It provides an overview of how a company's digital assets create **liability exposure.** Liability exposure refers to needless risk from the organization's failure to take action, which results in harm. Exposure accrues from the use of networked computers, ecommerce Websites, electronic records, automated transactions, digital signatures, and electronic contracting, –in short, things that all companies are doing. You will gain insight into the difficulty of evaluating and protecting digital assets and the consequences of failure.

This material serves as the foundation for understanding how to identify, qualify, and quantify risk of exposure to hackers and lawyers. We emphasize that the first step toward protecting digital assets is for management to take time to evaluate the value of data, and then the financial impact on business operations if specific systems become unavailable or compromised.

ASSESSING AND PROTECTING DIGITAL ASSETS

RISK ASSESSMENT

Before an organization commits its resources to security technologies, it must know which assets require protection and the real or perceived threats against them. A company can neither budget for nor manage the defenses needed to mitigate risks without an accurate assessment of risk. That assessment must reflect the organization's values as well as the nature of its business. Although these issues are discussed in detail in

⟨CASE ON POINT⟩

HACKERS

Two kingpins of Russian computer crime, Alexey Ivanov and Vasily Gorshkov, were found guilty of breaking into U.S. corporate information systems. They attacked through a known vulnerability in Windows NT. First they would steal sensitive information; then email company executives demanding payment in exchange for not exposing confidential customer data or destroying financial records. To execute their attacks and extortion attempts while hiding their identities, they used various free Hotmail email accounts, or company accounts they had hacked into.

Prior to their arrest by the FBI in Seattle, Washington, in November 2000, they had broken into the computers of at least 38 U.S. companies; stole financial data from computers of two banks; and were involved in the data theft of 300,000 credit cards from CD Universe's Website and 15,700 credit cards from Western Union's Website. Extortion demands followed their intrusions.[1]

Afterwards, it was learned that the victimized companies had not yet installed the patch that might have protected them from these intrusions. There are some who would hold these companies accountable for failing to protect against the hackers' exploits. However, in their defense, installing software patches is itself risky. Patches cannot be installed without first verifying that the "fix" won't cause more damage than hackers. Understandably, systems administrators are extremely reluctant to deploy patches that might disrupt critical business applications.

subsequent chapters, they are covered briefly here to illustrate the scope of the preliminaries.

Protecting computer networks from hackers and lawyers begins with a thorough understanding of

- The nature and location of all electronic data and knowledge assets and the extent to which they may be at risk; i.e., estimates of the extent of their exposure and the probability of attack from known threats.
- Appropriate responses to intrusions, or options if the company suffers a loss or causes another company to suffer a loss.
- The legal issues that can be triggered by release or corruption of those assets, Internet connectivity, electronic commerce, **electronic records,** and funds transfers. The **Uniform Electronic Transaction Act (UETA)** broadly defines an electronic record, or electronic document, as a record "created, generated, sent, communicated, received or stored by electronic means."
- The **opportunity costs** of disrupted business functions. Opportunity costs are measurements of missed or lost sales or profits or how long it might take to recover from an attack.

It is difficult to estimate financial impacts both before and after an incident. However, if a company bases its security investments on financial estimates of opportunity costs, it may have a much stronger position after an incident if it tries to recover costs through legal action.

⟨ **CASE ON POINT** ⟩

LAWYERS

New York Attorney General Eliot Spitzer issued subpoenas to Merrill Lynch, the largest U.S. brokerage, and five other Wall Street firms. He suspected they might have deliberately misled investors by making fraudulent stock recommendations in exchange for lucrative investment banking business. Citicorp chairman Sanford Weill was investigated by securities regulators wanting to know if he had influenced his company's research analysts to improve their ratings on certain companies' stocks. Allegedly, Weill had asked analyst Jack Grubman to reconsider bearish evaluations of AT&T. Investigators discovered emails that Grubman had sent to a friend saying that Weill wanted the support of AT&T's CEO, who was on the board of Citicorp at the time, in an internal power struggle. He went on to say that he was helping get one of Grubman's children into an exclusive preschool. Grubman claimed that his emails were groundless boasting.[2]

The focus of another investigation was Henry Blodget, Merrill's former star Internet analyst. At issue for investigators was whether Blodget or Merrill was criminally or civilly liable for securities fraud based on some of his stock recommendations under New York's Martin Act.[3] However "... an analyst's bad call coupled with an investment banking relationship between the analyst and the issuer does not in and of itself suggest criminal activity."[4] There is an important distinction between "intent to defraud" and "intent to mislead." Absent strong circumstantial evidence of intent and analysts' bad recommendations do not amount to criminally fraudulent misrepresentation even if the analyst or brokerage had a financial interest with the issuer.

In light of this, the Securities and Exchange Commission (SEC) and Spitzer investigated the firms' electronic records, looking for evidence of fraud. Spitzer discovered many incriminating internal emails written by Merrill's analysts. In these messages, analysts disparaged companies they were publicly recommending, describing them as "crap" or "junk." Key evidence against Merrill was Blodget's email wherein he slammed stocks that he was maintaining bullish ratings on.[5] Furthermore, several analysts had complained about the pressure they felt from the banking division. One typical statement: "I think we are off base on how we rate stocks and how much we bend backwards to accommodate banking," to cite a discovered email.[6]

⟨ **CYBERBRIEF** ⟩

MAJOR LOSSES FROM INTERNAL INTRUSIONS

An FBI study found that 70% of all computer attacks enter via the Internet, but 75% of all dollar losses stem from **internal intrusions.** Internal intrusions are those carried out by employees, or insiders. The focus needs to be on improving internal security, from passwords that are stuck to monitors to policies on acceptable use of network and email resources, what is and isn't appropriate to have on your computer, and what kind of dial-in and remote access procedures you have established.

Source: Statement for the Record of Louis J. Freeh, Director. Federal Bureau of Investigation, on Cybercrime Before the Senate Committee on Judiciary Subcommittee for Technology, Terrorism, and Government Information. Washington, D.C. http://www.fbi.gov/pressrm/congress/congress00/cyber032800.htm

< **CYBERBRIEF** >

TIME TO HOLD SOFTWARE COMPANIES LIABLE

Organizations are inserting language into licensing and purchase contracts to hold software companies liable for the costs of security breaches and hacker attacks that exploit weaknesses in their products. This shifts responsibility for viruses and attacks from IT staff to vendors.

Source: http://www.eweek.com, June 2002

INSUFFICIENT PROTECTION AGAINST AVOIDABLE LOSSES

There is considerable evidence that businesses and government agencies—despite all the recent publicity this subject has received—have not learned how to protect themselves against avoidable losses. A week rarely goes by without well-publicized accounts of successful network intrusions, virus infections, theft of customer data, lost laptops containing confidential information, or lost revenue from denial of Website services. As those who have not yet learned through the pain and expense of experience, a majority of these events are predictable and avoidable.

> **@LERT**
> Access that is easy and convenient for employees is also easy and convenient for hackers.

Today's standard corporate communication method has become email. This has made discovery of electronic communications a primary and remarkably persistent source of evidence in many criminal investigations and other legal matters.[7] As companies and litigators are learning, these records can be the evidence that makes or breaks a case in the eyes of the court as well as the public.

DIGITAL LIABILITY MANAGEMENT

Digital liability is another key concept to consider. It is defined as all the ways the information on computer devices and networks can actually hurt a company or individual. Digital liability so accurately represents the consequence and significance of cyber security that we coined the term *Digital Liability Management (DLM)* to refer to this methodology.

Managing the digital information that can create liability is much harder than it appears, even if all the risks are known. That's rare in practice. Even deleting it is very difficult, if not impossible, and occasionally illegal. Not surprisingly, illegal destruction of documents sets in motion another series of legal problems and possibly felony

---

File Creation

When a file is created and saved three things occur:

1. An entry is made into the File Allocation Table (FAT) that indicates where the actual file is stored in the Data Area of the hard drive or storage device. The FAT is an internal master index of all files on a hard drive.
2. A directory entry is made listing the file name, size, the link to the FAT, and other information.
3. The data is written to the Data Area of the hard drive.

File Deletion

When a file is deleted only two things occur:

1. The FAT entry for the file is zeroed out. This indicates to the computer that the space on the hard drive is available for use by a new file.
2. The first character of the Directory entry filename is changed to a special character (E5 HEX).

Nothing is done to the Data Area.

> Thus, when a file is deleted, the computer simply makes the space occupied by that file available for new files. The filename is removed from the Directory and FAT, but all or part of the file's content remains recoverable. The bytes that make up the file remain on the hard drive until they are overwritten by a new file or wiped out using utility software.

File Recovery

When a file is restored only two things need to be done:

1. The FAT entry for the file is relinked to the file's location in the Data Area where the file had been stored.
2. The first character of the Directory Entry filename is changed back to a legal (nonspecial) character.

Nothing is done to the Data Area.

> As long as the actual file in the Data Area is not overwritten by a new file or wiped, the deleted file can be recovered. When a hard drive is formatted, the Data Area is also left untouched. Normally, most of the original data can be recovered from formatted media.

FIGURE 2.1   How Files Are Created, Deleted, and Recovered

convictions. This became widely known in the wake of Andersen's document shredding activities in connection with the Enron debacle.

"Deleted" email and computer files have a habit of coming back at the most inopportune times, such as in the midst of a civil trial or SEC investigation. It is unfortunate that the term *deleted* was ever applied to digital content because the word connotes "unrecoverable" or "gone forever." This statement is seldom true of digital records.

ACTIVITIES THAT CAUSE DIGITAL LIABILITY

Digital liability will result from any illegal activity. However, digital liability can be triggered by unintentional actions as well. Several common causes of digital liability are

- Evidence of unlawful civil or criminal activity.
- Illegal possession of unlicensed software or other intellectual property.

<CYBERBRIEF>

POLICIES IN PLACE

A recent survey of Fortune 500 firms found that only 21% of respondents had formal digital security policies in place supported by documented procedures and guidelines for all users.

Source: The 2002 Ernst & Young Digital Security Overview.

- Theft of trade secrets and other privileged information.
- Theft of customer or partner information.
- Disclosure of confidential information.
- Deletion of records in violation of statutory or regulatory retention requirements.

@LERT
Proper information management means secure access to what should be available and denied access to what should not be available.

DIGITAL LIABILITY: POST-1999

Email-Borne Viruses

Since 1999, digital liability has intensified to the point of being out of control. That year **email-borne viruses** became prevalent and more potent with each new release. Previously, viruses were spread primarily via contaminated floppy disks. Then in 2002, hackers unleashed more insidious and infectious programs designed to disable software defenses and transmit themselves across networks. By 2003, driven by concern over genuine threats such as Klez and Bugbear, computer users were falling prey to false warnings of nonexistent viruses. Companies incurred the costs of wasted time and bandwidth as users forwarded these **hoaxes** to others.

"Dirty Laundry" Websites

Also appearing were Websites dedicated to criticizing companies or avenging their management. Internalmemos.com, for example, began posting internal memos containing everything from extremely sensitive corporate information to the corporate cafeteria food menu. Employees wishing to vent their frustrations in detail get the opportunity at sites such as Mybosssucks.com.

Self-Restraint

The behavior of employees plays a principal role in cyber security, and this behavior often supersedes that of any technical safeguards that may be in place. As most companies have learned, the perpetrator of cyber attacks is not solely the evil hacker. Honest individuals who open email messages indiscriminately or loyal employees who use their company account to access the Internet can detonate destruction. Unless endusers exercise self-restraint by deleting unsolicited attachments and email with

<LEGALBRIEF>

TWISTING IN THE WIND
OF POTENTIAL LIABILITY

Companies connected "to the Internet are twisting in the wind of potential liability . . . But because most hackers are presumed to be judgment-proof, there is a consensus that it is only a matter of time before companies that suffer damage from attacks start to move up the food chain."

Since hijacked Websites are both victims and the victimizers, the liability issue is whether they are victims that could have protected themselves.

Source: Shepherd, Ritchenya A. "Firms May Be Liable When Hackers 'Hijack' Computers." *New York Law Journal.* March 2, 2000. P. 5.

enticing subject lines, the organization's infrastructure will be at an unnecessarily heightened risk.

Employees' computer network accounts are, in effect, portals between hackers on the Internet and corporate networks. And sometimes those portals are wide open because **firewalls** and **antivirus (AV)** mechanisms do not detect, and therefore cannot deter, all viruses. Firewalls are hardware and software devices to protect a network or computer from exposure to other networks or computers. AV programs scan files to detect and deter viruses. These defense mechanisms will be discussed in detail in Chapter 8.

DAMAGE ESTIMATIONS

The joint 2001 **Computer Security Institute and FBI (CSI/FBI)** *Computer Crime and Security Survey* found that various cyber crimes accounted for losses of $378 million among the 186 companies that quantified their damages in 2001.[8] This average per company loss of $2 million was twice the average loss incurred during 2000. The exact amounts are less disturbing than the staggering 100% annual increase in losses that ensued despite increased investments in security hardware and software. The majority of the losses were attributed to theft of trade secrets, financial fraud, and damage from computer viruses. Virus damage alone cost firms over $13 billion in 2001.

The 2002 data showed no improvement. The CSI/FBI 2002 *Computer Crime and Security Survey* results confirmed that the threat from computer crime and other information security breaches continued unabated and that the financial toll continued to mount.[9] The two top types of losses were the same as in 2001—theft of proprietary information and financial fraud. In 2002, the third greatest loss was due to insider net abuse, which displaced viruses by a very narrow margin.

COMMON SOURCES OF RISK

USER IGNORANCE

Managers and users must be adequately trained to competently administer their own computer accounts. They need to learn how to recognize dangers and respond safely. Secure-use training can produce a very high **return on investment (ROI)** because the

⬡ CYBERBRIEF ⟩

HASTILY DRAFTED ELECTRONIC DOCUMENTS

Parties to litigation are beginning to realize that present sense impressions are indelibly captured in hastily drafted electronic documents. Companies are facing challenges as their employees' Internet and email usage subject them to liability.

_____

Source: Nimsger, Kristin M., and Michele C. S. Lange, "Computer Forensics Experts Play Crucial Role." *The Lawyers Weekly.* Vol. 2, No. 2. May 10, 2002.

savings exceed the costs. Consider that common high-risk practices are the indiscriminate opening of email, email forwarding, unprotected use of wireless devices, use of company email accounts to subscribe to external listservs, lack of discretion with email content and Web surfing, revealing passwords to strangers, and **instant messaging (IM).** The highly utilized IM programs let people chat in real time. With the added capability of exchanging file attachments and the constant server connections required, IM allow for greater exposure to bugs and vulnerabilities. Their ramifications can be disastrous, and all it takes is a single event.

There has been a migration of traditional crimes, including fraud and extortion, to electronic media, because online criminals can reach unsuspecting victims more quickly and easily. Ignorant employees make their jobs easier.

LACK OF ENFORCEABLE POLICY

When employees know, as a matter of company policy, that they cannot open email from unknown sources—no matter how enticing the subject—a hacker's easiest access to the corporate network is effectively eliminated.

Moreover, if employees are actively discouraged from sending or forwarding email indiscriminately, then disruptive civil rights discrimination or harassment suits may be avoided. Similar discipline must be applied to the composition of email or IM. Nothing should ever be written that a jury or judge would consider incriminating.

By conservative estimates, many companies could have saved themselves millions of dollars in damages and fees if they had implemented and enforced strict email **acceptable use policies (AUP).** These policies define acceptable uses of computing equipment and require little investment beyond what it takes to document the rules and communicate them effectively.

SOCIAL ENGINEERING

Due to ever more entrapping software, or **malware,** one of the greatest security risks occurs when employees are duped into being the conduit of cyber attacks. Malware refers to malicious software programs, such as viruses, worms, and Trojan horses. These programs will be discussed in detail in Chapter 3. Threats, such as email-spread viruses, achieve their destructive goal through **social engineering.** That is, by psychologically manipulating or tricking the enduser into doing something risky or damaging. Social engineering is highly successful because it is extremely easy to impersonate on the Internet.

This was the secret to success for several viruses. The **ILoveYou virus** spread rapidly because of its attention-grabbing email subject. It tricked and enticed recipients to open it, mostly at work, and unleash over a billion dollars of destruction in May 2000. Subsequent variations included a fake invoice, which lured recipients to open it to check a bill for unrecognized services, and a virus attachment disguised as an antivirus program.[10]

Klez.H, the most prevalent virus throughout January 2003, was successful due to its ability to send itself to addresses found on infected PCs within address books and documents, such as resumes. In this way, infected messages appeared to the recipients as coming from a familiar and trusted source.

From these infuriating events, a simple but profound lesson was learned—virus creators understand human vulnerabilities and exploit them just as viruses exploit software vulnerabilities.

@LERT
Security policy that is complex, obtrusive, and difficult to comply with is self-defeating, e.g., requiring overly frequent password changes or using unreliable swipe cards to unlock the doors. Under these circumstances, staff will tend to work around the policy by sharing the passwords or propping the doors open. With that organizational culture, employees are more likely to unknowingly help an intruder gain access to critical business information.

EXCESSIVE SHARING

Email and voicemail that contain jokes, including those with racial, gender, ethnic, or sexual content, tend to get widely distributed. Just as people tend to open all email they receive, they also seem compelled to share any joke they find amusing, regardless of content or consequence. People who want to share their funnies with co-workers can effortlessly, and without thinking, forward them via email or voicemail.

The potential liability implications are significant. Employees can violate the civil rights of anyone mentioned in the message. Communication that may be (mis)interpreted or construed as harassing or offensive creates legal exposure because of broad interpretations of the **Civil Rights Act of 1964.** This act prohibits any type of discrimination based on gender, race, national origin, or age. The act also requires employers to provide nonhostile, nonharassing workplaces and holds them legally responsible for failure to maintain such workplaces.

In a sexual harassment suit filed against Chevron, an email was forwarded among employees that listed *25 reasons why beer is better than women.* The email was discovered and used as evidence of a hostile workplace environment. Whether or not this message was intended to harass women was beside the point. The message became part of the damning evidence against Chevron because it illustrated that such illegal behavior was tolerated. The courts view the failure to implement controls to prevent such harassment as evidence that the behavior is, in effect, tolerated. In February 1995, Chevron agreed to pay $2.2 million to settle the women's claims, while denying the charges.

In contrast, to shield itself from liability, the *New York Times* fired 23 employees for distributing pornographic images by email, in violation of its email and Internet policies. The *Times'* December 1999 action resulted from an employee's complaint.

@LERT
Cyber security is neither nonintrusive nor user-friendly. It requires strong policy that is often irritating and inconvenient.

REVEALING CANDOR

As outlined in the introductory Cases on Point, the content of email can be used against a firm in civil or criminal cases. It is increasingly being used as evidence of **white-collar crime (WCC)** and **electronic fraud (efraud).** WCC is any nonviolent crime committed in a commercial context, for example, embezzlement, threats, or fraud. Efraud refers to the fraudulent use of electronic records, such as illegal interception or manipulation.

It is very risky to treat email like a telephone conversation when the content might be taken as evidence of wrongdoing. American Home Products was sued for problems associated with the diet drug Fen-Phen. After searching through over 33 million emails, plaintiffs' counsel discovered a message from someone in accounting who complained: "Do I have to look forward to spending my waning years writing checks to fat people worried about a silly lung problem?"[11] The company was being sued in part for reckless indifference to human life and settled the case for a record $3.75 billion.

The DOJ's "trial of the century" against Microsoft brought the connection between email and legal liability to everyone's attention. By collecting incriminating email records from Microsoft's computer networks, the DOJ was able to build a comprehensive and extended account of senior executives' activities violating antitrust laws. And as Bill Gates discovered, those records may not be refutable in court.

FACTORS EXACERBATING DIGITAL LIABILITY

Several disconcerting issues should now be apparent. Increasingly, digital records and communication are at the center of legal issues or used as supporting evidence. This has made employees' undisciplined computer practices or unregulated Internet access dangerous. Without fear of sanctions, it is unreasonable to expect employees to restrict their email and Internet activities to those of the business. The temptation is too great.

Risk exposure escalates when users assume that their cyber activities will remain undetectable. With false privacy expectations, users write things they would never even say aloud, much less knowingly save as a business record. As such, startlingly crude, off-the-cuff, offensive, or threatening comments might be made in email—exposing the company to lawsuits.

INTRACTABLE PROBLEMS

The intractable problem for businesses is that any email message sent by anyone with a company email account, regardless of whether it is personal or business in nature, may

- Be interpreted legally as the company's official corporate policy.
- Be used as evidence of company misconduct.
- Become ammunition against a company even if that message would have been disregarded by anyone with common sense and maturity at the company.[12]

LAGGING PRACTICES

The deployment of cyber security defenses lags significantly behind the discovery of threats. Investments aimed at changing user behavior lag investments in defensive technology for several reasons.

- Senior managers are not fully aware of the information security risks to their operations. They accept an unknown level of risk *by default* rather than consciously deciding what level of risk exposure is reasonable or tolerable.
- Employers and employees have a false sense of security, and rely on outdated cyber security and liability controls that may be ineffective against new threats.
- Managers do not have enough relevant information to make optimal investment decisions regarding cyber defenses and access controls.

BUSINESS AND LEGAL REASONS FOR CONCERN

We live in a society that emphasizes computer technology and litigation. This section contains an outline and summary of the compelling business and legal reasons for safeguarding digital assets.

BECAUSE OF ZERO-TOLERANCE ENVIRONMENTS

Companies are more thoroughly examining and assessing their partners' overall data security policies as well as their own. They are demanding that their business partners either maintain effective information security or terminate the collaborative relationship.[13] A growing number of businesses are also demanding extensive third-party audits, in part because of the demands of their insurance and fidelity companies.

During an information security audit, complete scans of the network, computing architecture, and application platforms are performed. There are reviews of the company's defenses against viruses, Trojan horses, and internal and external vulnerabilities. In addition threat assessments are conducted on the company's ability to identify, resist, and respond to intrusions and hack attacks. The data from these scans and assessments are analyzed and presented together with comprehensive

Internal Security Audit Assessments
Password and user-account policies
Backup and restore procedures
Disaster recovery plans
Network infrastructure vulnerabilities
Antivirus software and updates
Intrusion detection systems and updates
Network operating system configuration, upgrades, and patches
Physical security of vital company resources
Application security policies and procedures
Separation of duties by IT staff

External Security Audit Assessments
Risk factors that may compromise internal security
Servers that may be allow a security breach
Effectiveness of firewalls, their configuration, and rules
Effectiveness of wireless configuration
Effectiveness of email security and configurations
Application security policies and procedures
Remote access policies for dial-in, VPN, and Web access

FIGURE 2.2   Components of a Third-Party Information Security Audit

recommendations for improvements in policies and procedures. Figure 2.2 lists the specific assessments that are done in both internal and external audits.

BECAUSE THE COMPANY'S WELL-BEING IS AT STAKE

It is obvious that if a company's proprietary, financial, or customer information is stolen, exposed, or destroyed, the bottom line will suffer. What may be less obvious is the extent of the legal implications.

When estimating the cost of an intrusion for its own internal balance sheets, a company might be limited only by its own discretion. However, the real test of the cost of a computer crime comes in the court room.

The Standard of Reasonableness

Any attempt to recover damages from a perpetrator will involve defense attorneys, judges, or juries.[14] The courts will first look at the extent to which the company exercised reasonable diligence by safeguarding its own network and informational assets and treated them as being important. This legal **standard of reasonableness** that courts apply to such cases should not be underestimated. Competitive information and trade secrets that must not be divulged must be protected. Why? Because courts are likely to apply the same analysis as they do in trade secret cases or those involving physical assets. That is, if a company does not safeguard secret information from misconduct by employees or others, courts or insurers may deny action to recover those losses. If, for example, a company did not implement and enforce reasonable cyber security measures, it might not have any legal recourse if its confidential information was stolen by employees, hackers, or industrial spies.

Consequences When Reasonable Precautions Are Neglected

Without evidence of reasonable security measures, the potential detrimental consequences include

- Successful litigation by employees for breach of fiduciary responsibility or inability to seek injunctive relief for financial losses due to illegal disclosure.
- Personal injury lawsuits filed by customers, clients, or patients whose personal information has been disclosed or posted on Websites or in hackers' **chat rooms.** Chat rooms are real-time text-based teleconferences that can be private (entered by invitation only) or public (anyone can enter).
- Lost judgements based on damage caused by security breaches at business partners.
- Class-action lawsuits filed on behalf of irate stockholders.

FIGURE 2.3   Denial of Service Attack Launched by an Attacker Through Numerous Zombie Computers

Hacker instructs zombies to send millions of requests for access or service to a specific Web server.

The capacity of the target server is limited. the server cannot process and respond to an excessive number of requests—so it crashes.

In a typical DOS attack, an attacker will have installed backdoors on many PCs, turning them into zombies. Then the attacker can instruct those zombies to send millions of access requests to a specific Web server, overloading it. The attacking zombies will have different addresses, making it difficult to know where the actual attack is coming from.

<CYBERBRIEF>

THE PRUDENT MAN RULE

Computer virus **Goner** spread at a rate of 100,000 computers per minute. Goner, a level 4 virus—the highest level of destructiveness, proved that gullible users are a serious security risk. Goner arrived as an email with the subject "Hi." The message read, "How are you? When I saw this screen saver, I immediately thought about you . . . I promise you will love it!" It included an attachment called Gone.SCR, which appeared to be a screen saver. It was written in **Visual Basic Script (VBS)** but compressed into UPX format, an uncommon file format that neither firewalls nor AV software were programmed to detect. In this format, Goner bypassed AV software and corporate firewalls that had no filters to protect against it. When a user double-clicked it, Goner attempted to delete AV programs. Then it installed a **backdoor** on the infected PC to launch attacks against other networks or Websites. That is, the infected PC, which was remotely controlled by hackers, could perpetrate cyber attacks on other networks, computers, and Websites. When neither AV software nor firewalls proved to be effective, the only defense against Goner was to warn employees against opening suspicious attachments.

The **"prudent man rule"** imposes the duty to protect information assets as a prudent person would. Given current knowledge about how malware is transmitted and its destructive potential, a prudent organization would be expected to implement secure email practices that would have limited the spread of the Goner virus.

Source: Costello, Sam. "Goner Worm Spreads, Tries to Delete Firewalls." *InfoWorld.* December 4, 2001. http://www.infoworld.com/articles/hn/xml/01/12/04/011204hngoner.xml

BECAUSE OF PRIVILEGED INFORMATION

Organizations possess confidential or proprietary information belonging to third parties as well as their own. If their information was stolen, altered, or publicly disclosed and caused injury to its original owner, the firm may be liable for negligence.

For example, protecting **personally identifiable health information (PIHI)** requires awareness of technical and legal issues at every level at which health professionals handle confidential information. Anyone that HIPAA, the Health Insurance Portability and Accountability Act), defines as a health care provider—including doctors, nurses, medical technicians, pharmacists, and insurers—could face up to $250,000 in fines and up to 10 years in prison for "obtaining and disclosing protected health information with the intent to sell, transfer, or use it for personal gain, commercial advantage, or malicious harm."

TESTS OF NEGLIGENCE

The issue of industry standards constituting a sufficient defense against negligence and tests of negligence were addressed by Judge Learned Hand. Judge Hand outlined a standard for negligence and liability based on the **economic model of marginal cost-benefit analysis.**[15] According to marginal analysis, the firm is not negligent if and only if the marginal costs of safeguards are greater than the marginal benefits of those safeguards. That is, if a $1,000 investment in security training could prevent an estimated $1,000 or more in damages, that investment must be made. The benefits are calculated

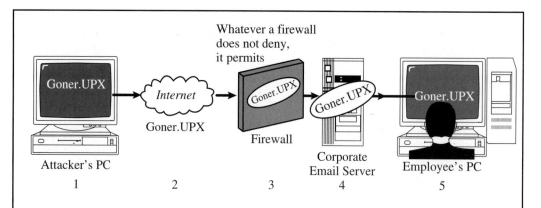

FIGURE 2.4   Illustration of How the Goner Virus Was Able to Infect Computers

by multiplying the estimated probability of a security breach by the expected average cost of damages. Despite the partially subjective estimations, Judge Hand's liability test "has received overwhelming acceptance in the courts."[16]

The potential for multimillion-dollar damage claims gives rise to another dilemma that the courts have yet to decide. If your firm fails to take prudent action to limit its exposure to network intrusion, it may become the victim of a denial of service (DOS) attack. This type of attack converts infected PCs into **zombies,** or computers that are controlled by the attacker. Often the hackers will use the zombie computers to infect and incapacitate other private or public networks.

Chapter Summary

There are no infallible security systems. There are cost-effective methods and procedures that can significantly reduce exposure to cyber risks. The reverse is also true—failure to implement stringent cyber security effectively leaves corporate assets vulnerable to both hackers and lawyers.

Adoption of these techniques has been painfully slow in commercial and governmental arenas. This delay has been very expensive, not to mention embarrassing for the victims of malicious or irresponsible actions of attackers or employees. How do we explain this lack of response to the threat on the part of management?

- They do not fully realize the value of the assets at risk that reside on their networks.
- They do not understand all the components of cyber risk.
- They place too much emphasis, investment, and reliance on technology to address the issue.

- They fail to educate themselves sufficiently to make the best available investments in technology.
- They fail to acknowledge the importance of people and their behavior in controlling exposure to cyber risk.

The DLM method is designed to facilitate the complete evaluation and comprehensive management of the risks inherent in a connected economy. It places equal weight upon its people, process, and technology foundations. These will be examined in detail in the chapters that follow.

Key Terms

- liability exposure
- internal intrusions
- electronic records
- Uniform Electronic Transaction Act (UETA)
- opportunity costs
- digital liability
- Digital Liability Management (DLM)
- email-borne viruses
- hoaxes
- firewalls
- Antivirus (AV)

- Computer Security Institute & FBI (CSI/FBI) *Computer Crime and Security Survey*
- Return on Investment (ROI)
- Instant Messaging (IM)
- Acceptable Use Policies (AUP)
- Malware
- social engineering
- ILoveYou virus
- Klez.H virus
- Civil Rights Act of 1964

- White-Collar Crime (WCC)
- electronic fraud (efraud)
- standard of reasonableness
- chat rooms
- Personally Identifiable Health Information (PIHI)
- economic model of marginal cost–benefit analysis
- zombies
- Goner virus
- Visual Basic Script (VBS)
- backdoor
- prudent man rule

Discussion Questions

1. What motivates hackers to crack corporate networks?
2. How does one estimate the probability of attack?
3. Which information assets are likely to be the most exposed?
4. What makes digital liability different from other sources of legal liability?
5. What is the government's responsibility in protecting businesses and consumers from cyber crime?
6. How do administrators strike the proper balance between security that is too lax and security that is too intrusive?
7. Some experts have argued that the cause of security problems is that the products just do not work the way we need, or want, or understand them to work. Do you agree or disagree with the validity of this argument? Why? What are some feasible supporting or counter arguments?
8. One generally accepted formula for estimating the financial impact of a security incident is computing the time spent fixing the damage. For example, if two system administrators,

with annual salaries of $90,000 each, spend 20 hours each disinfecting viruses from the network and applying security patches, what is the cost of the incident? Is this an accurate estimation of damage? Why or why not?

9. The stealth Melissa virus propagated itself by automatically emailing itself as an attachment to the first 50 addresses in the infected computer's email address book, if the victim used Microsoft Outlook for email. Based on its propagation method, list some of the digital liabilities or security incidents that this virus could trigger.

Endnotes

1. Brunker, Mike. "Cyberspace Evidence Seizure Upheld." *Cybercrime-Alerts.* June 3, 2001. http://www.mail-archive.com/cyber-crime-alerts@topica.com/msg00439.html

2. Bachman, Justin. "Scandals Made It Easy to Spot the Losers This Year." (AP) *The Buffalo News.* December 30, 2002.

3. Gasparino, Charles. "State Inquiry to Follow Close on Heels of Departing Merrill Lynch Analyst." *Wall Street Journal.* December 10, 2001.

4. Arkin, Stanley. "Analysts' Conflict of Interest: Where's the Crime?" *New York Law Journal.* February 14, 2002. P. 3.

5. Knox, Noelle. "5 More Wall Street Firms Subpoenaed." *USA Today.* April 11, 2002. P. B1.

6. Loomis, Tamara. "Electronic Mail: A Smoking Gun for Litigators." *New York Law Journal.* Vol. 227. May 16, 2002. P. 5.

7. Nimsger, Kristin M., and Michele C. S Lange. "Computer Forensics Experts Play Crucial Role." *The Lawyers Weekly.* Vol. 2, No. 2. May 10, 2002.

8. See the annual survey of the Computer Security Industry (CSI), the *CSI/FBI Computer Crime and Security Survey,* at http://www.gocsi.com; and Security Focus at http://www.securityfocus.com

9. Power, Richard. "2002 CSI/FBI Computer Crime and Security Survey." *Computer Security Journal.* Vol. XVIII, No. 2, Spring 2002.

10. Harley, David. "The Future of Malicious Code." *Information Security.* May 2002. P. 36.

11. Loomis, Tamara. "Electronic Mail: A Smoking Gun for Litigators." *New York Law Journal.* Vol. 227. May 16, 2002. P. 5.

12. Woodward, Victor. "It's the email, stupid!" December 1998. http://www.dominopower.com/issuesprint/issue199812/legal.html

13. Hulme, George V. "In Lockstep On Security." *InformationWeek.* March 18, 2002. http://www.informationweek.com/story/IWK20020315S0008

14. Conry-Murray, Andrew. "Deciphering the Cost of a Computer Crime." *Network Magazine.* April 1, 2002. P. 44.

15. See *United States v Carroll Towing Company,* 159 F. 2d 169, 173 (2d Cir. 1947).

16. Epstein, Richard A. *Cases and Materials on Torts,* 6th ed. Boston: Little, Brown & Co., 1995. P. 218.

CHAPTER 3
THREATS, VULNERABILITIES, AND RISK EXPOSURE

Learning Objectives

◆ Taxonomy of threats and vulnerabilities (TTV).

◆ Viruses, worms, Trojan horse programs, and hoaxes.

◆ Malware threats and vulnerabilities.

◆ Human-based threats and vulnerabilities.

◆ Internet protocol-based (IP-based) threats, vulnerabilities, and forgery.

◆ How to assess the severity of threats and mitigate risk exposure.

INTRODUCTION

An essential first step in security planning is to understand what the organization needs to protect against. That requires an awareness of the type and severity of threats and **vulnerabilities** confronting an organization's information systems. A vulnerability may be a weakness in hardware, software, people, or the Internet protocol (IP) that exposes a computer or user to an **exploit** or a threat, such as malware. Exploits are tools or techniques that take advantage of a vulnerability in order to exceed the user's authorized level of access. Malware refers to malicious programs such as viruses, worms, Trojan horse programs, and backdoors.

To better understand risks and how to mitigate risk exposure, this chapter introduces the **taxonomy of threats and vulnerabilities (TTV).** The TTV classifies the intruders and intrusions that organizations and users are exposed to. Threats and vulnerabilities are categorized according to their origin (e.g., external or internal) and type (directed or random); the reason for the intrusion and motive of the intruder; and the seriousness of the intrusion and sophistication of the intruder. We examine intruders, their exploits, and tools and methods of intrusion, and discuss reasons for their high success rate.

You will learn how vulnerabilities may lead to financial loss or the legal problems described in Chapters 1 and 2. Many examples in this chapter will show that threats and exploits are getting worse because of the trend toward connecting business processes across enterprises using shared and public networks in real time.

⟨ **CYBERBRIEF** ⟩

THE GROWING THREAT FROM COMPUTER DEPENDENCE

According to Howard Schmidt, vice president of President George W. Bush's Critical Infrastructure Protection Board, "Cyber-crime is costing the world economy billions of dollars and it is still on the increase. The more we depend on the system, the more we use the system, the more they will exploit it. . . . Cyber-related incidents are increasing in number, sophistication, severity, and cost."

Source: Reuters. "'Viruses Costing World Billions' says Bush Advisor." October 15, 2002. http://www.zdnet.com.au/newstech/security/story/0,2000024985,20269076,00.htm

⟨ **CASE ON POINT** ⟩

KLEZ AND SLAMMER CAUSE ELECTRONIC SIEGES FELT THROUGHOUT THE WORLD

Starting in 2002 and continuing in 2003, the **Klez worm** was the #1 malware circulating on the Internet. Within just 10 days, the Klez worm had infected thousands of systems worldwide via email, with some carrying **payloads** (instructions that control a computer) capable of destroying files. While still fighting Klez, the **SQL Slammer** (also called **Sapphire**) worm caused chaos around the world by sending out a flood of messages that jammed networks. This global traffic jam substantially slowed down the Internet in January 2003.[1]

Klez and Slammer differed in their modus operandi and purpose. But they both exploited known vulnerabilities and caused extensive disruption. Klez exploited the lack of user training, which contributes to email vulnerability. Slammer exploited the lack of preventive care, which contributed to the SQL database vulnerability. That is, Slammer took advantage of a flaw in Microsoft's SQL server that had not been **patched,** or repaired, by system administrators. While eradicating Slammer was as simple as turning the server computer off and then back on, Klez was virtually unstoppable because it exploited users' insecure habits.

Klez would send itself to email addresses stored in the infected users' address books. By forging the **SMTP (simple mail transfer protocol)** email header, the email (with attachment) appeared to have been sent by someone the recipient knew. Its forgery method was so good that it was extremely difficult to differentiate between infected email and legitimate email. Untrained (or unwarned) users assumed that the infected messages came from the email address listed in the from field—and opened them. Eventually, users were warned to be very cautious of unsolicited emails and not to open any attachments that they were not explicitly expecting.

Slammer did not destroy anything, but its geographical spread and disruption were debilitating. It infected server computers that were running unpatched **Microsoft SQL Server 2000** software. SQL servers store data that is accessed by Web users. Across Canada, Nigeria, Japan, South Korea, South Africa, and Finland, many people were unable to withdraw money from their banks. Chinese New Year celebrations were disrupted in Taiwan. In India, Web services were stopped. In Seattle, Washington, the computer-assisted 911 system, though not connected to the Internet, failed because it relied on servers that were connected to the Internet.

"The Slammer worm did not go hunting for personal information like credit card numbers. It was set on a random rampage throughout the Internet looking for unlocked doors, and had no instructions to steal data."[2] Until Slammer, viruses and worms, such as Klez, had targeted specific Websites or email programs. Security experts feared that Slammer might be a "proof of concept"—distributed ahead of a more malicious attack.[3] They believe that because details of the attack were sent around the world quickly, many were able to act before any serious disruption. An overriding worry is that too many system managers only fix problems as they occur, rather than keep their defenses up-to-date.

Microsoft servers were not the only ones attacked by worms. The Linux worm attacked Appache Web servers running on Linux systems, compromising more than 3,500 machines in September 2002.

FIGURE 3.1 Most Active Viruses in 2001

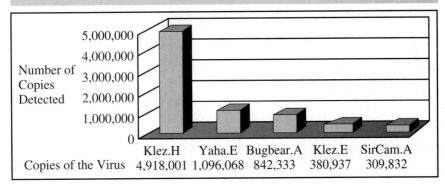

	Klez.H	Yaha.E	Bugbear.A	Klez.E	SirCam.A
Copies of the Virus	4,918,001	1,096,068	842,333	380,937	309,832

Source: The Register. http://www.theregister.co.uk/content/56/28585.html

FIGURE 3.2 Virus-Infected Email Increasing

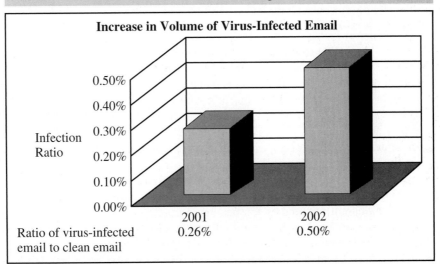

	2001	2002
Ratio of virus-infected email to clean email	0.26%	0.50%

Source: The Register. http://www.theregister.co.uk/content/56/28585.html

<CYBERBRIEF>

52 MILLION SECURITY EVENTS IN ONE WEEK

During the outbreak of Slammer, Alfred Huger, a senior director of engineering at Symantec Security Response, which monitors computer intrusions around the globe, revealed: "In the last seven days, we've seen 52 million security events." While most of these might be unsuccessful, the numbers suggest the breadth of the problem.

Source: Hafner, Katie, and John Briggs,. "In Net Attacks, Defining the Right to Know." *The New York Times.* January 30, 2003. (G) P. 1.

CLASSIFICATION OF COMPUTER THREATS AND VULNERABILITIES

We developed an extensive taxonomy of threats and vulnerabilities (TTV) that expose computer networks and applications to risk of intrusion. We use the term *intrusion* to refer to any type of intrusion, attack, or exploit. Vulnerabilities exist for two main reasons. The first is human error, such as using poor passwords or participating in chat rooms from business email accounts. The second is the complexity of software, that results in misconfiguration, programming errors, or flaws, such as those that allow malware like Slammer to disrupt network traffic.

Most intrusions fit into multiple categories. For example, a hacker (external intruder) may send an infected program (malware) in an email message to an employee (internal intermediary) who opens it because of an enticing subject (social engineering) that then installs a backdoor (malware) to gain access to customer records (deliberate attack) for financial gain (economic motive).

USES OF THE TTV

The TTV is a guide to understanding an organization's risk exposure that stems from weaknesses in cyber defenses and the powerful motives of intruders. The TTV can be used to estimate expected damages since threats and vulnerabilities in certain categories have higher expected costs. For example, intrusions that are not detected, allowing them to persist for an extended time period, have higher expected costs than those detected early. This is what makes the business case for investments in **intrusion detection systems (IDS).** An IDS, when properly deployed, can provide warnings indicating that the system is under attack.[4] An IDS sensor can be set to look at all traffic, into and out of the network, to stop internal and external intrusions.

There are also higher expected costs associated with targeted attacks, or directed attacks, that are motivated by financial gain than random acts of vandalism. The immediate costs associated with responding to security breaches and systems to cope with business interruptions also vary with the category of intrusion.

The diversity of threats represented in the TTV also provides the foundation for designing necessary defenses, such as education, training, strict acceptable-use policies, extensive auditing, and access controls. The TTV chart identifies the origins and types of threats and vulnerabilities, reasons for the intrusions, motives of the intruders, likelihood of detection, and escalation of the attack.

TAXONOMY OF THREATS AND VULNERABILITIES

FIGURE 3.3   Taxonomy of Threats and Vulnerabilities (TTV)

Origin of the Intrusion or Threat	
External	Malware, hackers, script kiddies, former employees, espionage, adversaries, terrorists
Internal	Management, employees, consultants, contract workers, maintenance crew, temporary staff
External threats with internal intervention	The external attack is able to occur because of inadvertent or deliberate help by insiders
Type of Threat	
Directed or focused	Hack attacks
	Industrial espionage
	Trophy hunting
	Extortion
Random or autonomous	Email viruses
	Worms
	Stealth Websites
	Bogus Websites enticing users to register
Reason Why the Intrusion Occurred	
Unintentional	Ignorance
	Lack of training
	Carelessness
	Disregard for security practice
Deliberate and directed	Focused attack by an adversary
	Focused attack for financial gain
	Focused attack for revenge or mischief
	For fame or notoriety
Deliberate, but random	Malware
	Script kiddies
	Proof of concept
Intent or Motive of the Intruder	
	For political or military objectives
	For retaliation or vengeance
	For ideological objectives
	For financial gain, extortion, or blackmail
	For curiosity or the thrill of vandalism
	For competitive advantage
	Focused attack against security companies for trophy hunting

(Continued)

FIGURE 3.3 *(Continued)*

Seriousness of the Intrusion or Sophistication of the Intruder

Level 0: Detected intrusions that cause little or no disruption

Level 1: Ostensibly benign activity that goes unnoticed, but ultimately proves to be disruptive; this category may escalate to higher levels

Level 2: Extensive disruption that is contained within a network or workgroup

Level 3: Widespread extensive disruption to multiple sites

Level 4: Total disruption of service or destruction of data

Likelihood of Detection of the Intrusion or Intruder

LOW	INTRUDER WANTS TO AVOID DETECTION
Stealth attack	• Information retrieval or theft
(human or viral)	• Espionage
	• Redirection of funds
	• Coverup of criminal activity
	• Coverup of negligence by altering data or records
HIGH	INTRUDER WANTS THE ATTACK TO BE NOTICED OR DETECTED
Visible or blatant intrusion	Many of these intrusions arise from the technology
(human or viral)	explosion, e.g., hacker tools.
	• Website defacement
	• Posting of damaging news or information
	• False postings in online bulletin boards or Usenet groups
	• Denial of Service (DOS) attack
	• Data corruption

Escalation of the Intrusion

No escalation beyond the initial state	Intruder gains some minimum access to the target system, but does not attempt further penetration. Popular among juveniles, disgruntled employees, or professional hackers who want to show off their skills. These offenders are motivated mostly by mischief, malice, or desire for fame rather than financial gain.
Escalate to higher penetration state, possibly to root access	Intruder gains administrative access to a network or application and then escalates the attack. This is the most potentially damaging scenario.

Source: Developed by Linda Volonino, Ph.D., 2003.

◁ **CYBERBRIEF** ▷

TROPHY HUNTING

Security companies, such as Symantec and McAfee, are targeted by intruders because of the inherent value in breaking into their Websites. Symantec has 3,000 or 4,000 people each day trying to break into its Website, with a lot of it trophy hunting by the intruder.

Source: Hafner, Katie, and John Briggs. "In Net Attacks, Defining the Right to Know." *The New York Times.* January 30, 2003. (G) P. 1.

⟨ **CYBERBRIEF** ⟩

CTO WARNS THAT ALL SERIOUS CRIME INVOLVES INSIDERS

According to Bruce Schneier, chief technology officer (CTO) at Counterpane Internet Security, "all serious crime involves insiders, and technical approaches to security generally presupposes bad guys are on the outside." He reinforced what is commonly known—that "internetworking vastly increases vulnerability by making one's own system dependent on the security of distant systems outside one's control."

Source: "Networks Won't Be Safe Till Business Faces Big Damages." *Washington Internet Daily.* Vol.3, No. 97. May 20, 2002.

ORIGIN OF THE INTRUSION OR THREAT

EXTERNAL THREATS AND VULNERABILITIES

Hackers

A common hack attack is the DOS attack, which can be launched in many ways. Regardless of the exact method, hackers constantly try to disrupt the servers where companies, universities, and governments store their Websites or applications by flooding, or overloading, them with useless information. When a server's memory buffer can be overloaded, it is vulnerable to what is called a **buffer overflow** attack. This type of vulnerability is a software flaw, or programming error, and has been known about for over 15 years. Many vulnerabilities that exist in Internet software systems are, in fact, buffer overflow vulnerabilities, which will be discussed in more detail in Chapter 8

The danger of buffer overflows, particularly in **IIS (Internet information server)**, is that these attacks can pass through a firewall undetected and not even appear in log files[5]. Log files, or logs, are access requests or other network activities recorded so that they can be analyzed for security purposes.

Sophisticated Hackers

Sophisticated hackers are capable of launching attacks at the **application level,** meaning that they can target flaws in specific commonly used programs that support business functions like accounting or marketing. They are able to do this while not disrupting business operations, so as to remain undetected. These expert hackers use various tools of intrusion. They will use **remote and local exploit tools** to gain high-level **privileged access** (**root access** to all other files and directories) to a company's network and systems. After gaining root access, they create **"hidden" directories,** which can be very difficult to detect, for storing files to escalate their attacks. The most common method for creating a hidden directory is to start the directory name with a dot (.) or two dots (..). They then may use **root tool kits,** such as Adore, to write scripts (programs) or hide their presence—that is, make their intrusion activities invisible to avoid detection. For example, the hacker can write a script to monitor traffic through various ports, such as port 423 (telnet), port 110 (email), and port 21 (ftp), and put it in the directory that runs Adore. As legitimate users access the network through any of these ports, the script writes those usernames and passwords to a file, which the hacker later accesses.

In addition, these experts utilize **log file cleaners** to eliminate any record of their activity from the log files and **sniffer** software to monitor traffic and activity on the network and install a backdoor for easy future access.

Script Kiddies

Script kiddies, or novice hackers, do not know enough to develop new viruses. But they can be just as disruptive and destructive as expert hackers. Readily available to them from hacker Websites and chat rooms are "hack tools" that are increasingly more potent and easy to use.

Script kiddies typically want to show off, so they may hack into a high-profile account, such as a microsoft.com account, and then brag about that username and password in a chat room.

Malware

Viruses Basically, a virus is a software program or computer code that consists of two parts: a **propagation mechanism** to sustain it and a payload that does the damage. Propagation consists of replication and migration, or the transport from one system to another.[6]

Virus infection is a multistep process. First, viruses infect computers by attaching themselves to programs or data files on hard drives. They also replicate themselves to be more resistant to eradication. Second, the viruses do damage, such as deleting files.

Descriptions of the common characteristics of viruses are

- *Propagation/Migration:* The way a virus replicates locally and over a network.
- *Payload:* The mechanism by which a virus causes damage, such as a computer command to delete files or send email. Payloads can be innocuous, minor annoyances, or cause severe file system corruption, including the deletion of critical operating system files.
- *Signature:* The identifier by which a virus is detected by AV software. In order for a virus to be detected, it must be identified and its signature established and incorporated into AV software.
- *Trigger:* The action that activates a virus. Many viruses are triggered when an unsuspecting user clicks on an attachment, often Visual Basic Script (VBS), assuming it is something nice (i.e., safe) from a friend or colleague. Because viruses often read users' address books, they will appear to be sent from people that the user knows.
- *Detection Avoidance:* The method by which a virus attempts to conceal or disguise itself. Many viruses try to hide themselves by inserting into unused space within a program so they do not change the size or other characteristics of the infected files. However, that would alter the file's **checksum.**

A checksum is a numeric value used to verify that a file has not been tampered with. It is calculated based on the contents of the file. It is a quick way to check whether anything in a file had been changed. If there is any change in the file's contents—even a single character or space—the checksum would be radically different. Thus, an infected file can be detected because of a change of its checksum. This method is not without drawbacks. When an existing file is modified, a new checksum must be created for that

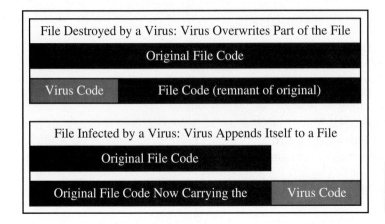

FIGURE 3.4
Virus File-Destruction
and Infection Techniques

newer version. This is often too inconvenient for users to do whenever they modify any file.

One particular type of virus, namely **application viruses,** may overwrite or append themselves to files, as shown in Figure 3.4. These methods serve the virus creator's intent to destroy or to become more resistant to extinction.

Worms A worm is a type of virus program that infects one computer and then "worms its way" through a network, infecting computers that are attached to it. This traffic often clogs the network or Internet. Automated worms, such as Slammer and **Linux,** can randomly probe the Internet on their own looking for vulnerable corporate networks or servers to victimize. Some viruses are hybrids having characteristics of both viruses and worms.

The **Melissa virus** was both a virus and worm. The worm component allowed Melissa to travel from system to system, while the virus component replicated itself on the local system and caused damage. The Melissa virus caused an estimated $1.2 billion worth of damage across the world.[7] Its creator–author, David Smith, was sentenced to 20 months in prison and fined $5,000 for releasing it.

The **SirCam worm** arrived as email with a random subject line that was identical to the attached filename and purported to be sent by a friend. Once activated, SirCam randomly attached itself to a document on the user's hard drive. It then sent that document to everyone in the user's email address book. SirCam was responsible for leaking corporate documents, password files, and even official FBI documents. The consequences of this type of intrusion are alarming since distribution of a confidential document might cause injury or harm and become the basis for a claim by the injured party. Regardless of whether or not a firm faces liability actions, the exposure power of SirCam for any organization with sensitive documents could adversely affect client relations or public image.

The **Anna Kournikova** email worm was created and sent by Jan de Wit, a 21-year-old Dutchman. De Wit was charged with spreading data via a computer network with the intent to cause damage, a crime punishable by four years in prison and a maximum fine of $40,000. His sentence for unleashing the Kournikova worm was 150 hours of community service. De Wit had used a worm-making tool kit to create Kournikova,

<CYBERBRIEF>

RAPID GROWTH IN INFECTION RATE OF MALWARE

The antivirus firm MessageLabs detected 50,000 copies of SirCam throughout all of November 2001. By contrast, within only 24 hours of Goner's appearance in December 2001, 40,000 copies of it were detected.

Source: McAuliffe, Wendy. "2001: The Year of the Virus." *ZDNet UK.* http://news.zdnet.co.uk/story/0,,t269-s2101493,,00.html

which spread rapidly under the guise of an email image of the Russian tennis star in February 2001. At his trial, De Wit claimed that he did not know what he was doing nor what the consequences of posting the virus in an Internet newsgroup could be. The judges did not believe his story since it was discovered that De Wit possessed over 7,200 computer viruses.[8]

Trojan Horses   The term "Trojan horse" is borrowed from Homer's *The Iliad*. For 10 years the Greeks besieged the walls of Troy, but could not break in. They finally resorted to a ruse and constructed a huge wooden horse that was too large to fit through the gates of Troy. The Trojans were enticed into bringing the spectacular horse statue into their city and tore down a portion of their protective wall. At night, the Greeks hiding in the horse came out and opened the gates for their comrades, who then destroyed Troy.

Like its namesake, a malware Trojan is an enticing, harmless-looking software program that can damage or destroy computers or steal information from them. Trojans can be sent as email attachments, as was Klez. When the recipient highlights or opens the infected email message, the stealth trojan can invisibly install itself on the computer. The speed with which worms can spread across the Internet makes them ideal delivery mechanisms for setting up Trojans on a network of PCs, which later can be exploited to launch coordinated cyber attacks.

Beginning in 2002, MessageLabs noticed a marked increase in crackers emailing Trojans in direct attacks against users. Although these attacks were relatively small in number, they signified a disturbing trend in malware.[9]

Backdoors   The most dangerous Trojans give the sender complete access and control over the PC or network that it has infected through a backdoor. Backdoors are used for quick remote access because they circumvent most security defenses, as was discussed in the section on sophisticated hackers.

The Back Orifice is one of many backdoor programs that attackers have used to access a computer system without anyone's knowledge or consent. Back Orifice 2000 allows complete remote administrative control of infected Windows 95/98/NT computers.[10]

Backdoors can be used to send unauthorized email, including altering files on the corporate network and then sending them as official documents. If a firm has not safeguarded against Trojans and backdoors being installed on its systems and becomes infected with a Trojan that enabled hackers to launch a cyber attack against other companies, the firm would not have a tenable defense against negligence.[11]

Web Hoaxes and Other Ruses   Many Internet users were caught up in the hype of the Xbox Web hoax, which tricked them into installing a Trojan horse on their PC.[12] A Trojan masqueraded as an Xbox emulator for the PC. What is most amazing is that there was no such thing as an Xbox. But widespread hype about the Xbox, together with Internet trickery, created strong demand among users who believed they were downloading an Xbox emulator. In reality, they were downloading a file called "EMU_xbox.exe," which installed a Trojan on their PCs. Once installed, the Trojan connected to a number of remote servers.

Malicious code can also be spread when users visit infected Web pages. In these incidents, users receive email that itself does not contain malicious code, but whose contents have links to malicious Websites. When those Websites are visited, it activates stealth downloads of destructive code to the visitor's PC.

These and other successful social engineering tricks show how amazingly simple it is to lure untrained users into actions that compromise or defeat an organization's security effort.

INTERNAL THREATS AND VULNERABILITIES

People—The Human Factor

Intrusions that are both deliberate and directed against organizations are on the increase. Most notably, those intrusions involve theft of customer or financial records, alteration or destruction of data, or acts of malice against network operations. As reported in numerous surveys and by the media, corporations lose millions of dollars every year to data theft. The question that every organization needs to address is: Who is actually stealing the data or secrets and for what purpose? Increasingly, it is not hackers, but company insiders who do the stealing. And their purpose is often some combination of resale to others, extortion, fraud, or retaliation.

Current and Former Managers and Employees   Surveys by computer security consulting companies @Stake and KPMG found that users' lack of knowledge was the single greatest cause of network security breaches, making employees the major source of risk.[13] Company workers caused almost half of the most serious security incidents that businesses suffered during 2001.[14] The same is true in the physical world. The *2001 National Retail Security Survey* indicated that employees stole more than shoplifters. Employee theft was responsible for over 46% of inventory shrinkage, which was far more than the 31% rate of theft by shoplifters.

Angry workers and disgruntled employees can access and destroy data, causing huge damages. The increased number of corporate sabotage incidents is attributed to former employees. Some studies report that as many as 70% of attacks are executed by someone within the organization or with inside information. The *Information Security Breaches Survey 2002* found that in small companies, 32% of the worst incidents were caused by insiders; in large companies, 48% of the worst incidents were caused by insiders. That survey was sponsored by the U.K. government's Department of Trade and Industry and prepared by PricewaterhouseCoopers.[15]

> **@LERT**
> Internal attacks can be extremely damaging because employees
> (insiders) typically have access and insight into where sensitive and
> important data reside. But company insiders and authorized users can
> be held legally liable for intentional damage to a protected computer
> regardless of whether or not the user had authorization to access the
> protected computer.

Problems in Dealing with Internal Threats   While most network administrators
(admins) diligently protect their networks from external attacks, they often disregard
the greater threat of internal attacks or malfeasance. This disregard is understandable,
particularly if network admins do not have senior management support. Unless
effective policies are in place, there is little basis for the rules most technology defenses
use to detect these potential threats or fraud.

Dealing with internal threats can be delicate, tricky to manage, and possibly offensive. The dilemma is that it is difficult to treat employees as though they are not
trusted, even though they *must not* be trusted. The following list of internal threats and
vulnerabilities stemming from employees or other insiders validates the need for initiatives for safer computing.

Internal threats stemming from employees or other insiders
- Using weak passwords or no password protection on network accounts, email, or
  portable devices.
- Allowing users access privileges they do not need to fulfill their job
  responsibilities.
- Allowing family or friends to use company email or network accounts.
- Using instant messaging (IM). Most popular and free IM applications do not use a
  secure layer for text messages, meaning that anyone could intercept and read
  those messages outside the corporate firewall.
- Using wireless devices and networks without encryption.
- Logging into the network remotely without AV and firewall protection on the
  remote computer. Using **broadband** (high-speed) connections from home to the
  office or **Virtual Private Network (VPN)** software without a firewall on the
  remote computer is dangerous. While VPN creates an encrypted "tunnel"
  between the computers to keep the data safe in transit, part of the broadband is
  not secure and open to viruses or other attacks.
- Abusing Internet access for Web surfing to potentially insecure Websites.
- Sending or forwarding potentially offensive jokes, indecent material, or harassing
  gossip, thus creating a hostile workplace environment.
- Using company email accounts for nonbusiness purposes, such as subscribing to
  external email distribution lists **(listservs),** participating in chat rooms or Usenet
  groups, or registering for contests, travel or financial news, adult content,
  auctions, etc.

⟨ **CYBERBRIEFS** ⟩

INSIDER THREATS

- Defense contractor Lockheed Martin's email system crashed for six hours after an employee sent 60,000 co-workers a personal email message containing a confirmation request. Lockheed, which posts 40 million emails each month, was forced to fly in a Microsoft rescue squad to repair the damage.
- A Hewlett-Packard (HP) employee sabotaged tests of a new HP computer server, giving it lower performance results. It cost millions of dollars in resources and lost sales, according to a lawsuit filed by HP. Just before he was fired, the employee reformatted important computer disks, cut cables to the test computer, and altered logs to hide his acts. HP also alleges that the employee copied email records, accessed private computer systems, and transferred confidential information outside the company. HP spent more than $1 million fixing the problems.
- A New York-suburb branch manager for H&R Block was indicted with three accomplices in an identity theft scheme. Personal information for 27 individuals from the branch tax return database was used to open bogus credit card accounts, which were then tapped using ATM machines. Card account statements and tax refund checks were redirected to the identity thieves using change-of-address notices filed with the Postal Service.

Sources: Huffman, Lisa, and James Hamilton. "Employee Revenge." June 4, 2002. http://www.techtv.com/cybercrime/features/story/0,23008,3386967,00.html; Hanley, Robert. "Former H&R Block Manager Accused in Identity-Theft Ring." *The New York Times.* January 3, 2003.

- Opening unexpected email attachments, particularly from unknown senders.
- Using the "reply all" feature to respond to email carelessly or inappropriately.
- Using **telnet** (a program that lets users connect to other computers on the Internet). Telnet passes (sends) usernames and passwords in **clear text** (unencrypted) so it is easy to **sniff,** or monitor, as it travels over the Internet.
- Listing the systems administrator's name, email address (which is also his/her username), and other contact information when the company Website is registered. This information is available to everyone who does a search of the company's domain name in the **Whois database**.
- Allowing employees to use **peer-to-peer (P2P)** file-sharing networks, such as **KaZaa** and **Gnutella**. Many KaZaa users were infected by the Benjamin worm disguised as popular film, song, and game titles.[16] Gnutella users also suffered similar virus threats. The Trojan **SubSeven** was rampant in those networks and could open company networks to backdoor script kiddie attacks. The danger of allowing employees to use P2P file-sharing networks also encourages the hosting of illegal copies of copyrighted material.

WIRELESS THREATS AND VULNERABILITIES

The requirement to provide ubiquitous access to enterprise information has led to the support of remote wireline and wireless access to private networks, email systems, intranets, and databases from laptops, public terminals, and handheld devices. This trend toward portability of information has heightened the risk of exposure by several orders of magnitude.

There has been widespread adoption of wireless networks throughout corporate America, but it has come without sufficient attention to protection against their inherent weaknesses. Many firms have rolled out their wireless networks so quickly or under such time demands that wireless security issues were neglected.

Wireless networking is especially vulnerable because the current technology standard is insecure by design. In a large-scale test of urban wireless networks done by Riptech, experts could not find a corporate wireless network they *could not* break into. This is an open invitation to intrusion.

Hackers are spying on corporate wireless networks, scanning email and documents. Next, they will be stealing data or using attack tools, or malicious software, to take down networks.[17] Hackers can breach a company's unguarded wireless network simply by sitting nearby (e.g., in the parking lot) with a laptop equipped with an antenna to pick up radio signals that transmit company data.

EXTERNAL THREATS WITH INTERNAL INTERVENTION

In this classification, the external attack is able to occur because of inadvertent or deliberate help from insiders. There have been many examples of this type of intrusion throughout these chapters. Typically, these intrusions involve social engineering. But they also can result from passwords written on notes visible to others or having too much information revealed on company Websites.

Social Engineering

Most expert hackers depend on employees to inadvertently help them attack company networks or databases through social engineering techniques. Social engineering is, in effect, a network intrusion technique based on trickery. Hackers use it to fool someone into revealing access codes, passwords, or other confidential information and then break into a system. Basically, it is an elaborate term for fraudulently obtaining information to gain access.

Websites are also an outstanding resource for hackers. Telephone numbers, job responsibilities, and email addresses—which tend to double as account usernames—of employees and admins are often listed on company Websites. Those disclosures are a blatant security risk.

Social engineering works most easily where people do not know each other well. Organizations with high staff turnover are generally at greater risk than those with staff longevity. People who have worked together over time become familiar with the normal responsibilities and work patterns of their peers. Deviation from normal behavior is easier to notice. Employees of long standing tend to be more loyal and protective of company property, and more suspicious of outsiders.

Some of the most notorious and successful hackers, such as **Kevin Mitnick,** not to mention unscrupulous private investigators, rely most heavily on social engineering over technology to access private data. Mitnick had been under strict probation until

2003 after being released from federal prison in 2000. He had been arrested in 1995, barred from contact with computers, and not allowed to access the Internet for eight years. He was accused of costing companies millions of dollars by stealing software and altering computer information. His victims included Motorola, Novell, Nokia, and Sun Microsystems.

Whois Database of Domain Names

Another hacker standard for inside information is the Whois database. Whois is an online database of domain names that can be queried by anyone to find out information or identities of the owners of those domain names. The database reveals information such as company domains, networks, and host servers. Also listed are the name, address, telephone, fax, and email of the administrator of each domain. The data revealed by Whois is commonly used for social engineering or to gain access to the system administrator's network account. The data that is provided when registering a domain name is a serious security leak. It can be avoided by using generic email (e.g., info@companyname.com) and other indirect contact information.

@LERT

According to the CERT® Coordination Center at Carnegie Mellon University, the number of reported computer intrusions, including worms and hacker attacks, soared from 3,734 in 1998 to 82,094 in 2003 as more computers were linked to the Internet.

INTERNET PROTOCOL VULNERABILITIES AND THREATS

It is well established that the Internet, the world's most popular network, is highly vulnerable. A major weakness is its susceptibility to **Internet protocol (IP) forgery.**

IP Address Forgery

IP addresses, like physical addresses, are used as the basis for delivering information across the Internet. The IP provides for only two functions. It defines a **datagram** that can be routed through the Internet, and provides a means for fragmenting those datagrams into **packets** for transport across the Internet and then reassemble them into the original datagrams at the destination computer. As such, the IP is specifically limited in scope to provide only the functions necessary to deliver a package of bits (datagram) from a source computer to a destination computer over an interconnected system of networks.

Note that there are no mechanisms to ensure end-to-end data reliability, flow control, sequencing, or other services commonly found in host-to-host protocols. That is the inherent cause of the Internet's vulnerability.

Figure 3.5 represents an IP datagram, which is generally referred to as a packet. Note that the fourth line of the description calls for the Source Address of the packet. In the simplest form of IP address forgery, the forger only needs to create a packet that contains a false Source Address and insert it into the Internet. This is

Version	Header version	Type of Service	Length, in bytes	
Identification			Flag	Fragment Offset
Time to Live		Protocol	Header Checksum	
Source IP Address				
Destination IP Address				
Options			Padding	
DATA (variable length)				

FIGURE 3.5
Components of an Internet Protocol (IP) Packet

Source: Shinder, Debra Littlejohn. *Computer Networking Essentials.*
Indianapolis, IN: Cisco Press, 2001, p. 249.

done by writing the packet into the output device that is used to send information out to the Internet. For the nonexpert forger, there is a tool called **iptest,** which is part of the free and publicly available ipfilter security package that automatically forges packets for the purpose of testing configurations or routers and other IP security setups.

The infrastructure of the Internet consists primarily of a set of gateway computers and packet routers. These systems have multiple hardware interfaces. They maintain routing tables to let them decide which output interface to send a packet out on, based on the input interface that it came in on, and the destination IP address specified in the packet. When a forged packet arrives at a gateway or router, it will faithfully route the packet toward the destination address, exactly as it would a legitimate packet.

How Can IP Address Forgery Be Used?

Fundamentally, IP address forgery is a method of deception, and thus it can be used in much the same way as other forms of deception. Some ways IP address forgery might be used are:

- *To Conceal:* IP address forgery is commonly used to conceal the identity of an attacker, especially in DOS attacks.
- *To Camouflage:* IP address forgery is used to make one site appear to be another as a way to convince the victim that an attack is from a legitimate source when it might be from an intruder, such as a competitor.
- *To Deceive:* IP address forgery can be used to trick the victim into believing that an intrusion is somewhere else. This is a way to misdirect the victimized organization into wasting limited resources.

SUCCESS OF HACKERS AND MALWARE

Massive investments in perimeter defenses, such as firewalls and IDS, have failed to protect even the leading high-tech companies from significant losses due to hackers. Citibank, Microsoft, Visa International, Amazon.com, E-Trade, and Western Union Financial Services Inc. have all been victims. When hackers revealed the credit card and debit card numbers of 16,000 of Western Union online customers, it brought attention to the risks of eCommerce.

The hackers, including Ivanov and Gorshkov, who launched DOS attacks against the Websites of Amazon.com, Buy.com, CNN, eBay, Excite, and Yahoo!, had used university computers. Today, hackers and virus creators use all types of networks to orchestrate their attacks—commercial, educational, government, and personal.

INTRUDERS EXPAND THEIR OPTIONS

Hackers have also expanded into other types of systems that they exploit, such as **PBX (private branch exchange)** and voicemail systems. A PBX is a private telephone network operated by an organization. PBX—or voicemail—hackers can steal trade secrets or competitive information, expose financial data or employee information, exploit customer billing and credit data, or shut down voicemail entirely. These risks are easily underestimated. Think about how much vital secret data is transmitted over phone lines in business.[18] PBXs, voicemail, voice-response units, and other network devices can all retain and expose information for use in fraud or extortion attempts.

COMPLEXITY OF SOFTWARE AND CONFIGURATIONS

There is considerable overlap and synergy between malware and human threats. This exacerbates information security risks. Much of the success of malicious programs, however, can be attributed to faulty software and the settings used in the installation of that software. IT professionals know that the first step in securing a system is to configure it to comply with company policies and install only what is needed. Yet there are many services installed using the default settings. Since the values of default passwords are widely known (e.g., the default username and password for network administration rights may be "*admin*"), they become an excellent educated guess for would-be intruders. The result is a state that is highly vulnerable to the malware threats described next.

WHY HACK ATTACKS SUCCEED SO OFTEN

Network Security Technologies and Internet Security Systems (ISS) report that there's almost a 100% success rate with social engineering.[19] Social engineering enabled crackers to break into user accounts at America Online. The breaches were caused by the most basic of procedural lapses— customer service representatives who failed to get adequate proof of identity from people phoning in.[20]

The reasons why many hacker attacks succeed represent the entire range from simple to sophisticated.

- Cross-organizational security is complex, expensive, and not an overriding priority.
- Firewalls and security systems "out of the box" are easy to set up, but they don't protect until they've been configured correctly.

- Companies have poor intrusion detection due to lack of expertise or sloppy administration.
- Cyber security systems degrade over time because software gets out of date. The flaws of old software are well known to hackers, who can play on them to crash a system or gain access to confidential data.
- Changes to production systems or upgrades that are unknown to security administrators and that go unprotected as a result.
- Many administrators don't keep up with the latest updates. Most hacks that CERT® hears about would have been prevented if the advisories had been followed. Also, CERT® doesn't know about hacks until after they have happened.
- After a hacker attacks, most ecommerce Websites do not change the way they do business.

THREATS, VULNERABILITIES, AND FIRST-PARTY AND THIRD-PARTY RISKS

There are two types of risks that need to be taken into consideration. These are **first-party risks,** which concern the company itself; and **third-party risks,** which are threats to the company's customers, suppliers, business partners, or competitors that may seek legal redress by lawsuit. A breach of professional service, breach of contract, or security negligence may be a cause of action and source of potential legal liability. Details of these risks are as follows:

FIRST-PARTY RISKS

- Risks to company information assets, such as the theft of customer data, proprietary business processes, and internally or custom-developed software applications.
- Business interruption risks, including attacks to ecommerce Websites or destruction of critical data.
- Fraud, efraud, and other computer-mediated crimes, such as disbursement fraud, embezzlement, theft, or misuse of **digital certificates** or **digital signatures** (dig sigs). A digital signature is the equivalent of a physical signature on a document or message. It verifies that the encrypted message or document originated from the person whose signature is attached to it. Digital signatures issued by a company are also referred to as digital certificates.

THIRD-PARTY RISKS

- Risks related to the infringement of intellectual property rights.
- Risk of loss incurred by customers or trading partners due to your online service disruptions.
- Risks related to privacy violations, such as theft or unauthorized disclosure of confidential information.
- Risks from the propagation of cyber attacks through the information systems of customers and partners.
- Liability risks related to Websites, email, or other media.

FIRST- AND THIRD-PARTY DAMAGES

Not only are potential legal damages high, so are the damages due to customers' resentment and bad publicity. Consider what happened to Eli Lilly Inc., held liable for the unauthorized disclosure of sensitive personal information. From March 2000 to June 2001, Lilly offered a Medi-messenger email reminder service for their Prozac customers. Customers who used Medi-messenger received personal email messages to remind them to take or refill their antidepression medication. But on June 27, an employee unintentionally disclosed personal information of Prozac users. That privacy breach led to an FTC complaint. The FTC alleged that Lilly's claim of privacy and confidentiality was deceptive because the company failed to maintain or implement appropriate internal measures to protect consumer information.

Chapter Summary

The TTV offers a classification system for identifying threats and vulnerabilities to intrusions and intruders. It highlights many cyber security risks that are often overlooked by organizations. The TTV helps build the business case for investments in a comprehensive defensive infrastructure.

The issues that get great media attention— hackers, viruses, and Net attacks— represent only one dimension of business risks. Hackers, while a very serious threat, are not typically a company's greatest security threat. Employees' actions, deliberate or mistaken, easily rival the damage done by hackers. Employees are the greatest financial risk, and as is always the case with people, the best defenses are education, training, forewarnings, and persuasive compliance incentives.

Although technology attracts most of the attention and investment in IT security, people and their behavior play an equally important role in the overall risk profile of any enterprise.

Repeatedly, the most expensive and elaborate security measures have been undone by a company's failure to get employees to observe relatively basic precautions.

A cyber defense system is weak, possibly useless, unless all users are made acutely aware of

- The importance of computer security to be able both to do and keep their jobs.
- Hackers, hired hackers or industrial spies, ruthless marketers, or other employees who might try and

manipulate them to gain access to organizational networks or reveal confidential information.

- Management's commitment to strict enforcement procedures, including penalties for noncompliance.
- System administrators' commitment to monitor management's strict enforcement procedures.

Key Terms

- vulnerabilities
- exploit
- Taxonomy of Threats and Vulnerabilities (TTV)
- Klez worm
- payload
- SQL Slammer
- sapphire
- patched
- SMTP (Simple Mail Transfer Protocol)
- Microsoft SQL Server 2000
- Intrusion Detection System (IDS)
- buffer overflow
- IIS (Internet Information Server)
- application level

- remote and local exploit tools
- privileged access
- root access
- hidden directory
- root tool kits
- log file cleaners
- sniffer
- propagation mechanism
- checksum
- application viruses
- Linux worm
- Melissa Virus
- SirCam worm
- Anna Kournikova
- back orifice
- broadband
- Virtual Private Network (VPN)

- Listservs
- Telnet
- clear text
- Whois database
- Peer-to-peer (P2P)
- KaZaa
- Gnutella
- SubSeven
- Internet Protocol (IP) forgery
- datagram
- packet
- Iptest
- PBX (private branch exchange)
- first-party risks
- third-party risks
- digital certificates
- digital signatures

Discussion Questions

1. Research and classify at least five recent threats and vulnerabilities according to the TTV. Which category do most threats and vulnerabilities fit into?
2. Search for Websites that provide detailed descriptions of tools to help secure a system and deter break-ins. Examples include http://www.cert.org/tech_tips/security_tools.html or http://www.foundstone.com/rdlabs/proddesc/ntlast.html, Describe those tools and their strengths and weaknesses.
3. Since email attachments are so potentially dangerous, why don't organizations prohibit them altogether? How might users be motivated to not open email attachments?
4. What or who are the most potentially dangerous internal and external threats to an organization? How might those threats be minimized?
5. Describe the differences among a virus, worm, and Trojan. Which of these types of malware can be the most dangerous to a company? Why?
6. How can malware pass through AV software or IDS undetected? What can be done to prevent malware from infecting a network?

7. Why should users be concerned about IP address forgery? What are some ways to protect against it?

8. Distinguish between first-party risks and third-party risks. Give two security breach examples of each.

9. Check the information that is revealed in the Whois database for four organizations. (It can be found by doing an Internet search for Whois database.) What security risks do you recognize? What information should be listed in the Whois database instead?

Endnotes

1. O'Harrow, Jr., Robert, and Ariana Eunjung Cha. "Internet Worm Unearths New Holes; Attack Reveals Flaws in How Critical Systems Are Connected." *The Washington Post.* January 29, 2003. P. A01.

2. Hafner, Katie, and John Briggs,. "In Net Attacks, Defining the Right to Know." *The New York Times.* January 30, 2003. (G) P. 1.

3. Lebihan, Rachel. "Business Braced For Worm Onslaught." *Australian Financial Review.* January 28, 2003. P. 29.

4. McHugh, John, Alan Christie, and Julia Allen. "Defending Yourself: The Role of Intrusion Detection Systems." *IEEE Software.* September/October 2000. P. 42.

5. "Technology; Group Test; Intrusion Detection Systems." *Network News.* March 27, 2002. P. 19.

6. Henry-Stocker, Sandra. "Analysis: Understanding Viruses." *CNN.* January 2001. http://www.cnn.com/2001/TECH/ computing/01/30/understanding.viruses.idg/ index.html

7. Lee, Chris. "US Approves Tougher Cybercrime Penalties." May 9, 2002. http://www.vnunet.com/News/1131635.

8. Evers, Joris. "'Kournikova' Virus Writer Appeals Sentence." May 6, 2002. http://europe.cnn.com/2002/TECH/ internet/05/06/kournikova.sentence.idg/ index.html

9. http://www.theregister.co.uk/ content/56/28585.html

10. http://www.iss.net/security_center/ static/2343.php

11. For the latest backdoor threats and vulnerabilities, visit the Internet Security Systems (ISS) Website at http://www.iss.net or https://gtoc.iss.net/

12. Middleton, James. "Xbox Web Hoax Installs Trojan Horse." May 10, 2002. http://www.vnunet.com/

13. Knight, Will. "Staff Oblivious to Computer Security Threats." May 2, 2001. http://news.nwfusion.com/newsletters/file-share/2001/00768553.html

14. Ward, Mark. "Employees Seen as Computer Saboteurs." *BBC News Online.* April 29, 2002.

15. Loney, Matt. "Your Worst Security Threat: Employees?" ZDNet (UK). April 23, 2002. http://zdnet.com.com/ 2100-1105-889542.html

16. Vamosi, Robert. "Instant Messaging: The Next Hacker Target." *Anchor Desk.com.* May 29, 2002.

17. Iwata, Edward. "Hackers Scope Out New Prey: Wireless Users." *USA Today.* July 16, 2001. http://www.newsbytes.com/news/01/ 167981.html

18. Jainschigg, John. "Securing Your Switch; Your Phone System and Its Peripherals May Be an Achilles Heel." *Communications Convergence.* Vol. 10. No. 4. April 1, 2002. P. 55.

19. http://www.iss.net/

20. Oram, Andy. "Cyber Hygience, Not Cyber Fortress Protects Our Networks." June 2, 1998. American Reporter. http://www.oreilly.com/~andyo/ar/ cyber_hygiene.html

CHAPTER 4
AN AFFIRMATIVE MODEL OF DEFENSE: DIGITAL LIABILITY MANAGEMENT

Learning Objectives

◆ Understanding the need for a preemptive defense.

◆ The digital liability management model and methodology.

◆ Benefits of the top-down approach to implementation.

◆ The role of people, process, and technology in security.

◆ Practical application of the DLM defense model.

INTRODUCTION

This chapter presents the four defensive tiers of the digital liability management (DLM) model. Those tiers are senior management support, acceptable-use policies, secure-use procedures, and technology tools. The objective of this approach is to protect against the occurrence of intrusion and incidents—and to provide an affirmative defense when they occur. These defenses are organizational solutions to the challenges posed by the threats and vulnerabilities that were outlined in the TTV discussed in Chapter 3.

DLM is a top-down model in which the first tier emphasizes the need for the highest-ranking members of the organization to think through the importance of information security to the overall business plan. This approach is needed to align the information security plan and objectives with those of the organization as a whole. Once this is achieved and well communicated, the actual implementation of the security plan's policies, practices, and technology can begin.

THE INFORMATION SECURITY CHALLENGE IS NOT BEING MET

Despite substantial progress, the information security challenge is not being met effectively. The problem stems from the limitations of technology and vulnerabilities of networks, lack of executive support, and lack of understanding of the true cost of resource requirements.[2]

Information security strategies that are either technology-centric or policy-centric will fail. Technology-centric strategies are weak without strong policies and practices. Policy-centric strategies are ineffective without technology to monitor and enforce them. What is needed is a comprehensive multifaceted approach based on senior

CASE ON POINT

U.S. CHARGES ENGINEER WITH COMPUTER INTRUSION AND DESTRUCTION OF A DATABASE

Richard Eitelberg was arrested and charged in Manhattan federal court with the unauthorized invasion of the computer network of his former employer, MP Limited LLC, an apparel manufacturer based in Manhattan.[1]

According to the federal complaint, Eitelberg was hired as the controller at MP in September 2001. He was given the password to remotely access the MP computer system from his home. On that system, MP manages various business databases, including its customers' orders.

On February 1, 2002, Eitelberg stopped working at MP. On April 11, 2002, an MP employee accessed the customer orders database and found that the records of all of MP's orders were gone. The computer records allegedly indicated that someone accessed the MP computer system using a password from about 9:21 PM until about 9:46 PM April 10, 2002, and that orders in the database were deleted during that session.

The complaint also stated that AT&T phone records indicated that between February 27, 2002, and April 10, 2002, the phone line registered to the wife of Eitelberg and located at the Eitelberg residence was used to call MP's modem connection approximately 13 times, including the call made at about 9:24 PM on April 10, 2002. Eitelberg's computer account at MP had not been terminated, allowing him continued access.

management support, policy, process, and technology, because all play a vital role in the proper execution of the program.

THE IMPORTANCE OF EXECUTION

Anyone doing business in the twenty-first century knows that one of the current watchwords of commerce is **execution.** According to a widely reprinted *Harvard Business Review* article, most companies do not fail for lack of talent or strategic

CYBERBRIEF

RECENT INFORMATION SECURITY NEWS HEADLINES

- "Cost of Cyberattacks Rises Sharply"
- "Worldwide Corporations Compromise on IT Security"
- "Security Training Still a Business Afterthought"
- "Little Corporate Emphasis on Security Post-9/11"
- "Configuration Errors Still Prevalent"
- "Corporate Attacks by Insiders Deemed the Most Dangerous"
- "Government Agencies Fail Computer Security Review"

Sources: USAtoday.com; Computerworld.com; informationweek.com

---

⟨ **CYBERBRIEF** ⟩

TOP MOST-STOLEN DIGITAL ASSETS

The top digital assets that are stolen from firms include financial statistics, research and development data, strategic plans, and customer lists, according to the results of a survey of 138 companies, including both Fortune 1000 and small and midsize businesses, conducted by ASIS and PricewaterhouseCoopers.

Source: "Trends in Proprietary Information Loss." http://www.asisonline.org/pdf/spi2.pdf

---

vision, but rather for lack of execution.[3] Execution refers to how effectively the firm's strategic vision is communicated to its employees and customers and how that message changes behavior to effect a positive financial result over time. Successful execution is the end result of performing multidisciplinary tasks effectively.

HALLMARKS OF PROPER EXECUTION

The hallmarks of proper execution that are needed for security initiatives are the following:

- A clear and powerful mandate from the senior leaders of the organization.
- Communication and adoption of the strategic vision from senior management throughout every level of the organization.
- A commitment to continuous two-way communication about policy and procedures.
- An ongoing commitment to training employees about policies, practices, and procedures.
- A system that monitors compliance with security practices.
- Prudent investment in technology to implement and enforce best practices.

THE RISK AND REWARD OF NEW INITIATIVES

Popular strategic business initiatives, such as **Total Quality Management (TQM)** and **Customer Relationship Management (CRM),** have several things in common. While they require significant investment up front, they will alter the way many employees perform their jobs, and they can encounter significant resistance. Too often, they fail, but when they are executed correctly, they can produce spectacular results.

The fiercely competitive 1990s placed a high value on profitable delivery of superior products and customer services. This remains the case, but reaction to current events is adding several new standards, namely security, integrity, and privacy. A survey of 8,100 global technology and security professionals polled by *InformationWeek* indicates that these standards are far from becoming universal. The survey found that only 18% report intrusions to watchdogs such as CERT® or government authorities, while only 14% inform their business partners when there is a security lapse.

⟨ **CYBERBRIEF** ⟩

SECURITY IN THE DIGITAL WORLD VS. THE PHYSICAL WORLD

If the typical information security strategy were applied to the physical security world at a bank, "we would wind up with a large building equipped with titanium reinforced doors. However, those doors would remain ajar, and burglar alarms would squawk at every tenth customer. Inside would be tables piled high with cash, appropriately marked 'please do not touch.'"

Source: Shipley, Greg. "Secure To The Core." *Network Computing.* January 23, 2003. P. 34.

HIGHER STANDARDS OF SECURITY

There is ample evidence that investors, regulators, customers, and partners are demanding that companies they associate with initiate and maintain higher standards of security and integrity with regard to digital assets and confidential information. Fines for inadequate security and failures can be expensive. In 2001, subscriber data that included credit card numbers were stolen from one of Ziff Davis's (ZD) magazine promotion Websites. New York State Attorney General Eliot Spitzer found ZD's privacy policy and interpretation of "reasonable security controls" inadequate. As part of the agreement in August 2002, ZD paid $100,000 in state fines and $500 per credit card lost, ok payable to the victims.[4]

WHY IS INFORMATION SECURITY POORLY EXECUTED?

Given the current business climate, why do investments in information security and the management of digital assets remain largely misunderstood, underfinanced, and most of all, poorly executed? The problem is that most of them are lacking in one or more of the essential ingredients of effective execution.

In a cost-conscious economy, organizations need more effective security controls, not more expensive ones. The most common mistake is to address the issue by funding the acquisition of technology defenses championed by IT staff in a knee-jerk response to a well-publicized threat or intrusion. This approach is problematic for several reasons.

- It shows little senior management commitment.
- It has no specific economic justification.
- It requires little or no active participation from employees.
- It often gets defeated by faulty configuration of the tools, neglected maintenance, or a process failure, such as the failure to close out the network IDs of terminated employees, as described in the opening case of this chapter.

THE DLM DEFENSE MODEL

The DLM defense model lays out a four-tiered approach to cyber security that raises the discipline from a *technology tactic* to the higher standards that are applied to a *strategic business initiative.* The four tiers, each of which is addressed in detail in subsequent chapters, are designed to ensure that all of the elements of successful execution are addressed.

Some of the milestones within the DLM approach include:

- Email and Internet-use AUPs.
- Secure-use practices.
- Monitoring and enforcement of compliance with AUPs and secure-use practices.
- Guidelines for a technology architecture.
- Intrusion response protocols.
- Periodic audits to validate that policies and procedures are being followed.

The proactive nature and documentation provided by the DLM approach are clear evidence that the business is managing the risks inherent in networked business transactions.

With increasing legal and regulatory actions, that evidence is a necessary defense in the event of litigation. Organizations that continue to operate with negligent controls can expect to face lawsuits, significant financial loss, negative publicity, and reduced customer confidence. Furthermore, information security efforts should be audited externally. The importance of this effort is described by Theodore Claypoole, an attorney and former legal counsel for Bank of America and CompuServe. He stated: "If you have a third party come in and review [your information security], then it helps prove your case. You can say, 'Look, we spent money to have a reputable company review our procedures; we took those suggestions, and we made those changes.'"[5]

THE DLM MODEL

The DLM Defense model (see Table 4.1) describes the four key components of an affirmative defense as a tiered structure. Each tier is discussed in detail in later chapters, but they are covered here in brief.

TIER 1: SENIOR MANAGEMENT COMMITMENT AND SUPPORT

The first tier of the model focuses on senior management commitment and support in building a strong mandate for necessary security changes and investments. Senior management needs to send an emphatic and visible message that information security and

TABLE 4.1	DLM Defense Infrastructure
Tier 1	Senior management commitment and support
Tier 2	Acceptable use policies and other statements of practice
Tier 3	Secure use procedures
Tier 4	Hardware, software, and network security tools

> **Intranet/Portal Application Programmer**
>
> Requires basic concepts of Web application development, Working knowledge of XML, Working knowledge of Oracle Applications and Databases, Understanding of SEI CMM Level II/III, Programming in Sun UNIX Environment.

FIGURE 4.1
Too Much Information Revealed in Monster.com Help-Wanted Ad

Source: Monster.com Online Ads. http://www.monster.com

digital risk management are core values and vital to all aspects of the business. They also need to set examples of acceptable use. Employees and staff cannot be expected to change their behavior if they do not observe respect for security concerns among their superiors.

By virtue of their responsibilities, senior executives tend to have access to the most sensitive information and are often in a position to be compromised. They approve company Websites that often include news of major projects, merger and acquisition activities, expansion plans, personnel names, and other information that hackers can use to guide their attacks.

They invest in **data warehouse** initiatives that are designed to provide integrated access to information about customers, finances, and operations. Because data warehouse applications are often not considered mission-critical, they might not be designed with sufficient security safeguards. This is something hackers know and look to take advantage of when these projects are publicized.

Even Help-Wanted ads placed in technical newsgroups or online job boards can provide useful clues for the potential network intruder, as shown in Figure 4.1. This Monster.com ad is a good example of how such ads can reveal the company's network infrastructure.

SECURITY AWARENESS BEGINS AND ENDS IN THE BOARDROOM

Information security has not been a high priority at the board level. When the mandate is to get the systems working, or integrated after a merger/acquisition, security concerns are downplayed—as hackers know. Today, however, corporate governance demands that executives undertake a duty of care to employees, customers, shareholders, and other stakeholders.

It is becoming clear to publicly held companies that cyber security has become a strategic issue to be addressed in boardrooms (see Figure 4.2). It was never a strictly technical issue that could be delegated to network administrators. If the issue does not find its way into the boardroom, the consequences most likely will.

When lawsuits occur alleging mismanagement, violation of security laws, or other wrongful acts, corporations, directors, and officers may be directly at risk. These risks can be expected to increase as U.S. security laws get tougher and compliance with privacy standards, either legislated or otherwise mandated, becomes more prevalent.

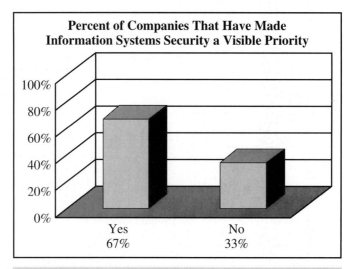

FIGURE 4.2 Priority of Information Systems Security

Source: From *Global Computer Security Survey 2002.*
http://www.redsiren.com/survey.html

OVERCOMING OBJECTIONS AND ADVERSARIES

Security Is Unpopular

Executives who have had success in implementing major strategic initiatives know that they cut across departments, force people to change the way they work, and involve complex and expensive technological challenges. This kind of organizational change requires power and patience. If it is not championed and sold by senior management, it will not happen.

Basically, the power of senior management is needed to set and maintain unpopular, nonnegotiable security practices and priorities (see Figure 4.3). Their constant support is needed to back up those responsible for eliminating bad habits, as in the situation of a network administrator who lamented: "After I reconfigured my company's password policy to disallow blank passwords, the help desk was flooded with complaints." Inconvenienced users must learn that new security procedures will not be subject to debate or their discretion. Compliance rates increase when people understand the rules, the enforcement mechanisms, and perhaps most importantly, the consequences of violation.

> **@LERT**
> One company president supported the rule that prohibited any forwarding of email originating from outside the company. Employees learned that this rule was in effect to prevent the spread of viruses, jokes, and content that might be offensive time-wasters. The penalty for violators was immediate termination. This kind of draconian enforcement is generally not required, but it did ensure immediate, universal compliance.

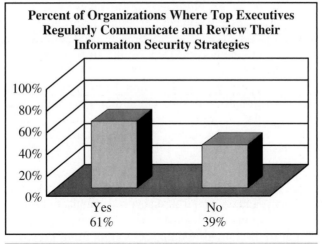

FIGURE 4.3 Executive Reviews of Information Security Strategies

Source: From *Global Computer Security Survey 2002.*
http://www.redsiren.com/survey.html

Security Requires a Strong Mediator to Resolve Conflicts

The same dynamic applies when it becomes time to allocate scarce resources in the budgeting and planning process. Good security can be expensive, and will often require funds that would otherwise go to projects with strong political support.

The computer security administrator's relationship with users and network administrators tends to be adversarial. Users want fast and unfettered access, but security measures slow down response times and limit access. Senior management needs to apply its influence proactively to decide the outcome of these power struggles.

TIER 2: ACCEPTABLE-USE POLICIES AND OTHER STATEMENTS OF PRACTICE

AUPS DEFINE ACCEPTABLE AND UNACCEPTABLE BEHAVIOR

Employers have two primary concerns in designing an effective acceptable-use policy: preventing system misuse and avoiding exposure to subsequent liability. An AUP should define the responsibilities of every user by specifying both acceptable and unacceptable actions and the consequences of noncompliance.

Email, Internet, and computer AUPs should be thought of as extensions of other, more traditional corporate policies, such as those that address equal opportunity and sexual harassment. They exist to protect the rights of employees, as well as limit the liability of the employer.

STAKEHOLDERS INVOLVED IN AUPS

All of the traditional stakeholders should be involved in writing and implementing the AUP, including human resources (HR) managers and legal counsel, who are aided by

IT and those responsible for physical security. Likewise, accountants and auditors are concerned with practices and policies pertaining to efraud. Ecommerce managers have a strong vested interest since a security breach could seriously undermine their ability to market to their customers and their ability to recruit security-conscious business partners.

Like other HR policies, an AUP should require that every employee explicitly acknowledge in writing his or her understanding and compliance with the policy.

AUPS DEFINE EXPECTATIONS AND DEMONSTRATE DUE DILIGENCE

The AUP specifies what is expected of all employees when they use company networks and computing devices, including PCs, handheld devices, telephones, voicemail, remote and wireless services, faxes, email, and access to public and private networks. AUPs set employees' expectations with regard to violation consequences and privacy.

In addition to discouraging dangerous computing practices, a well-crafted AUP demonstrates to business partners and the court, if necessary, that the company is taking a proactive stance toward digital security and risk management and that there is one set of rules that are universally applied and fairly enforced. Examples of AUPs are the topic of Chapter 6.

EVERYONE MUST PRACTICE INFORMATION SECURITY

Another best practice is to make information security part of everyone's job description whether or not they use computers routinely as part of their job function. This not only will boost their self-perceived status but will make the staff more vigilant and likely to report all suspicious behavior, not just that which is computer-related. For those who use the network routinely, making them responsible for ensuring acceptable practice creates an environment of mutual support and trust.

MAINTENANCE IS IMPORTANT

It is important to emphasize that simply having policies in place is not enough. Deficient or obsolete AUPs and practice statements put the organization at risk. The issues, regulations, and technologies surrounding security are highly dynamic. So it is reasonable to expect that companies will need to review and reissue these policy statements periodically. A recent survey of 1,000 businesses in the United Kingdom showed that only 27% had a documented security policy. Of those that did, however, 76% updated it at least annually, and 31% did so every six months.[6]

TIER 3: SECURE-USE PROCEDURES

The third tier in the DLM model is where the transition occurs from documents and statements of policy to the actual day-to-day application of policy within the context of business operations. This tier, outlined fully in Chapter 7, provides detailed examples of practices to be encouraged, as well as those to be discouraged, or totally prohibited, such as use of file-sharing networks and insecure instant messaging.

It also includes many lessons learned in the field to help plan and guide the application of policy. Much of the discussion is focused on planning and organizational activities. This is the direct result of early experience that has taught us that many information security programs have failed as a direct result of organizational issues, such as lack of a powerful sponsor and failure to directly tie the goals of the program to the strategic priorities of the business. Ongoing administrative staffing and maintenance concerns play a critical role as well. A proactive approach to testing, benchmarking, and updating defenses requires dedicated resources, but it is the only way to avoid quick obsolescence.

Secure-use procedures require a survey and evaluation of digital assets at risk, along with estimates of the probability of loss. This discipline is fundamental to all types of risk management but is rarely practiced with intangible digital assets. As a result, the value of these assets, particularly as defined by the cost of replacement, tends to be seriously underestimated, and underinsured. Underestimated replacement costs make it difficult to justify large investments in the protection of these assets.

Once the most valuable assets are identified and the areas of greatest vulnerability are located, defensive resources, as well as physical security, can be focused where the risks are greatest.

The other major area of focus in Tier 3 is preparation of the appropriate response to a major security event when it occurs. The extent of the damage from a major breach is affected by the quality of the reaction to that event. Reactions need to be immediate and properly targeted to limit exposure, damages, and legal liability.

TIER 4: HARDWARE, SOFTWARE, AND NETWORK SECURITY TOOLS

Once the strategy, policy, and practice tiers are in place, then the software, hardware, and netware defenses needed to support implementation of the policy and the enforcement of practice can be put in place. The selection of technology is a very complicated task because the market is full of immature products and devoid of universally adopted technology standards.

There are many products that address a portion of the overall set of needs, but none comprise a complete solution by themselves. In such a market, one is forced to choose between a **product suite** from one vendor that works together well but does not represent the best technology available or a combination of tools from different sources that may be superior individually but do not integrate well.

As is always the case with technology, there is no one solution. Each situation requires a complete assessment of the requirements, as defined within the top three layers of the model. In Chapter 8, we outline the basic building blocks of an information security technology architecture.

Chapter Summary

The DLM model emphasizes people, practices, and technology because all three play a vital role in the complete execution of the program. Such execution requires a clear and visible mandate from senior manage-ment that the goals and objectives of information security are completely aligned with, and essential to, those of the business as a whole. With such a mandate, and an ongoing commitment to the program, it is possible to overcome the obstacles and adversaries that often come with the implementation of rigorous security policies.

These policies, which must be documented completely and communicated frequently, define what is considered accept-able and unacceptable practice as it relates to network usage. After the policies are defined and the practices accepted, they form the basis for sound investment decisions in the technology that is available to enforce and enable them.

Key Terms

- execution
- Total Quality Management (TQM)
- Customer Relationship Management (CRM)
- data warehouse
- product suite

Discussion Questions

1. What is driving higher standards of security?
2. List some reasons why information security might be poorly executed in a large organization? In a small organization?
3. Why might it be difficult to secure adequate funding for information security? What business operations might be perceived as more important investments?
4. Where in the organization should the ultimate responsibility for information security lie? Where does it tend to be?
5. What criteria should be used to evaluate the effectiveness of a cyber security program?
6. What is the function of risk assessment and external audits?
7. What are the primary purposes of an AUP? Why should AUPs be signed by all employees?
8. What are the major barriers to the implementation of a DLM defense model?
9. Why are insiders often the greatest security threats?

Endnotes

1. Press release. http://www.cybercrime.gov/eitelbergArrest.htm
2. Shipley, Greg. "Secure To The Core." *Network Computing*. January 23, 2003. P. 34.
3. Rodgers, T. J. "No Excuses Management." *Harvard Business Review*. July/August 1990. Vol. 68, Issue 4. P. 84.
4. http://www.oag.state.ny.us/press/2002/aug/aug28a_02.html
5. Scalet, Sarah D. "See You in Court." *CIO Magazine*. November 1, 2001. http://www.cio.com/archive/110101/court.html
6. *The U.K. Dept. of Trade & Industry—PricewaterhouseCoopers Information Security Breaches Survey—2002*. P. 17.

CHAPTER 5
MODELS FOR ESTIMATING RISK AND OPTIMIZING THE RETURN ON SECURITY INVESTMENT

Learning Objectives

◆ Using risk assessment methods to estimate security investments.

◆ Categorizing risks in the Risk Assessment Cube.

◆ Calculating an expected value of loss (expected loss).

◆ Optimizing the return on investment for security.

◆ Creating a complete organizational risk profile.

INTRODUCTION

Information security is a business problem that can be assessed with the same analytic methods that are used for other business-related risks and consequences (outcomes). The purpose of **risk analysis** is to fully identify and assess risk factors, then to balance the expected costs (damages) of incidents with the cost of defenses needed to avoid incidents. The deliverable from risk analysis is a budget plan to minimize overall cost and maximize defenses.

Quantitative models are routinely used for making business decisions under conditions of risk or uncertainty. These models are **expected value,** which gauges uncertainty about the financial impact of an outcome, and **marginal analysis,** which estimates the investment in security defenses. These models form the basis for estimating the cost of a loss and appraising an organization's risk exposure. The risk analysis methods discussed in this chapter are extremely important for business and legal reasons. It shows business partners and customers that the company has identified and assessed its risk exposure and made prudent security investments. It provides rigorous documentation that a company had not been negligent.

THE IMPORTANCE OF RISK ASSESSMENT

GETTING MANAGEMENT'S ATTENTION

The factor that most gets the attention of executives is how much a security breach can directly cost a company in terms of cash, not just embarrassment. A related factor is the

◁**CASES ON POINT**▷

SABOTAGE AND RETRIBUTION AGAINST FORMER EMPLOYERS

OMEGA ENGINEERING INC.

Timothy Lloyd was a chief network program designer at Omega Engineering Inc., a manufacturer of high-tech measurement and control devices used by the U.S. Navy and NASA.[1] Lloyd had been terminated from Omega on July 10, 1996, after working for the company for approximately 11 years. In 2000, he was convicted of hiding and later detonating a software "time bomb" that deleted critical files in Omega's computer system 20 days after being fired. Once detonated, the time bomb deleted Omega's design and production programs and paralyzed its networks. Omega's damages included $10 million in lost sales and contracts.[2]

On May 9, 2000, a federal jury in Newark convicted Lloyd on one count of fraud. He was charged with intentionally causing irreparable damage to Omega's financial position by activating a time bomb that permanently deleted all of the company's sophisticated manufacturing software programs. He was sentenced to 41 months in prison. This case was one of the most expensive computer sabotage cases to date in U.S.

Secret Service history, according to Special Agent C. Danny Spriggs.

FORBES INC.

In 1997, George Parente was arrested for deliberately causing five network servers at the publishing company Forbes, Inc., to crash. Parente was a former Forbes computer technician who had been terminated from temporary employment. In what appears to have been a vengeful act against the company and his supervisors, Parente dialed into the Forbes computer system from his residence and gained access through a co-worker's log-in and password. Once online, he caused five of the eight Forbes computer network servers to crash and erased all of the server volume on each of the affected servers. No data could be restored.[3] As a result of this one act of sabotage, Forbes was forced to shut down its New York operations for two days, sustaining losses in excess of $100,000.[4] Parente pleaded guilty to one count of violating the Computer Fraud and Abuse Act, Title 18 U.S.C. 1030.

probability of those attacks. In 2001, it was estimated that up to 4,000 U.S. business Websites were victims of DOS attacks *each week*—including Microsoft, Amazon, the FBI, and Yahoo! Yahoo! suffered a $1 billion loss in its share price directly following their DOS incident.[5] The costs of recent targeted attacks are available at the U.S. government's cyber crime Website at http://www.cybercrime.gov. These actual figures help illustrate and estimate both the cost and frequency, or probability, of various types of attacks.

According to the *InformationWeek Research Global Information Security Survey,* in 2002, the amount of computer network downtime increased, more companies had outages, and those outages lasted longer.[6] In 2001, 28% of U.S. companies had not suffered downtime from attacks, and in 2002 only 16% avoided downtime. Approximately 45% of companies were able to recover within eight hours in 2002, but 39% of the companies had downtime lasting eight hours or more in 2002, which was a 13% increase from 2001.

A February 2003 report on cyber attacks published by Symantec Corp. stated that the frequency of attacks on Internet-connected machines had decreased over the past six months, but the number of software vulnerabilities continued to skyrocket. The company said it recorded more than 2,500 newly identified vulnerabilities in various software products during all of 2002, an 81.5% increase over 2001.[7]

RISK ASSESSMENT: A BASIC REQUIREMENT OF ISO 17799

There are vast differences in organizations' security needs because of differences in their size, attractiveness to attackers, and dependence on networks. These differences are explicitly recognized in the **ISO 17799,** an international standard for *best practices in information security.*[8] Risk analysis, or assessment, is a basic requirement of this standard, as is the establishment of a security policy.

ISO 17799 was introduced by the International Organization for Standardization in 2000. Its origin was British Standard 7799, which is the most widely recognized security standard in the world. All U.K. government departments have to be compliant with BS 7799 in their key business systems in 2003.[9] BS 7799 is built from a pyramid of 127 controls, starting at the top with policy based on risk.

RAISING THE STATUS OF INFORMATION SECURITY BUDGETS

Hard quantitative estimations are necessary because security administrators have difficulty getting their projects funded in the face of competing or more compelling business priorities. In the budgeting process, raising the priority of security investments is best done by calculating credible estimates of the expected loss from intrusions, negligence, or subsequent litigation, that is, by using risk management methods.

The application of risk management techniques to IT investments is an increasingly common approach. Furthermore, these techniques enable business decision makers to tackle information security policy even if they do not know very much about technology.[10]

ASSESSING THE EXPECTED (AVERAGE) COST OF A LOSS

Computer security is essentially about risk management. Before making decisions about security spending or policy rules, the first thing to do is make a hard-headed risk assessment.[11]

Expected value is a basic concept commonly used by managers to make decisions when there is uncertainty about the financial impact of an outcome,[12] such as theft of a trade secret, if some particular event should occur, e.g., a stealth network intrusion. The

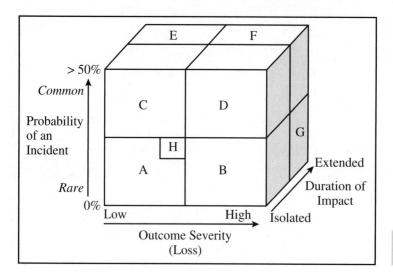

FIGURE 5.1
Risk Assessment Cube

type of expected value method that is relevant to security is **expected loss** (further discussion will follow). The expected loss model provides an important benchmark against which to assess and justify investments in digital security.

Marginal cost–benefit analysis is also applicable because it is used to estimate the investment in security defenses that optimizes ROI. The purpose of marginal analysis is to minimize overinvestment or underinvestment. Marginal analysis has been used since the 1940s by the courts as a measure of due diligence in assessing negligence,[13] as was discussed in Chapter 2.

RISK ASSESSMENT CUBE

The Risk Assessment Cube in Figure 5.1 provides a structure for categorizing risks along three dimensions. Those dimensions are

1. *The Probability of an Incident.* Probability is the likelihood or frequency of an event. Probability ranges from 0 to 100%, or from rare to common.
2. *The Severity of the Outcome or Loss.* Outcomes include all of the direct and indirect financial impacts if an incident should occur. The severity of outcomes ranges from low to high.
3. *The Duration of the Impact.* Duration ranges from isolated incidents that can be contained to those that extend over longer periods of time, such as when a company loses loyal customers because of a confidentiality breach.

Figure 5.2 is helpful in categorizing intrusions or incidents, but the expected losses from diverse situations like these need to be standardized for comparison. This is done using expected value methods. Those calculations involve estimations of loss and the probability of a loss and are demonstrated next.

Segment	Probability of an Incident	Severity of Outcome or Loss	Duration of Impact	Examples (These vary according to industry and company attractiveness.)
A	Rare	Low	Isolated	Retaliation or vengeance, civil lawsuit brought by an employee for harassment or discrimination
B	Rare	High	Isolated	Nonsophisticated hacker or DOS attacks, criminal or class action lawsuits for negligence or violation of employee civil rights
C	Common	Low	Isolated	Spam and some malware, possession of unlicensed software
D	Common	High	Isolated	Disruptive or destructive malware
E	Common	Low	Extended	Electronic fraud or extortion
F	Common	High	Extended	Insider theft and exposure of confidential financial, customer, or competitive information
G	Rare	Low	Extended	Quickly recoverable disruption of customer databases or other mission-critical systems, employee use of company email for distribution of child pornography
H	Rare	High	Extended	Nonrecoverable destruction of customer databases or other mission-critical systems

FIGURE 5.2   Characteristics of Segments in the Risk Assessment Cube

EXPECTED LOSS VALUE ESTIMATIONS

EXPECTED LOSS COMPUTATION

Expected value of either a gain (e.g., expected profit) or loss (e.g., expected cost) is used extensively to evaluate the consequences of business decisions during a particular time segment, which is usually one year. Expected loss is defined as the amount of the loss multiplied by the probability of its occurrence. (Note that *loss* and *cost* are used interchangeably). The formula is

$$\text{Expected loss} = (\text{Amount of loss}) * (\text{Probability of loss})$$

where Amount of loss is the average cost for such an incident.

Incident in Segment B of the Risk Assessment Cube

To demonstrate this formula, assume that there is a low probability of 5% that a large company will be faced with one class action lawsuit for failure to maintain a non-hostile workplace environment in the following year. The typical cost for investigation, legal fees, judgments, compensation, and punitive damages ranges between $500,000 to $1,500,000 to resolve or settle out of court. The calculations to estimate the annual expected loss from that risk is as follows:

$$\text{Average cost} = [\$500,000 + \$1,500,000]/2$$
$$= \$1,000,000$$

Annual expected loss [$\epsilon(\text{loss})$] is then calculated as

$$\text{Expected loss} = .05 * \$1,000,000$$
$$\epsilon(\text{loss}) = \$50,000$$

Incident in Segment C of the Risk Assessment Cube

In contrast, if there were a 20% probability of a virus that would result in a $250,000 loss of revenue per year, the expected loss would also be $50,000.

$$\text{Expected loss} = .20 * \$250,000$$
$$\epsilon(\text{loss}) = \$50,000$$

With expected loss estimates, security investments are not based solely on the damages caused by the incident. The estimate, and therefore the investment, takes into consideration the probability of an incident. The time interval for risk assessments is usually one year because budgeting decisions are made annually.

A benefit of the expected loss method is the ability to standardize the costs of incidents for comparison purposes. This method provides hard data to substantiate the priority of security investments.

Businesses commonly apply this expectation principle when they invest in door locks, alarm systems, and safety devices to protect against loss from break-in, fire, casualty, and legal liability. They work with insurance companies to appraise the value of their assets, assess their risk factors, and improve their preparedness. This decreases the likelihood of loss and lowers premium costs.

MARGINAL COST–BENEFIT ANALYSIS—AN APPLICATION OF EXPECTED VALUE

The issue of industry standards and defenses against negligence was addressed by Judge Learned Hand in 1947. Judge Hand outlined his standard for negligence and liability based on the economic model of marginal cost–benefit analysis in his decision in *US vs Carroll Towing Company* (2d Cir. 1947). According to marginal analysis, the firm is negligent if and only if the marginal costs of safeguards are greater than the marginal benefits of those safeguards. Expected costs and benefits are calculated using the expected value method—that is, by multiplying the probability of a security breach (or benefit) by the average expected loss or benefit, respectively. Judge Hand's liability test continues to be used today in the courts.[14]

<CYBERBRIEF>

KNOW WHAT RISKS
TO ACCEPT OR TRANSFER

According to Alan Liddle, the technical director at the British ecommerce security consultancy Trustis, "First, crucially, you have to know what your risks are. Then for each one you have a management decision to make: can you accept the risk, and if not, what action should you take? Don't let the technologists assume that every hole has to be plugged—that would be far too expensive."

Source: "Business IT Strategy—Calculating Risks." *Accountancy.* December 27, 2001. P. 56.

BALANCING EXPECTED LOSS WITH THE COST OF SECURITY DEFENSES

Expected losses from an incident can be a benchmark for investments in defenses to defend against them. There are several standard methods for managing business risk. Three common approaches are

1. To try to mitigate the loss by implementing preventive measures, such as those in tier 2 through 4 of the DLM defensive infrastructure.
2. To transfer the risk to another party by outsourcing the secure management of a network, mission-critical databases, or ecommerce application.
3. To transfer the remaining risk using insurance. This cost of this approach will depend on security investments and audits that the organization has already implemented.

CHALLENGES IN ESTIMATING LOSS OF DIGITAL ASSETS

INTANGIBLE ASSETS

Digital assets are intangible, so their value may only become fully understood in the actual event of loss. For example, one of the most valuable business assets is information maintained in the customer databases. Assume that these data are stolen and get used for identity theft, causing customers serious problems. While the data replacement cost can be estimated with some precision, the impact on potential revenues would be much harder to quantify. Those costs could go on for years and the lost business might not be fully calculated. For these reasons, all types of businesses tend dangerously to underestimate the expected value of their digital assets.

They also fail to take into account the variety of ways these assets can come under attack, which increases the probability of a loss. This leads to poor investment decisions with regard to protecting those assets using security technology, insurance, and expertise.

@LERT

Corporate software piracy is a federal offense. Typically, it becomes known through anonymous tips from irate workers, former employees, or vendors. Anyone getting caught with illegally duplicated, or pirated, software can face fines up to $150,000 per title infringed.

REPLICATION INCREASES EXPOSURE AND PROBABILITY OF A LOSS

Physical assets tend to exist in only one place and therefore must only be protected in one instance. Ironically, one of the ways in which we protect digital assets is to retain multiple backup copies. This is an effective way to protect against accidental destruction but increases the opportunities for theft.

The adoption of client–server and distributed computing architectures has created an environment in which documents are stored on many networked devices. A common example is a confidential report for a new product stored on

- The central database server
- The desktop PC of an analyst who prepared the report
- The laptop PC of the manager who received the report via email
- The company email server that sent the email, and
- The PDA of another executive who was copied on the email.

FIGURE 5.3 Message Replication

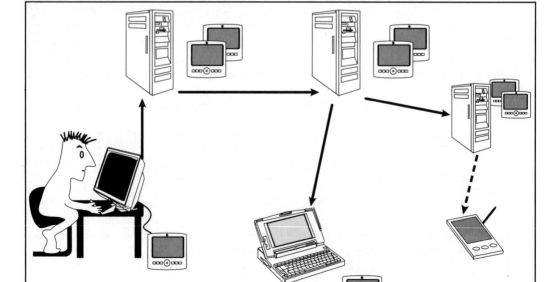

CYBERBRIEF

CREATOR OF THE MELISSA VIRUS PLEADED GUILTY TO CAUSING $80 MILLION IN DAMAGE

A tip received by the New Jersey State Police from America Online and their follow-up investigation with the FBI's Newark Division led to the April 1, 1999, arrest of David L. Smith. Smith pleaded guilty in federal court to one count of violating 18 U.S.C. § 1030 and to four state felony counts for releasing the Melissa virus. As part of his guilty plea, Smith stipulated to affecting one million computer systems and causing $80 million in damage.

Source: Statement for the Record of Louis J. Freeh, Director FBI, on cyber crime before the Senate Committee on Judiciary Subcommittee for Technology, Terrorism, and Government Information. Washington, DC March 28, 2000. http://www.fbi.gov/pressrm/congress/congress00/cyber032800.htm

Any one of these devices may have the report stored in several places as a result of backup activity or in **cache,** which are temporary file copies to enhance system performance. Each one of these copies, on any one of these devices, is potentially vulnerable (see Figure 5.3). Thus the information is only as safe as it is on the device with the weakest set of defenses.

OUTSOURCING PLACES DATA AND DOCUMENTS OUT OF CONTROL

If business operations are outsourced or conducted in cooperation with a business partner, valuable information often must reside on networks that lie outside of organizational control. This creates a situation in which one is reliant on the efforts of that partner to protect the shared asset. This practice is very widespread, considering that anyone who uses a free Web email service relies on that service to protect any confidential information that may be contained in messages routed through its service.

KNOWLEDGE ASSETS ARE DIFFICULT TO REPLACE

Digital assets come in many forms. Some have direct monetary value like an account balance in a bank account. Others have indirect value derived from their associated knowledge or goodwill. The information most commonly resident on computers and networks is structured data (see Figure 5.4). Structured data is expressed as numbers with defined attributes, such as "Activity_amount = $2,389.91 for Transaction_date = 01/09."

Transaction_date	*Activity_Amount*	*Transaction_type*
01/09	$2,389.91	Deposit
01/10	$300.00	Debit
01/19	$850.00	Check

FIGURE 5.4
Structured Data

<CYBERBRIEF>

THE COST OF
ELECTRONIC FRAUD (EFRAUD)

Fraud cost etailers $700 million in lost merchandise in 2002. Some large Internet retailers have software that screens transactions and refuses to sell to customers who appear suspicious. It is estimated that this costs Web stores between 5 and 8% of sales.

Source: Gartner Group. http://news.com.com/2009-1017-912708.html

It is now common to capture and store unstructured information through the use of what is known as **Knowledge Management (KM).** KM assets, by their nature, are much harder to identify, inventory, and most of all, replace if lost. Many firms, particularly those in service industries, know that most of their value is derived from the knowledge that resides within their employee base. These firms use KM techniques like electronic document management systems to track and share these documents among employees and make better use of knowledge. These systems also provide a hedge against the loss of knowledge caused by the departure of a key employee with many years of training and experience.

New-product design documents are important knowledge assets. Individuals exercise KM when they manage and maintain a list of professional contacts in their address books. The value of these assets often defies quantification but must be considered in estimating expected value.

MISSION-CRITICAL SOFTWARE APPLICATIONS

Beyond data and knowledge, customized software can have significant value. If a business has made a major investment in a proprietary customer contact application, that asset could be exposed in two ways. If it provides a competitive advantage, its design could be learned and copied by a competitor. Or an employee or hacker could disable it. Therefore, such an asset has value not only from the point of view of development costs but also from the expected loss of revenue if it was sabotaged.

Another direct economic risk involves the potential for fines and other penalties that could result if a business is found to be negligent with regard to information security in a manner that violates state or federal law. These issues of privacy and legal liability will be examined in detail in Parts III and IV.

DENIAL OF SERVICE RISK

As our economy makes more and better use of networks as productivity tools and becomes more reliant on them to perform our work, the denial of these services looms as an ever larger risk. Often the most direct economic impact of a digital attack is the significant loss of productivity that can result from even the more "benign" forms of malware. Worms like Code Red did not actually destroy data, rather they paralyzed networks and services through self-replication, creating enormous network "traffic jams" that made it impossible for legitimate traffic to get through. As previously discussed, between the denial of services and the resulting cleanup, it was estimated that the Code Red incident cost global businesses over $2 billion.[15]

VALUATION OF DIGITAL ASSETS AND RISK

With tangible assets, like buildings and equipment, it is easy to calculate replacement costs as our basis for estimating expected loss and justifying investments in insurance and technology. There are two main ways to assign economic value to these investments. One is to examine their impact on revenues and the other is to focus on loss prevention.

SOFTWARE ASSETS

The risk here is not the actual loss of software itself. Even when application software becomes corrupted and inoperable as a result of an attack, it can be restored from offline storage. What is lost is the use of that software for as long as it takes to do the restoration. For a retail business with a Web storefront, the potential loss is estimated by tracking the average revenue generated by the Website per hour. That average revenue amount is multiplied by the downtime to calculate total loss.

Other software applications are designed to enhance productivity. One way to quantify their potential loss is to use the cost-saving estimations that went into justifying the original purchase of the application, if available. For example, if a wireless email server application is purchased based on an estimated 10% productivity improvement in the mobile workforce, then the expected loss for a worm that disables the server for one day would be 10% of the total daily payroll for all mobile workers.

KNOWLEDGE ASSETS

When appraising the value of knowledge assets, it is important to remember that it is the *unique* knowledge and data within an organization that creates value at risk. With adequate backups in place, corrupted databases and knowledge stores can be restored quickly. The danger lies in what the attackers do with stolen information. Trade secrets and customer lists can be used by competitors, or employees, to steal revenue. Theft of sensitive partner data may become the basis for litigation.

Breaches of privacy policies may become cause for punitive damages (for punishment or deterrence) that may be awarded if the company's conduct was reckless.[16] Businesses that operate out of physical sites in other countries are familiar with the complex compliance issues that result.[17]

As the Internet gives local businesses a global presence, their managers are finding out they may be subject to local regulation. For example, the purchase of copyrighted material by a customer in France from a U.S.-based company's Website operating over a European network can lead to highly ambiguous jurisdiction issues and conflicts of policy with regard to privacy, intellectual property protection, banking regulations, etc.

GOODWILL

Goodwill may be an extremely valuable asset, particularly for service businesses. Accounting issues aside, goodwill is largely the result of accumulated knowledge, experience, public image, and body of customer relationships the firm has developed over its lifetime. The more reliant the firm is on technology to manage its knowledge and face its markets, the more vulnerable is goodwill to digital assault.

Highly automated businesses that act in a custodial capacity, such as financial institutions, need to be trusted by others. That is, they must be perceived as having well-developed security defenses for their customers' peace of mind. To some extent, this is true of all businesses that manage and use information about their customers and partners. As such, any and all goodwill that they carry is at digital risk, and the value of that goodwill should figure into the DLM investment model.[18]

SOURCES OF INFORMATION FOR RISK ESTIMATIONS

RESEARCH AND CONSULTING FIRMS

There are several credible sources of information that can be drawn upon with regard to the history of cyber crime incidents. Many leading IT research and consulting firms publish research on the subject. See the Appendix for a listing of their Websites.

More specialized firms, such as the CSI, in conjunction with the FBI publish an annual survey of over 500 firms with detailed breakdowns by industry, type of attack, magnitude of loss, and so on. In addition, there are other public sources of valuable information, including the **CERT® Coordination Center.** CERT® is a federally funded research and development center operated by Carnegie Mellon University dedicated to information security monitoring and alerts.[19]

Other resources include **Infragard,** an alliance of the public and private sectors formed by the FBI to share knowledge and coordinate defenses against cyber terror. Software vendors that specialize in information security also provide some valuable expertise based on their experiences in implementation. They, as well as independent consulting firms, will provide comprehensive risk assessment services that can serve to expedite the process and compare your company's status to established benchmarks.

TECHNICAL TOOLS

Firewalls, intrusion detection technology, and network administration tools keep detailed logs of activity that has either been permitted or denied. Analysis of these logs can provide significant insight as to the frequency and nature of attempted break-ins and other unauthorized activity. Resources most often attacked, housing the most valuable information, can then become the focus of protective investments.

BUSINESS PARTNERS AND INDUSTRY GROUPS

Business partners may also be valuable sources of information to gauge areas of vulnerability. They may share their experience in an attempt to coordinate security around common data and processes. Various industry groups are also collecting this kind of data

<CYBERBRIEF>

SYMANTEC'S *INTERNET SECURITY THREAT REPORT*

According to *Symantec's Internet Security Threat Report,* banking and utilities are at risk from cyber attack. Banking and utilities are the most at-risk sectors for threat of attack by malicious code, such as hacks, worms, and viruses. Both industries have the finances to protect their systems, and the most to lose if they don't. They are the greatest challenges and sources of fame for the hacker or virus writer that breaches their defenses.

During the second half of 2002, Symantec, an Internet technology security company, recorded an average of 987 attacks per company in the power and energy sector. Nonprofit organizations had an average of 869 attacks per company; telecoms had 845; high-tech had 753; banking and finance had 689.

In terms of severity of the attacks, the top three were power and energy, banking and finance, and nonprofit. Almost 70% of attacks targeted at power and energy companies were severe. For banking and nonprofit organizations, 48% and 30% were severe, respectively.

Source: ZDnet. February 3, 2003. http://news.zdnet.co.uk/story/0,,t269-s2129944,00.html

for the benefit of their members. Several insurance companies have expanded their coverage in this area. They actively collect data regarding the incidence of cyber losses to help them set rates and develop mitigation strategies for their customers.

OVERALL RISK EVALUATION PROFILE

After calculating annual expected losses for digital assets, a risk profile can be documented. For each class of asset, such as customer data and new-product research and development (R&D) documentation, an approximate level of risk can be specified. Figure 5.5 demonstrates a risk profile.

ASSESS THE CURRENT SITUATION

One of the most important aspects of the DLM model is that it stresses the people, process, and policy components of security as much as the technology. Many well-intentioned digital security initiatives, including those that were well funded, did not completely succeed because too much weight was placed on the technology.

FIGURE 5.5   Risk Profile

Asset Class	Risk of Loss of the Asset	Risk of Lost Revenue	Current Exposure	Investment Priority
Customer Account Data	High	High	Moderate	High
New Product R&D Documents	Moderate	High	Moderate	High
Supplier Transaction History	Moderate	Low	Moderate	Low
Employee Benefits Data	Low	Low	Low	Low

It has been estimated that over 90% of successful cyber attacks could have been prevented by the technology available at the time. But it was inadequate human attention that contributed to the technology failure. Numerous examples of this have been well documented and chronicled in this book. Patches to repair security flaws in widely used software are not applied. Updates to virus-scanning software are not made so viruses like Klez are allowed to spread for a period long after the patch was released. Passwords are often left at their well-known default values set by the vendor. Social engineering is used to dupe employees into divulging passwords to strangers. The list, unfortunately, goes on.

The key to successful DLM is to establish a culture and a process that fosters investment in defense against the greatest risks and maintains their effectiveness. This is the necessary objective, but the path to that objective cannot be established without a risk assessment.

@LERT

Hacking is not a spectator sport, so hackers can fulfill their craving for notoriety with high-profile exploits.

POLICY AND PROCESS PERSPECTIVE

The effectiveness of the policy and auditing tools for managing and mitigating risk needs to be tested. All policy documents related to information security, such as an AUP, should be examined for completeness, clarity, and compliance as part of the audit. Audit results can make the policy far more defensible if it becomes evidence in a legal action. Other policies that are usually included pertain to privacy, outsourcing of processes that involve sensitive data, password maintenance, and remote access to company networks.

Testing the security awareness of the workforce can gauge the effectiveness of current training and documentation efforts. Many companies with strong policies are staffed by people who have never read them. This is evidenced by the continued successful introduction of email-borne viruses into corporate networks.

ORGANIZATIONAL PERSPECTIVE

Assigning responsibility for DLM-related issues is also part of the picture. This can be a problem issue in larger firms where this responsibility has become fragmented. It is not uncommon for a company to have a network administrator and a network security administrator, with the latter reporting to the former. Although this approach aligns well with the technical demands of the task, it can weaken DLM responsibility.

Regardless of whether or not responsibility for network security and physical security is combined in the organization, the two are interrelated and should be assessed together. We have seen several situations where servers that control access to highly secure data sit in closets with little or no physical security. One routine sweep revealed that doors to equipment rooms were propped open every night by maintenance personnel and left unattended for hours, available to anyone who happened to be in the building.

⬡ **CYBERBRIEF** ⬡

INEFFECTIVE INTERNAL
SECURITY POLICY

Microsoft took a public file server offline after Internet users discovered that the system contained scores of internal Microsoft documents, including a huge customer database with millions of entries. This particular server was intended to enable Microsoft customers to download drivers, software patches, and other files. Due to what experts say was ineffective internal security policy, the public was able to have full access to folders containing confidential company presentations, spreadsheets, and other information, including a 1 GB database containing millions of customer names and mailing addresses. The data was kept in a compressed archive, was protected with the password "dbms," and was easily opened with freely available password-cracking software.

Source: http://www.wired.com/news/infostructure/0,1377,56481,00.html

TECHNOLOGY PERSPECTIVE

The easiest aspect of the overall risk profile is to assess technology. This task is relatively well defined through extensive work by industry, governments, and academia. A more complete review of available defensive technology is presented in Chapter 8.

AUDITS WITH TRADING PARTNERS AND CUSTOMERS

If business operations demand network connections to partners and customers, then their levels of information security are equally important. Thus, it makes sense to undertake a cooperative effort and test the integrity of the interconnected network. Some larger concerns may require and subsidize an audit and enhancements to the security infrastructure to meet their standards.

For many businesses, a proper assessment can only come with the help of a complete audit of the current security infrastructure using a reputable and qualified third party. Why use a third party when the technical expertise is available in-house? Because objectivity is as important as it is difficult to achieve. A proper audit needs to examine all aspects of the current state of preparedness, as discussed above.

Some companies stage an unannounced attack using known hacker methods or **white hat hackers** hired for the purpose. White hat hackers are ethical hackers who search for weaknesses in computer systems or business applications. This may include the introduction of specially designed examples of malware, such as backdoors or benign viruses, to test whether they were detected by the defensive technology.

Chapter Summary

The bottom line is that security needs to be managed in the context of the business. The most important reasons that most information security programs are underfunded are that most enterprises do not know what they have to lose and do not appreciate all the ways they can lose it. The only way to properly justify DLM investments is to fund them based on the anticipated economic return. The key is to properly identify and quantify all value at risk within the enterprise and estimate the probability of loss by creating an overall risk-exposure profile. With these in hand, a reasonable estimate of expected loss can be calculated that forms the basis of a justifiable DLM budget.

A risk-based approach, with senior management involvement and business awareness on the part of IT people, can optimize the return of security investments. Security depends on balancing cost and risk through the appropriate use of both technology and policy.

Key Terms

- risk analysis
- expected value
- marginal analysis
- ISO 17799

- expected loss
- cache
- knowledge management (KM)

- CERT® coordination center
- infragard
- white hat hackers

Discussion Questions

1. What is the purpose of risk analysis? How does the financial analysis for determining adequate investments for information security differ from determining investments in another functional area, such as marketing or new-product development?
2. Why are there vast differences in organizations' security needs? What is ISO 17799, and what is its purpose? What is a basic requirement of the ISO 17799 standard?
3. Are hard quantitative estimations necessary? Why or why not?
4. What is expected value? What is expected loss? What is the expected loss formula?
5. Assume that there is a 35% probability that a company will suffer a disruptive worm like Slammer within the year. The estimated costs from downtime and restoring the network range from $2,500 to $4,500. Calculate the annual expected loss from that risk. If the probability increases to 50% the following year, what would be the annual expected loss?
6. Why is marginal cost–benefit analysis important in determining the level of investment in information security?
7. Visit the U.S. government's cyber crime Website at http://www.cybercrime.gov. What companies have been recent targets of cyber attacks? What were the damages or costs of those intrusions?
8. What are four of the most valuable assets for businesses engaged in ecommerce? Classify them using the Risk Assessment Cube.
9. Identify and define the three dimensions for categorizing risks.
10. Where might duplicate copies of files be stored? How do duplicate copies increase security risk? How do duplicate copies decrease security risk?
11. What tends to characterize organizations at the highest risk of insider attack? What tends to characterize organizations at the highest risk of hacker attack?
12. What is the advantage of hiring a third party to perform a security audit? Do you think that white hat hackers should be used to verify cyber security? Why or why not?

Endnotes

1. Tahmincioglu, Eve. "Management: Vigilance In the Face Of Layoff Rage; Employer Miscues Can Breed Retaliation." *The New York Times*. August 1, 2001. Section C. P. 1.

2. "Former Computer Network Administrator at New Jersey High-Tech Firm Sentenced to 41 Months for Unleashing $10 Million Computer 'Time Bomb.'" U.S. Department of Justice, United States Attorney, District of New Jersey. February 26, 2002. http://www.cybercrime.gov/lloydSent.htm

3. Statement for the Record of Louis J. Freeh, Director Federal Bureau of Investigation, on *Cybercrime* before the Senate Committee on Judiciary Subcommittee for Technology, Terrorism, and Government Information. Washington, DC, March 28, 2000. http://www.fbi.gov/pressrm/congress/congress00/cyber032800.htm

4. *Los Angeles Times*. February 4, 2001. http://www.rtmark.com/more/articles/latimes20010204.html

5. Burkitt, Mike. "Security Strategy Must Go Beyond Technology." *Computing*. March 28, 2002. P. 35.

6. Hulme, George V. "Guarded Optimism— Even as Companies Plug More Holes, the Threats Grow More Sophisticated." *InformationWeek*. July 8, 2002. P. 36.

7. Fisher, Dennis. "Cyber Attacks Decline; Vulnerabilities Surge" *eWeek*. February 03, 2003. http://www.eweek.com/article2/0,3959,857004,00.asp

8. "Putting it All Together." *The Economist*. October 26, 2002 U.S. Edition. Section: Survey.

9. Loney, Matt. "Your Worst Security Threat: Employees?" *ZDNet (UK)*. April 23, 2002. http://zdnet.com.com/2100-1105-889542.html

10. "Business IT Strategy—Calculating Risks." *Accountancy*. December 27, 2001. P. 56.

11. "Putting it All Together." *The Economist*. October 26, 2002 U.S. Edition. Section: Survey.

12. Pappas, James L., and Eugene F. Brigham. "Risk Analysis." *Managerial Economics*, 3rd ed. Boston: The Dryden Press. 1979. Pp. 73–82.

13. Epstein, Richard A. *Cases and Materials on Torts*, 6th ed. Boston: Little, Brown & Co., 1995, P. 218.

14. Epstein, Richard A. *Cases and Materials on Torts*, 6th ed. Boston: Little, Brown & Co, 1995, P. 218.

15. Waite, Beverly. "Malicious Code Attacks Had $13.2 Billion Economic Impact in 2001." *Computer Economics*. January 4, 2002. http://www.computereconomics.com/article.cfm?id-133

16. Gleim, Invin N. and Jordan B. Ray, with Eugene P. O'Connor. *Business Law/Legal Studies*. Gainsville, FL: Gleim Publications, Inc., 1992.

17. Armstrong, Illena. "Computer Forensics." *SC Magazine*. April 2001. http://www.scmagazine.com/scmagazine/2001_04/cover/cover.html

18. Scalet, Sarah. "Fear Factor." *CIO Magazine*. October 15, 2002.

19. See http://www.cert.org for further information.

CHAPTER 6
ACCEPTABLE-USE POLICIES: HUMAN DEFENSES

Learning Objectives

◆ Acceptable-use policy as a security and legal necessity.

◆ Balancing safety with privacy concerns.

◆ User accountability and responsibilities.

◆ Corporate accountability and responsibilities.

◆ Characteristics of an effective AUP.

◆ Template for creating a comprehensive AUP.

In Part I, information security threats, digital liabilities, and risk management techniques were discussed to provide a broad foundation on what is at risk. In Part II, the focus is on the specific defenses that are needed to prevent incidents—and to protect against their consequences when prevention methods fail. These defenses are needed for business and legal reasons, particularly **duty of care** obligations. In general, a duty of care simply means that a company or person cannot create unreasonable risk of harm to others.[1]

INTRODUCTION

An AUP helps the organization fulfill its "duty of care" to provide employees with a nonhostile working environment. A nonhostile environment is one in which employees are not subject to content or actions that may be morally, racially, ethnically, or religiously offensive. Their other civil rights, such as privacy and free speech, also need to be protected, as required by law.

With more workers connecting to the Internet each year, the potential for offensive behavior and waste of company resources is getting worse. In 2003, it was reported that 30 to 40% of workplace Internet use is not related to business, according to IDC Research, based in Framingham, Mass.[2] Cyber slacking costs U.S. corporations over $85 billion annually in lost productivity, according to Websense, an employee Internet management software company.

In this chapter, we discuss why companies need to implement and enforce AUPs (acceptable-use policies) that focus on accountability by all users.[3] AUP training and documentation are also essential to provide evidence that policies have been in force. The nature of the provisions needed in an AUP is best understood by example and a generic AUP is provided at the end of the chapter. Although there is no universal AUP

◁ CASE ON POINT ▷

ALLSTATE INSURANCE CO.'S EMPLOYEES ILLEGALLY ACCESS AND USE CONFIDENTIAL INFORMATION

In February 2003, the California Department of Motor Vehicles (DMV) cut off Allstate Insurance Co.'s access to digital driving records. Their investigation revealed that company employees had been accessing confidential state computer records on over 100 occasions for illegitimate reasons.[4] DMV Director Steven Gourley charged Allstate with fostering a "corporate culture that disregarded security and privacy" after a nine–month investigation that found many violations of state rules governing handling of DMV information. Audits conducted in nine Southern California Allstate offices showed that employees had regularly obtained driving records and car registration information for friends or relatives. Employees had been using fake claim numbers to gain unauthorized access to driving records.[5]

Gourley said the DMV initiated its investigation after a complaint that "an Allstate customer's confidential address had been released, which resulted in a written threat to that person." In this case, an Allstate employee revealed the woman's home address, which enabled a road-raged driver to send her a threatening message.[6]

Investigators could not identify the Allstate employee who facilitated the threat, but they found 131 violations of confidentiality rules. Allstate employees were sharing computer passwords instead of using individual passwords. Many Allstate personnel had not signed the necessary paperwork promising to follow confidentiality rules. "It indicates to me that many of their employees were either not trained at all about security issues or had never had it emphasized to them that security issues were very serious," Gourley said.[7]

Allstate acknowledged in a statement that security and customer confidentiality procedures had been breached, but not whether the employee had been fired. The DMV Director said he would ask the state attorney general's office to seek fines against Allstate and would file a civil lawsuit against Allstate outlining the specific instances of improper behavior. Accessing DMV information under false pretenses carries up to a $100,000 fine for each violation.[8] Release of DMV records was restricted in 1989 after an obsessed fan of actress Rebecca Schaeffer hired a private investigator to get her home address from the DMV, went to her home, and shot and killed her.

template since provisions must be specific to the organization, effective AUPs have common characteristics.

> **@LERT**
> The most readily calculable cost of an outdated or incomplete AUP is the lawsuit—as is the payoff from implementing an effective one.

MCIWORLDCOM'S AUP LEADS TO EARLY DISMISSAL OF LAWSUIT

Two employees had filed an employment discrimination lawsuit against the major telecommunications company MCIWorldcom in a Texas federal court.[9] The plaintiffs

< **CYBERBRIEF** >

SURVEY OF DOCUMENTATION OF SECURITY POLICIES

Ninety-one Fortune 500 firms answered the following question: "How would you characterize your information security policies with regard to being supported by documented procedures and guidelines for all users?" The answers, by industry, were as shown in Figure 6.1.

FIGURE 6.1   How Well Security Policies Are Documented, by Industry

	Auto/ Man	Energy	Financial Services	Life Sciences	Tech/ Media	Telecom	All
They are documented, implemented, and followed.	9%	9%	31%	30%	29%	30%	21%
They are documented, some implemented, and followed.	64%	46%	50%	10%	41%	50%	45%
They are documented, not implemented or followed.	0%	18%	0%	20%	0%	20%	9%
Some documented, implemented, and followed.	27%	27%	13%	40%	24%	0%	22%
They are not documented.	0%	0%	6%	0%	6%	0%	3%
	100%	100%	100%	100%	100%	100%	100%

Source: Ernst & Young *Digital Security Overview.* April 2002.

maintained that another employee had sent four email jokes that constituted racial harassment. The plaintiffs claimed that their employer had been negligent by allowing the corporate email system to be used for harassment and that the defendant retaliated against them for using the jokes in the suit.

The court dismissed the plaintiffs' claims of negligence against MCIWorldcom. The three reasons for the dismissal cited by the court were that the employer

1. Had an established email acceptable–use policy that expressly prohibited discriminatory email, and
2. Had acted consistently in enforcing the policy against the employee who had sent the email messages, and
3. Had taken remedial action to enforce its written email policy.

Together these strict actions that MCIWorldCom had taken were sufficient to defend the company against liability under that federal law. This is in sharp contrast to the lax attitude that led to the impending lawsuits that Allstate faces without strong defense.

TABLE 6.1	DLM Defense Infrastructure
Tier 1	Senior management commitment and support
Tier 2	**Acceptable-use policies and other statements of practice**
Tier 3	Secure-use procedures
Tier 4	Hardware, software, and network security tools

THE AUP: THE DISCIPLINE AND DILIGENCE DEFENSE TIER

AUPs, the second DLM defense tier, inform employees of their responsibilities and rules regarding use of company computer equipment. In effect, they tell employees that the company is paying for the computer networks and security, and that violators will pay if they are out of compliance.

Despite the increase in litigation from email or computer misuse, policies to govern employees' use of company computer networks are rarely current, comprehensive, or strict enough to ensure high levels of productivity and legal protection. We repeatedly see reminders that huge investments in information security technology are ineffective unless there is a strong commitment from employees, as well as their managers, to comply with acceptable use of IT resources.

Unfortunately, users must be made to operate within the constraints of the AUP even though that diligence and discipline is inconvenient to them. After years of irresponsible email and Internet use, users have developed high-risk habits that will not be changed easily. The only way to bring about that change is through AUP training, reminders, and enforcement. AUPs should be integrated with other employee policies and control systems.[10]

DUAL FUNCTIONS OF THE AUP

With the tremendous increase in technology usage, companies must implement and mandate AUPs for email, Web access, and other technology applications.[11] Without a doubt, Internet, computer, and email AUPs are necessities for security and legal reasons. That is, their dual functions are to prevent misuses from occurring and to protect the organization when prevention techniques fail.

SECURITY BREACH PREVENTION

Companies are reporting more frequent instances of unauthorized and unwanted conduct being committed over or through their computer networks.[12] Their AUPs can help

1. To inform employees what they can and cannot do to reduce inappropriate or risky use of technology, thus preventing damage to a company's competitive, financial, legal, or ethical position.
2. To clarify expectations about personal use of company equipment, privacy, and user responsibility.
3. To warn employees that their activities will be monitored.
4. To outline the consequences of noncompliance.

Employees are more likely to abuse their Internet privileges when organizations have not made it clear that such behavior is not allowed. Organizations that have set their employees' expectations regarding acceptable use and privacy issues through an AUP usually have fewer problems.[13]

The basic position of the courts has been that if a company does not take action to prevent a hostile workplace environment, then it is guilty of promoting such an environment. That is, any misuse that the company does not proactively try to prevent is viewed by the courts as having been allowed. That is why monitoring is so important as a preventive measure. Sixty-three percent of U.S. companies monitor employees' Internet activities. For larger firms, that ratio rises to 80%, according to surveys conducted by the ePolicy Institute, the American Management Association (AMA), and *U.S. News & World Report*. Workers might object, but the courts typically side with the employers.

There is a difficult and fine line between allowing employees the freedom to function to their full proficiency and maintaining sufficient management controls to protect the company, its reputation, executives, and resources. With employees' email and Internet records being used during the discovery process in most lawsuits against a company, prevention has become more critical, as will be discussed in Chapter 9.

@LERT

The following scenario describes the circumstances under which an AUP would be rendered useless.

The company has a well-written email AUP stating that staff should not use company email systems for private use. This policy is widely ignored from the managing director downwards. The management structure and system for implementing the AUP is in place, but the system is *not* enforced.

LEGAL PROTECTION

Defensively, a uniformly enforced AUP is supporting evidence that the organization exercised its legal duty to safeguard employees from workplace hostility or violations of their civil rights. Corporate scandals of 2001–2003 have alerted employers to the fact that inappropriate actions of employees can have negative impacts.

As many companies have learned, not only is the email policy useless in court as a defense against liability lawsuits, it can instill a culture of *ignoring the company policy* regarding Internet and email usage.

There are two legal doctrines that are especially relevant to employer liability. Because of their importance to AUPs, they are detailed in the next section.

LEGAL THEORIES AND EMPLOYER LIABILITY ISSUES

Employers' liability stems from two longstanding legal doctrines. They are *respondeat superior* and negligent supervision and duty of care.

⬡ **CYBERBRIEF** ⬡

DUTY OF CARE

The court has stated that directors have a duty of oversight beyond merely being reasonably informed.

"[A] director's obligation includes a duty to attempt in good faith to assure that a corporation's information and reporting system, which the board considers adequate, exists, and the failure to do so may . . . render . . . a director liable."

Now the risk of legal liability is greater for directors and officers if they fail to protect key systems because risks to those systems are foreseeable.

Sources: "Now More than Ever, Cybersecurity Audits are Key." *National Law Journal.* Section: News. Vol. 24. No. 27. P. C8. March 11, 2002. Also *In re Caremark International Inc. Derivative Litigation.* 1996.

RESPONDEAT SUPERIOR DOCTRINE AND LIABILITY

Respondeat superior is a doctrine that holds employers liable for misconduct of their employees that occurs within the **scope of their employment.** The conduct of an employee is generally considered to be *within the scope of employment* if it occurs substantially within the authorized time and space limits of the job. Of course, with mobile workers and wireless technologies, it is increasingly difficult to define that scope.

On Nov. 23, 2001, the United States joined 29 other countries in signing the **Convention on Cybercrime,** an international treaty designed to improve international cyber crime prevention.[14] Among its provisions, the Cybercrime Convention seeks to ensure that when a corporation fails to properly supervise employees in leading positions, and that failure makes certain computer crimes possible, the corporation itself will be held liable for the cyber crimes committed for its benefit, even if such crimes were committed without its knowledge, consent, or approval.[15] The treaty would require Congress to pass legislation that imposes *respondeat superior* liability on a company for not diligently monitoring the cyber activities of its employees.

NEGLIGENT SUPERVISION AND DUTY OF CARE

An employer may also be liable for damages that result from **negligent supervision** of its employees' activities. Under the theory of negligent supervision, the employer's duty of care and liability may extend to actions **outside the scope of employment.** Under the doctrine of duty of care, directors and officers have a fiduciary obligation to use reasonable care to protect their company's business operations.[16]

In the case of a security breach, the risk stemming from these doctrines is a lawsuit against corporate directors and officers claiming that they failed to fulfill their duty of care by not ensuring adequate protection.[17]

Businesses can no longer rely on *force majeure* (i.e., "force of nature" or "beyond human control") claims to protect themselves against damages from hacker attack claims since widespread hacking incidents have made those attacks foreseeable.

CHARACTERISTICS OF EFFECTIVE AUPS

COMPREHENSIVE SCOPE

The scope of the AUP must explicitly apply to *all* company-provided IT resources that access the Internet. This includes desktop and laptop computers, personal digital assistants (PDA), and other wireless devices. It also includes employee-owned devices accessing the Net via company-owned network resources, including virtual private networks. It applies to *all* users of company-provided resources and imposes specific limitations on other potential users, such as families, friends, or partners.

CLEAR LANGUAGE

To be effective, the AUP must be clear and concise and explain the company's commitment to enforcement. It must address any unique aspects of the firm's business, as well as the employee's role in the firm. The language must be narrow and specific enough to address known threats while including statements that are broad enough to cover new or unanticipated dangers and events.

ADAPTIVE CONTENT

AUPs must be dynamic documents that are subject to constant revision to adapt to inevitable changes in the business, technological, and legal environments and cyber risks. A mechanism for distributing and acknowledging updates to the policy needs to be in place.

EXTENSION TO OTHER COMPANY POLICIES

Provisions in the AUP must manage employees' expectations with regard to their right to privacy. It should also reinforce the idea that the use of company technology is an extension of the physical workplace. As a result, all other primary provisions of company policy, such as protection of intellectual property and prohibition of harassment, also apply in the **virtual workplace,** for example, any place where company business is being conducted using company-provided equipment. Those activities need to be monitored at all times for compliance.

ENFORCEMENT PROVISIONS

AUPs must be maintained and enforced consistently. An obsolete, informal, or randomly enforced policy can be at least as dangerous as no policy at all because it can be seen as evidence of negligence or discrimination.

An effective AUP removes any ambiguity as to the manner in which compliance will be monitored and enforced. If, for example, network traffic will be monitored for the presence of trade-secret information, this should be spelled out. Penalties for specific types of violations should be listed, and the process for administration and potential appeal outlined.

CONSENT

Acceptance and adoption of an AUP should not be passive. Acknowledgment of responsibilities, enforcement procedures, and penalties should require an action on the part of the user such as his or her signed agreement. This is referred to as **expressed consent,** in contrast to implied consent. Implied consent occurs when users see a notice on the log–in screen informing them that by using the company account they are, by implicit consent, agreeing to comply.

ACCOUNTABILITY

Although responsibility for development, administration, and enforcement of an AUP is typically assigned to the IT organization, it requires direct and ongoing involvement from legal, human resources, and senior line management. In practice, specific individuals will have responsibility for monitoring compliance and enforcement activity. These individuals should be named within the AUP, along with contact information to help users get answers to questions about the policies themselves or the manner in which they will be enforced.[18]

AUP TEMPLATE

The sample AUP that follows serves two purposes: It explicitly identifies key security issues to be addressed within an AUP and can be used as a basis for developing a new AUP.

Managers should review their company's current AUP and update it with relevant specifications from this template. For those lacking an AUP, the template can be customized to meet a company's particular business needs. It is not intended to be used as is, nor is it a substitute for professional advice regarding legal compliance and liability.

The concept of a policy regarding the regulation and monitoring of email and Internet use is relatively new to some companies. Acceptance cannot be assured, or even expected, without an effort to educate users as to the necessity of such a policy and the protection it provides to all concerned. With changing technology and legislation, AUPs can become outdated quickly and they require review at least annually. There is no boilerplate template for constructing a well-crafted AUP. Managers must assess their IT resources, infrastructure, culture, and business needs in order to compose a relevant and feasible AUP.

This sample AUP does not allow any personal use of email or the Internet on company time. It does allow for personal use on personal time on a noninterference–with–business basis. This is a stringent but realistic position. However, companies must decide how much personal email or Internet use to allow at any time. For example, the AUP could specify that the company's email system and other technology assets can be used for incidental personal purposes only, such that it does not require a substantial amount of time or violate other provisions of the company's AUP (e.g., use must be business appropriate and nonharassing).

SAMPLE ACCEPTABLE-USE POLICY (AUP)

PURPOSE AND SCOPE

This policy addresses issues related to the access and use of the company's computer and information systems, telecommunications infrastructure including the Internet, Intranet, email, voice mail, facsimile (fax) transmissions, computer networks, servers, desktops, hardware, and software (IT resources). It is intended to promote employee productivity and safety, while recognizing that technology alone cannot provide adequate assurance against external or internal threats to company resources and assets. It requires the combination of well-informed and trained employees applying diligence, judgement, and the best available technology to provide that insurance.

The policy's key objectives are to (a) maintain a nonhostile workplace environment; (b) prevent sexual, racial, and other forms of discrimination, copyright infringement, software piracy, and any other misuse of company resources; (c) protect the company against computer crimes, viruses, worms, hackers, hoaxes, cyber pranks, denial of service attacks (DOS), cyber terrorist threats, and other civil wrongs or criminal offenses; (d) protect proprietary company information, employee and customer data, trade secrets, and other protected or privileged material; and restrict use of company IT resources to authorized users for legitimate company purposes; and (e) maintain a productive workplace use of company IT resources.

This policy is intended to clearly describe enforcement and compliance procedures and potential penalties and align expectations with regard to employee privileges and responsibilities with regard to company IT resources.

The company's performance and survival depends on the security measures specified in this AUP. Many people's jobs are dependent on the company's ability to conduct business without interruption or destruction due to computer security breaches or workplace misconduct.

AUP GUIDELINES

The company's IT resources are company property for use only by those individuals who are specifically authorized in writing by the company. Use by anyone other than these users, including spouses, partners, children, or other family members, is not permitted at any time.

The company's IT resources are to be used only for company business purposes. Occasional personal Internet access is allowed only to the extent that this use is restricted to personal time, is business appropriate, does not interfere with company business, and does not violate this AUP.

The company's IT resources are to be used in compliance with all applicable laws.

Network capacity is a scarce resource. Excessive consumption by any one user will degrade the performance of the entire network for all other users. As such, all highly resource-intensive activities (e.g., large object transfers and streaming video) should be minimized and confined to off–peak hours whenever possible.

The creation or transmission of any offensive, obscene, or indecent images, data, or other material designed or likely to offend, annoy, inconvenience, or cause anxiety is not permitted.

Any employee and nonemployee using the company IT resources does so subject to the company's right to monitor such use and are advised that if monitoring reveals possible evidence of criminal activity, the company may provide this information to law enforcement officials. Users have no expectation of privacy in anything they create, store, send, or receive on company IT resources.

One of the most important aspects of email and other electronic material is that they constitute company records. All users are responsible for managing these records according to the company's electronic records management (ERM) policy and with the same confidentiality and care as paper-based company records.

PROVISIONS AND PROHIBITIONS

Company email accounts, including email usernames and passwords, are not to be used for any purposes other than those of the company's business. They are not to be used for chat rooms, bulletin boards, instant messaging, peer-to-peer file transfers (such as music downloads), online auctions, newsgroups, or other nonbusiness-related activities. They are not to be used to subscribe to news services, travel services, financial services, online banking, games, prizes, or other Web-based nonbusiness-related forms or printed material. They are not to be used to subscribe to educational listservs, including college or university course listservs, even if the company is offering or providing tuition assistance.

Users are responsible for ensuring the accuracy of distribution lists and that messages and information are transmitted only to the intended recipients and those who have a business-related need to receive them.

Users should check email daily, delete unwanted messages, and keep remaining messages in the mailbox to a minimum. In most cases, messages should be deleted after one month, after which they may be archived to offline storage. Email attachments that exceed a preset size limit will not be permitted.

Users are not to save, forward, or send email chain letters.

Users are not to use company IT resources for personal gain not related to the company's business.

Company facilities are not be used for unauthorized political, commercial, or religious activity, including seeking employment outside of the company.

Email is not to be used for anonymous postings to online discussion forums or other online systems.

Sending or posting messages that imply or state that the user's views represent the views of the company without permission of an authorized member of management is prohibited.

Users are to honor all applicable intellectual property and licensing rights of software and Web-content manufacturers at all times. Unauthorized duplication, installation, or use of protected materials, including software, images, text, presentations, etc., is expressly prohibited.

Installation of any freely distributed software known to be incompatible with essential company-provided tools, facilities, or services is expressly prohibited. An updated list of such software is provided at (Website).

All information sent, received, created, or stored by or through company IT resources is the property of the company.

Users must scan all files and other material copied or downloaded from the Internet or noncompany computers, diskettes, or networks for viruses and other destructive programs before being accessed or saved on company-owned hardware.

All updates to company-provided software, including vendor-supplied patches, virus definition updates, etc., are to be applied in timely fashion per instructions posted by the IT department.

The creation, downloading, posting, or dissemination of harassing, threatening, discriminatory, or defamatory messages, information or materials (including those relating to sex, gender, race, national origin, veteran status, disability, marital status, religion, age, or any other classification protected by state, federal, or local law) on company IT resources is strictly prohibited. This misuse of the company's IT resources is a violation of the company's antidiscrimination/harassment policy and will not be tolerated. This misconduct will result in discipline up to and including termination. Employees should refer to the company's antidiscrimination/harassment policies for additional information.

Use of company IT resources for hacking, cracking, bugging, virus, or self-replicating program distribution, and accessing or tampering with government or private data without authorization, is prohibited.

Deleting any sent or received email messages, faxes, or computer files after the company's digital records have been subpoenaed is prohibited.

Falsely representing your position or job responsibilities to obtain information or access to trading partners, competitors, or any other party is prohibited.

Any posting, transmittal, dissemination, or receipt of classified information via the Internet or an insecure network is prohibited.

Because of export restrictions, programs or files containing encryption technology are not to be placed on the Internet or transmitted in any way outside the United States without prior written authorization from company management.

Users are to access the Internet only through the approved company's Internet firewall. Accessing the Internet directly, by modem, is strictly prohibited unless (a) the accessing computer is not physically connected to the company's network and (b) the user has received written authorizations from the IT department for any connection outside of the company's network.

Only authorized employees are allowed to access the company's network remotely. Remote access is only allowed from computers with an up-to-date, properly configured, and functioning firewall with virus protection. Security precautions must be taken whenever logging into company networks, including the protection of passwords and data pertaining to the company. Such transmissions must be encrypted or confined to private networks.

COMPLIANCE

The company may choose to monitor or review all use of its IT resources, including but not limited to

- email sent and received
- Internet usage
- computer files, documents, and faxes created, stored, deleted, or distributed
- any files that contain images, text, video, or audio for content-installed software for licensing

Be aware that all computer activities create audit trails. Deleted, edited, and overwritten computer files often cannot be erased or may be recovered using computer forensics techniques.

Users will not view another user's email without permission; send, create, or receive email or other information or material under another user's name; or tamper with, reveal, or change another user's password.

> ## EXPLICIT STATEMENT OF ACKNOWLEDGEMENT
>
> This signifies that I have read and understand the policy. I agree to comply with all of its terms and conditions. My signed acknowledgement is to be kept in my Personnel file.
>
> User's Name: _____
>
> Date: _____
>
> Witnessed by: _____
>
> Date: _____

Users are to report any violation of this AUP to [*insert name(s), contact information,* or *positions*].

The company will not be liable for the actions of users of its IT resources. All users assume full liability for their own actions. The company also takes no responsibility for any information or material transferred using company IT resources or personal equipment.

Users release the company from any and all liabilities or claims relating to the company's IT resources.

Complaints about use of the company's IT resources should be directed to [*insert name(s)*] in writing. All complaints will be handled in a professional, thorough, fair, and prompt manner.

Any use of the company's IT resources that is not in strict compliance with this AUP can result in disciplinary action up to and including immediate termination and/or legal action.

This policy may be amended or revised as necessary by the company.

Chapter Summary

To take a preemptive strike at loss and liability, an employer must exercise due diligence and reasonable care to prevent employees from causing harm. Due diligence requires implementing an up-to-date Internet and email AUP in various languages, monitoring/filtering email as part of the enforcement procedure, and providing training sessions to inform all employees of the AUP and the consequences of noncompliance.

AUPs are not silver bullets. No matter how comprehensive and well written, an AUP alone is insufficient protection against misuse, abuse, and liability. This situation is no different from mandated antiharassment and antidiscrimination policies, which extend to AUPs.

Employers who have an effective, well-publicized AUP that is enforced with proper monitoring and violation procedures have a better chance of escaping liability and damages resulting from employee abuse. Those who do not are risking liability because *employers* have the burden of proving an affirmative defense in court. Consequently, the company needs to have a visible set of control mechanisms in place with which to minimize misuse and substantiate its due diligence and reasonable care. Security controls must be applied in a fair, uniform, consistent, and unbiased way to mitigate against claims of privacy invasion, harassment, discrimination, retaliation, etc.[19]

Offensive conduct can take several forms, but email is one of the more recognized means. Inform all employees that discrimination, whether directed at them or toward others, should be promptly reported. Designate at least two individuals to receive complaints. An employee who was told to report discriminatory incidents to one specific person faces a dilemma should that individual be the alleged harasser or someone having close ties to the accused. Laws favor multiple channels for complaint reporting.

In the past few years, the courts have expanded the reasonable care standard to create a duty of oversight requiring directors and officers to act affirmatively to make sure that adequate information and compliance systems are in place.

If prevention and protection attempts fail, the computer forensic trails left behind by the unethical or disgruntled employee may be very damaging to the company, as will be discussed in Chapters 9 and 10. Employees who believe they can delete evidence of wrongdoing are wrong.

Key Terms

- duty of care
- *respondeat superior*
- scope of employment
- convention on cybercrime
- negligent supervision
- outside the scope of employment
- virtual workplace
- expressed consent

Discussion Questions

1. Compare and contrast the Allstate case to the MCIWorldcom case. What losses can Allstate expect to incur?
2. What are the dual functions of an AUP? Why is an AUP a vital security defense? Why is it a necessary legal defense?
3. What are the responsibilities imposed by the *respondeat superior* doctrine?
4. What are two examples of employee's activities that might make an employer liable for damages according to the negligent supervision doctrine?
5. What are the key characteristics of an effective AUP?
6. List five activities that need to be covered in an AUP?
7. What are some of the foreseeable violations and potential penalties that should be addressed in an AUP?
8. When, or under what circumstances, should an AUP be updated?
9. How can compliance be monitored? Does that violate employees' right to privacy? Why or why not?
10. List three activities that should be expressly prohibited in an AUP.

Endnotes

1. Gleim, Irvin N., and Jordan B. Ray, with Eugene P. O'Connor. *Business Law/Legal Studies.* Gainsville, FL: Gleim Publications, Inc. 1992.

2. Myers, Jr., George. "Keeping Eye on Workers: Monitoring Software Used to Help Restrain Growth of Internet Abuse at Office." *The Columbus Dispatch.* January 21, 2003. P. 01C.

3. Etzioni, Amitai. "Implications of Select New Technologies for Individual Rights and Public Safety." *Harvard Journal of Law & Technology.* (15 Harv. J. Law & Tec 257). Spring 2002.

4. Martin, Mark. "DMV Cuts Off Allstate Access to Digital Records." *The San Francisco Chronicle.* January 17, 2003. P. B2.

5. Lohse, Deborah. "Illegal Snooping Costs Allstate Access to Online DMV Records." *San Jose Mercury News.* January 16, 2003. http://www.siliconvalley.com/mld/siliconvalley/4965810.htm

6. Ibid. Martin.

7. Ibid. Martin.

8. Reich, Kenneth, "Allstate Loses Access to DMV Computer Data." *Los Angeles Times.* January 17, 2003. Part 2. P. 8.

9. *Daniels and Ballou v Worldcom Corporation, et al.,* U.S. District, Lexis 2335 (ND Texas 1998).

10. Andress, Mandy. "An Overview of Security Policies." http://searchsecurity.techtarget.com/originalContent/0,289142,sid14_gci822681,00.html

11. Arkfeld, Michael R. "Policing Your Firm's Technology: Address Missteps before They Occur." *Arizona Attorney.* (37 AZ Attorney 10) June 2001.

12. Zwillinger, Marc J. "Cybercrime Developing a Computer Policy Framework: What Every General Counsel Should Know." *The Internet Newsletter including legal.online.* Vol. 6, No. 3. June 2001.

13. Myers, Jr., George. "Keeping an Eye on Workers: Monitoring Software Used to Help Restrain Growth of Internet Abuse at Office." *The Columbus Dispatch.* January 21, 2003. P. 01C.

14. See *Convention on Cybercrime*, November 23, 2001. http://conventions.coe.int/Treaty/en/treaties/html/185.htm.

15. "Now More than Ever, Cybersecurity Audits are Key." *National Law Journal.* Secton: News. Vol. 24. No. 27. March 11, 2002. P. C8.

16. Ibid.

17. For example, see *In re Logue Mechanical Contracting Corp.*, 106 B.R. 436, 439 (Bankr. W.D. Pa. 1989).

18. Lawrence, Patti. "Acceptable Use: Whose Responsibility Is It?" *SANS Institute.* http://www.sans.org/rr/acceptable/responsibility.php

19. For additional resources on acceptable use and employee awareness programs, see: http://www.sans.org/rr/aware/

CHAPTER 7
SECURE-USE PRACTICES: DEFENSIVE BEST PRACTICES

Learning Objectives

- ◆ Understanding internal threats.
- ◆ Defining the managerial aspects of information security.
- ◆ Reinforcing the importance of training in secure-use practices.
- ◆ Applying best secure practices.
- ◆ Avoiding common, but insecure practices.

INTRODUCTION

This chapter focuses on what companies must do to protect themselves from internal risks. Long before hackers and the Internet, businesses were vulnerable to disgruntled and corrupted employees, careless administrators, and hostile managers. Often, serious internal security breaches are not the result of malice, but the result of loyal employees acting carelessly or out of ignorance.

Current technology and telecommunications amplify security threats that stem from dysfunctional or imprudent organizational practices. In many cases, threats defy a technological safeguard and must be addressed by changing users' practices. The most effective countermeasure can be adoption of secure-use practices and user training.

SECURE USE PRACTICES: POLICIES

MAJOR RISK FACTORS

All available evidence indicates that the most likely sources of cyber threats continue to come from within the company.[3] These threats take the form of current or former employees who abuse the network out of ignorance or intent or who actively engage in sabotage. Insider abuse can defeat even the most hardened defensive technology.

The tendency is to look at unknown and unseen hackers and thieves as the major risk factors. It is difficult to accept the reality that a majority of cyber security incidents are traced to company insiders. Moreover, most external attacks cannot succeed without some kind of help from the inside, as outlined in the TTV. Several examples follow.

- An unwitting employee may spread infected email or be tricked into revealing information through a popular hacker technique—social engineering. Manipulating authorized users into disclosing passwords is an effective method

CASE ON POINT

THE EMAIL PRANK
WITH SPOOFED SENDER

As a prank, an employee of a large New England bank composed an offensive email message and clicked *Send*. Immediately the *you have new mail* message flashed on his PC screen. When the employee opened the email message, he saw that he had sent the offensive message not only to his intended readers but to everyone in the office. His carelessly judged prank had gone wrong.[1]

In the email message, he'd poked fun at the bank's controller and written personal innuendoes and offensive jokes. More damaging, the employee had changed the name and email address to make it appear as though the controller had sent the message—a trick known as **spoofing**. This fiasco, like many other email disasters, was caused because he had mistakenly clicked *Reply to All* instead of *Reply*. Because of that mistake, he routed the message to the entire office, including the person he was ridiculing. The email was easily and quickly traced to the actual sender, who was subsequently fired.

Preventing cyber pranks, and other dangerous email, is yet another reason for implementing information security procedures, user training, and periodic reminders to everyone with access to company networks and email.

CASE ON POINT

POINT: EMAIL CREATES WORLDWIDE
PUBLIC HUMILIATION

In 2001, an email incident became known worldwide. A newly hired analyst for a British investment firm decided to boast to his friends and colleagues about the lifestyle advantages offered by his relocation to Korea. Excerpts from his message read as follows:

```
From: Peter Chung
Subject: LIVING LIKE A KING
Date: Tue, 15 May 2001 20:26:21 -0400

So I've been in Korea for about a week
and a half now and what can I say, LIFE
IS GOOD....
I've got a spanking brand new 2000 sq.
foot 3 bedroom apt. with a 200 sq. foot
terrace running the entire length of my
apartment with a view overlooking
Korea's main river and nightline ... I
go out to Korea's finest clubs, bars
and lounges pretty much every other
night on the weekdays and everyday on
the weekends to (I think in about 2
months, after I learn a little bit of
the buyside business I'll probably go
out every night on the weekdays). I
```

```
know I was a stud in NYC but I pretty
much get about, on average, 5-8 phone
numbers a night and at least 3 hot
chicks that say that they want to go
home with me every night I go out. I
love the buyside, ... I have bankers
calling me everyday with opportunities
and they pretty much cater to my every
whim - you know (golfing events, lavish
dinners, a night out clubbing). The
guys I work with are also all chill - I
live in the same apt building as my VP
and he drives me around in his Porsche
(1 of 3 in all of Korea) to work and
when we go out. What can I say,....
live is good, ... CHUNG is KING of his
domain here in Seoul.....
```

Within hours, the entire "Chung is King" email message had circulated throughout the world to almost every major investment and banking firm and to senior executives at Chung's own firm. The mere act of firing him did little to relieve the embarrassment and negative publicity this message caused the firm.[2]

TABLE 7.1	DLM Defense Infrastructure
Tier 1	Senior management commitment and support
Tier 2	Acceptable-use policies and other statements of practice
Tier 3	**Secure-use procedures**
Tier 4	Hardware, software, and network security tools

for gaining access to a network. This type of exploit is extremely difficult to prevent using technological solutions.

- Administrators may be unable or unwilling to apply software patches to fix known vulnerabilities. Hackers possess the technology to scan hundreds of thousands of servers a day over the Internet looking for security holes in operating systems or Web servers. Unpatched servers enabled Slammer to paralyze network services, including ATMs and stock trading worldwide.[4]

Effective DLM requires proper management and motivation of people. Activity on internal networks is best controlled through thoroughly documented, communicated, and enforced secure-use practices and procedures. There are limits on the extent to which these risk factors can be controlled, however.

LIMITS ON THE EXTENT TO WHICH RISK FACTORS CAN BE CONTROLLED

A complete set of updated, well-documented policies and training in security procedures can be time-consuming. And they are not without risk. In fact, some legal and HR advisors actually fear the consequences of AUP and monitoring with some justification:

- Having a policy that is selectively enforced can be worse than having none at all. If an employee files a grievance against the company claiming that he or she was treated differently, the courts will look upon selective enforcement as an unfair and self-serving mechanism for getting rid of unwanted employees.
- If the company monitors the content of employee communications and an employee sends threatening messages to others, the company has a duty of care to take action to prevent harm. If the company fails to notify law enforcement authorities as required, it can be held liable for negligence.

Risks of this nature can be mitigated through proper design and consistent enforcement of a secure-use procedures program. Moreover, they are far outweighed by the risks of allowing unrestricted and unsupervised Internet access.

ENFORCEMENT OF SECURE-USE PRACTICES MUST BE CONSISTENT WITH THE AUP

Assume that employees waste time and resources sending IM to friends, managing stock portfolios, posting political messages on Internet news groups, searching for jobs, or watching streaming videos. The IT staff notices that networks are responding slowly because of extreme bandwidth demands.

An audit of network usage reveals excessive use on the part of certain employees. Those employees admit to their activities when confronted with the evidence. To stop abuse of company property, some employees are terminated even though the company had not implemented an AUP or training in secure-use practices. The terminated employees may file a claim for millions of dollars in compensatory damages for wrongful termination. They may have a strong legal argument that the company had no right to terminate them because of the lack of formal notification or AUP training that explicitly prohibited the activities for which they were fired.[5]

Such a lawsuit may or may not succeed, but it would certainly be disruptive and expensive in the event of a settlement. This outcome cannot be blamed on any failing in the technology. The fact that it was monitoring technology that led to litigation explains why companies fear it. But this loss may have been avoided if the company had a clear written AUP and documentation of confirmation from employees that they had read, understood, and agreed to its terms.

These scenarios typify the mutual dependency among people, process, and technology in proper information security practice. Acquiring and implementing the right defensive technology is important. People and their practices are what make technology effective or render it useless.

The tools and techniques used to prevent abuse will vary, but it is always critical to have a cyber security policy in evidence. This will serve as a planning guide and, once implemented, as a template with which to measure compliance.[6]

KEY SECURE-USE PROCEDURES AND PRACTICES

INTRODUCING A SECURITY FOCUS IN THE ORGANIZATIONAL PLANNING PROCESS

All organizations operate with a business plan that defines goals, objectives, strategy, and priorities. Once the overall direction is set, individual departments and staff functions develop their plans in support of the strategic objectives. Organizations and budgets are restructured when they are found to be inconsistent with those objectives. However, this process is not always followed with information security planning. Managers may let external events, current threats, technical considerations, or trends dictate security initiatives. Although it is important to be responsive to changes in the environment, a strong connection to the business plan must be maintained.

ESTABLISHING SECURITY AS A BUSINESS FUNCTION

Profound changes in behavior and attitude are required to make security a priority. This cannot be accomplished without clear and consistent evidence that top management is committed to implementing and enforcing sound information security behavior throughout the organization. Security *as a business function* must achieve the same status as sales, marketing, and finance. One way that this is accomplished is to centralize accountability within a single office and to make the position visible and powerful. It needs to be coordinated with the other forms of risk management, including the physical security, insurance, and legal functions.

INTEGRATING SECURITY AND BUSINESS PLANS

Another key step toward establishing a cyber-secure culture is to ensure that the security plan is developed in conjunction with the overall strategic and operational plans of the firm. This will ensure that the most strategic informational assets receive the most protection. It will also reinforce the notion that security is as fundamental to the success of the business plan as any other business function. This emphasis on integration into the planning process will ensure that information security initiatives receive an allocation of resources that is consistent with their importance to the success of the business. Failure to do this creates the impression that information security policy is out of sync with the business plan, and hence not to be taken seriously.

DEPLOYING INFORMATION SECURITY STANDARDS

Once the plan is in place, and the priorities set, the actual standards and practices can be developed and documented or revised. In addition to the AUP discussed in Chapter 6, formal policy and standards documents should be developed for other basic cybersecurity functions and facilities, such as

- Firewall and gateway configuration
- Remote access procedures
- Wireless and handheld devices
- Archival storage
- Roles and permissions
- Password maintenance

It is imperative that all of these be developed together and continuously maintained to ensure consistency and currency with changes in the technology as well as the business environment. Technology standards must govern all technology purchases to ensure that automated facilities can be properly integrated and administered efficiently.

One example is the use of standard **directory protocols,** such as **Lightweight Directory Access Protocol (LDAP).** These standards make it possible to maintain or remove an employee's set of access privileges in one place and have those settings apply across all systems that are impacted.

⟨ **CYBERBRIEF** ⟩

THE COST OF VIRUS INFECTIONS

With the creation of 50 new computer viruses weekly and the increasing sophistication of hackers, the FBI estimates that actual losses by businesses across the United States reach well beyond the $7 billion mark.

Source: Veta, D. Jean, Paul W. Schmidt, and Rochelle E. Rubin, "Is Your Company Protected? Developing a Comprehensive Cyber-Security Plan to Mitigate Legal Exposure From Cyber-Crime." *Cyberspace Lawyer,* Vol. 7, No. 5. July 2002/August 2002.

DOCUMENTATION AND TRAINING

One common mistake made with regard to information security spending is that documentation and training budgets are set at a level that is below what is consistent with technology expenditures. Given the principle that human behavior is a far more critical success factor, this tendency to starve the education budget will tend to subvert the entire program.

In addition to informing employees of their own rights and responsibilities, a complete training program also points out how to recognize and react to actions on the part of others that compromise cyber security. Once everyone realizes their stake in a secure workplace, policies are more likely to be enforced in a communal fashion, which is usually the most effective method.

INCIDENT RESPONSE POLICY AND INCIDENT RESPONSE TEAMS

People need to know how to respond promptly and properly to detected or suspected attacks. Before an incident occurs, companies need to design an incident response policy and team, educate everyone as to their roles, and conduct tests to validate the plan's effectiveness.

Richard P. Salgado, senior counsel with the Computer Crime and Intellectual Property Section (CCIPS) of the Criminal Division of the DOJ, encourages companies to have a well-crafted and simple **incident response policy.** The incident response policy needs to be clear and simple so that people can follow it under very stressful conditions. An incident response policy is very important because it

- Provides guidance on what to do when faced with an attack on the system, which may have legal consequences.
- Defines the scope of the powers, authority, and discretion that the team has in responding to the attack.
- Focuses management's attention on security and response issues.[7]

Recent experience has demonstrated that the impact of certain events, like the outbreak of viruses, varies widely. The eventual outcome depends on the level of preparedness of the target firm. In 2001, there were several reported incidents of firms shutting down their email systems completely for several hours in response to what turned out to be a benign hoax.[8] At the other extreme, accomplished hackers continue exploiting security holes to which security updates have not been applied, even though updates may have been available for a long time.

DEVELOPING A NOTIFICATION PLAN

A comprehensive cyber-security plan must contain protocols for determining whom to notify in the event of a security incident. Such notification might apply to

- Law enforcement
- Regulatory authorities
- Clearinghouse organizations, such as CERT
- Business partners
- Bugtraq

In most cases, this decision is up to the victimized firm. In specific industries, such as financial services and health care, notification requirements are explicitly defined by regulation. A complete security plan should contain guidance on identifying when a hacker attack or other cyber crime triggers regulatory reporting requirements. Failure to comply with such requirements can lead to the imposition of civil monetary penalties as well as unwanted regulatory oversight and negative publicity.

The 2002 CSI/FBI Computer Crime and Security Survey reported that only 60% of known intrusions were reported to anyone not directly involved and only 34% were reported to law enforcement.[9] These figures are probably conservative. In making the decision whether to report an event, companies must balance conflicting considerations. Some companies may be reluctant to report a network breach because of perceived publicity concerns, risk of liability, and the potential for delays and costs in the event of a formal investigation.

There are also compelling arguments for selective disclosure, particularly if such communication can help limit legal liability or the spread of a successful attack across the Internet.[10] Regardless of the policy that is adopted on this sensitive issue, it should be clearly defined and understood by the response team and approved executive management.

The response plan should include detailed information on the appropriate law enforcement agency to contact, how to work with that agency to limit publicity, and how to cooperate with the agency in a way that protects the interests of all impacted parties, including customers and partners.

SECURE-USE PROCEDURES: TECHNOLOGY

Once the security goals, standards, and reporting protocols have been determined, the focus shifts to measuring where the organization stands against those standards and taking remedial action where necessary. This is a fundamental best practice. If it is not done proactively and repeatedly, a hacker, lawyer, or regulator may end up doing it instead. What follows is a list of proven techniques that will harden the defenses of a private network.

SHUT DOWN UNNECESSARY SERVICES

Network administrators should review all active **ports** to exposed servers and shut down those that are no longer necessary or justifiable. Ports are interfaces, or entry/exit points, to a network. They are numbered and usually associated with a specific process.

The same discipline applies to any physical connections that are available to the network. The strongest available network security can be defeated by a single telephone modem or wireless access point physically attached to a PC inside the firewall.

SET UP AND MAINTAIN PERMISSIONS SECURELY

With all software applications and services on a network, and employees who have access, there are numerous potential **permissions** (one user to one application) that have to be maintained. Permissions are privileges granted to each user that control what data and applications that user is allowed to access. The system administrator controls permissions.

Most applications have various tiers of privileges, ranging from basic read-only ability to full administrator functions. Ideally, everyone gets precisely the correct set of privileges consistent with their responsibilities and skills. In reality, that is far from the case because of the extraordinary time and high clearance or authority needed to administer changes in permissions.

In practice, given a choice of dealing with the hassle of being overly restrictive and denying access to essential functions or granting excessive permissions and keeping users content and productive, it is more expedient to choose the latter. This often does not create a problem because most honest employees will not actively explore the limits of what they are allowed to do. This is *security by ignorance.* A dishonest employee may test the extent of his/her permissions and then seek to exploit them for illicit purposes.

An effective way to manage permissions and access rights is to divide users into **roles,** or access-level categories, as shown in Figures 7.1 and 7.2. Roles are assigned specific access levels to the server. Each role corresponds to a job description such as "analyst" or "executive" or "sales." For each role, a complete set of privileges can be assigned to correspond to the employee's responsibilities. Individuals can then be

FIGURE 7.1 Example of Roles Assigned According to Responsibilities

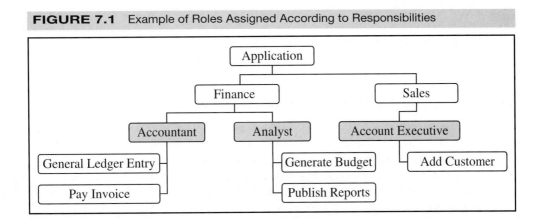

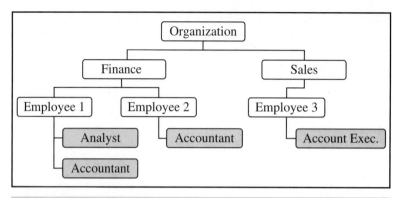

FIGURE 7.2 Example of Roles Assigned According to Employees' Job Descriptions

assigned to roles and given the access associated with that role. This way, only the roles need to be maintained when there are changes in the network.

CONDUCT BACKGROUND CHECKS

A thorough background investigation of everyone being considered for system administration positions should be conducted rigorously prior to employment. Another good security practice is to rotate responsibilities among several people to make it more difficult to hide any illicit, fraudulent, or irresponsible activity.

ENFORCE STRONG PASSWORDS

Passwords vary in effectiveness from strong to weak depending on their length, construction, and how often they are changed. There are several rules to increase the strength of password protection:

- Never install any application or service with default passwords.
- Make all passwords at least 10 characters long.
- Use numbers, letters, and symbols, such as $,* if possible.
- Do not use words. Avoid any word in the English and Klingon (from the cult TV series *Star Trek*) dictionary.
- Avoid names of sports teams, social security numbers, first names, and family names (including pets) that may reside on personnel files or be displayed on the wall.
- Change passwords at least once every four months.
- Memorize passwords and keep them secret at all times.
- Lists of passwords to be retained should be encrypted.

REVIEW PARTNER CONTRACTS

The networks of business partners become an extension of the business's own network so their level of security is critical for everyone. It is essential to take steps to protect against lapses in security on the part of business partners. One protection is to ask for third-party certification of information security practices before taking on electronic partners. At Goodrich Corp., a Charlotte, NC aerospace company, the IT team must be convinced that security is good enough that there's almost no chance of a partner having a security breach. Furthermore, it sets up a detailed procedure in case there is a breach. Goodrich requires partners to assign a response team that knows what to do and whom to contact at Goodrich if there's a security lapse.

Another step is to build provisions into partnership contracts that provide protection in the event that breaches of a partner's security result in network exposure or release of sensitive information. Special attention must be paid to contracts with outsourcers who have extensive access to vital business information.

AUDIT AND UPDATE

One area of liability that is often ignored is the use of unlicensed software. This is not limited to the use of illegally copied CDs or pirated downloads. Many commercial software applications are distributed to customers on CDs that can be installed on a limitless number of computers, but the applicable licenses are restricted to the number of purchased CDs.

Software vendors are entitled to conduct audits to ensure license compliance. One large bank had such an audit and received an unexpected bill for several million dollars to compensate for excessive installations and maintenance in arrears. The best protection is to survey all computers for illegal applications proactively. This can be done automatically over the network using special tools designed for the purpose.

As we have discussed previously, much of the vulnerability to hacking we currently see is the direct result of a failure to address known vulnerabilities in commercial software that have been identified, publicized, and repaired by the vendors. People who do not pay for software do not or cannot maintain it. This includes updates to patch security holes.

@LERT
System administrators are often very reluctant to apply security patches to key infrastructure components like operating systems and databases for one simple reason. In a complex environment, these patches have been known to cause previously functional services to break down in unexpected ways. This process is known as **regression.** Regression testing is generally used to certify all updates to key components before application, but this process can be costly and time-consuming. It is often impractical given the frequency with which these patches are released.

PHYSICAL SECURITY

Although most businesses recognize the need for physical security, it is generally applied unevenly. Some companies protect data centers like Fort Knox, only to put routers in

⟨ **CYBERBRIEF** ⟩

RECYCLED HARD DRIVES EXPOSE SENSITIVE DATA

Recently, MIT graduate students Simson Garfinkel and Abhi Shalat discovered and documented the vulnerability created by hard disk drives that are not disposed of properly. They purchased 158 recycled units from local dealers and over eBay. Of these, 129 were still working. Some of what they recovered from these drives included

- thousands of active credit card numbers.
- pharmaceutical and health records.
- legal correspondence.
- sensitive corporate memoranda.
- pornographic images.

Only 12 had been thoroughly cleaned and were completely free of recoverable data.

Source: Junnarkar, Sandeep. "Old Hard Drives Yield Data Bonanza." *C\net News.com.* January 15, 2003. http://news.com.com/2100-1040-980824.html

unlocked closets within publicly accessible rooms. Thousands of laptops and PDAs that contain highly sensitive, unprotected information are lost at airports every year.

Here are some basic steps to take to keep information physically secure:

- Keep offline storage devices like portable hard drives, floppies, zip disks, printed documents, and reports, etc., locked.
- Use passwords to protect laptop sign-on and any folders containing sensitive data.
- Consider using encryption on all offline storage of sensitive data, including backup and archives.
- Make sure network devices in the field are in a physically secure space.
- Dispose of old computers with extreme care. Uninstall and erase all software and data so that it cannot be recovered. This also applies to removable media, including backups. Dumpster diving is not just about paper.
- Scan the network for any undocumented devices or external connections such as modems or wireless access points.

⟨ **CYBERBRIEF** ⟩

STOLEN LAPTOPS

In a survey of 503 security professionals, 134 reported instances of laptop theft, with a dollar loss of $11,766,500, or nearly $88,000 per incident, with most damage from the loss of proprietary information.

Source: "Cyber Crime Bleeds U.S. Corporations, Survey Shows; Financial Losses from Attacks Climb Third Year in a Row." *Computer Security Institute Press Release.* April 7, 2002. http://www.gocsi.com/press/20020407.html

AUDIT AND TEST

Audits demonstrate diligence to current and potential partners, customers, and investors. They may deter potential legal adversaries, who know that they are less likely to win a case if the company can demonstrate ongoing attention to effective information security. **Security audits,** like financial audits, work best when they are conducted both internally and certified by a recognized third-party expert.

Security audits should include all aspects of the security program, including technology, procedures, documentation, training, and personnel in some cases. A complete audit includes simulated attack drills to test the response of both the defensive technology and the designated response team. This activity should be coordinated with a conventional disaster recovery test, as these plans share many of the same personnel, processes, and resources. Backup sites require the same standards as the main operating facilities, as it is accepted practice among hackers to attack backup sites when they are known to be in use after a publicized disaster.

OTHER SECURE PRINCIPLES AND PRACTICES

INSURANCE

The insurance industry has begun to address the new business risks associated with information security within a connected enterprise. Among the specific cyber risks that can now be explicitly covered are

- Liability from virus transmission.
- Loss of income from a denial of service attack.
- Business interruption stemming from destruction of software or data.
- Liability resulting from the release of confidential information.
- Fraud resulting directly from the abuse of electronic credentials.
- Breach of intellectual property rights.

Just as important, the insurance companies are taking the lead in working with their customers to develop new and effective ways to manage cyber risk on an ongoing basis, just as they do with conventional risks.

⟨ CYBERBRIEF ⟩

HACKER INSURANCE

Hacker insurance, or "network risk insurance," is expected to reach $2.5 billion in volume by 2005, according to industry projections. This is, in part, the result of the expiration of existing commercial general liability policies that are being replaced by policies that contain explicit exclusions for hacker-related losses. Some hacker insurance includes extortion coverage, a reward for information leading to the conviction of cyber criminals, and money to hire a public relations firm for image repair.

Source: Reuters. January 27, 2003.

⟨ **CYBERBRIEF** ⟩

COMMON HOAXES

- **The Jdbgmgr (Teddy Bear Virus) Hoax:**
  This urgent warning comes from a friend
  telling you to delete a program called
  jdbmgr.exe. In reality, it is the Java Debugger
  Manager that comes with Windows and has
  an icon that looks like a Teddy Bear.

- **Bill Gates Wants You:** Impossible as it
  may seem, Bill Gates is contacting you, personally. Not only that, he wants to pay you
  hundreds of dollars to help test some new
  software.

- **Money for Nothing in Nigeria:** You
  receive an urgent, confidential message
  from a Nigerian government official who
  wants to stash millions of dollars in your
  bank account to get around a local bureau-
  cratic snafu. Just respond with your name
  and bank account number.

- **Save Big Bird:** We are often reminded that
  PBS needs public support to keep delivering
  its programming. So it comes as no surprise
  when you receive a professionally written
  plea warning that the system is in danger.
  You don't even have to send money, just forward the message to all your friends.

- **Help a Sick Child:** This one appeals to the
  parent in all of us and promises a donation
  to a charity for sick children for every person who forwards the message to a parent.

- **Let the Good Times Roll:** Frightened
  recipients frantically forward a bogus advi-
  sory to everyone they know. One of the
  earliest warned recipients not to read or
  download any files with the name Good
  Times. Of course, the message spread like a
  virus, clogging mail servers.

Source: The Big List of Internet Hoaxes. http://Hoaxbusters.org/

STAYING CURRENT

According to a recent survey, 75% of companies that have information security policies in place do not keep them current; and only 9% of employees understand what
their companies' security policies are.[11] The rapid pace of change in the business climate and the relatively immature nature of security technology ensure that policies
and procedures tend to have a very short shelf life. Not only must the policies themselves be kept up-to-date but the employees entrusted with the application of policy
must also be kept current and aware of the most current threats and hoaxes.

REINFORCING SECURE-USE PROCEDURES

One way to keep users aware of their role in cyber security is to put reminders and
warnings in the log-on process. Of course, their effectiveness depends on employees'
beliefs about the importance of reading those reminders. When employees log in, the
first thing they should see is a *warning* message and not a welcome message.
Employees cannot be disciplined or fired for if they have "welcome" access to proprietary information. The courts have found that providing employees with a "welcome"
type of message implies that they are authorized to access that network.

REWARDING SECURE BEHAVIOR

Positive reinforcement is always an effective way to build good security practice. This
requires that everyone understand they have a key role to play in maintaining the

safety of the firm's assets that are directly tied to overall success. Acknowledging participation in good security practices is as important as responding swiftly to risky or unacceptable behavior.

WORST PRACTICES

Just as there are best practices to be encouraged, there are also some particularly dangerous worst practices that should specifically be avoided. The following are among the most prevalent.

DANGEROUS EMAIL PRACTICES

Email forwarding

It seems many people cannot resist reading something funny or informative in email, then forwarding it on to others. This practice propagates viruses, hoaxes, social engineering schemes, malicious humor, and cyber fraud. Forwarding of email should not be allowed to or from company email accounts.

Auto Reply

Auto reply or **auto responders** are an email feature that allows the system to send a prepared message automatically to every email message it receives. This is often considered a courtesy to inform senders that the recipient is unavailable to read messages at the current time. This also informs hackers that this email account is available for use since no one is using it. Auto replies also guarantee that **spammers,** who send junk email, will receive a response to their messages. This validates the victim's address on their lists. Generally, it is best to avoid using this feature.

HTML eMail

HTML email makes it possible to enhance text with color, bolding, italics, images, and links to Websites. It also makes it possible to remotely invoke malicious programs designed, among other things, to contact secret Websites with information about you without your knowledge. As a result, many firms filter out all HTML messages at their email gateways. Most email programs give the user a choice as to whether to compose messages in HTML or plain text.

Instant Messaging

Many people find IM a convenient way to stay in close contact with friends and business contacts. Most IM applications are insecure by design, and messages are subject to interception by outsiders. IM activity over the Internet can, in some cases, be used as a backdoor into an otherwise secure network. There are some secure IM applications on the market, but they must be configured correctly. For all IM allowed on the network, guidelines for its use should be covered in the AUP.

DANGEROUS SHARING PRACTICES

Sharing resources may be considered virtuous in a civilized society, but it is generally a very bad practice when applied to networked digital assets. Some specific examples include the following.

<⟩ **CYBERBRIEF** ⟨

A SPREADSHEET REVEALS CONFIDENTIAL DATA

A helpful, but careless, HR person sent an employee phone extension list to everyone at her company. The spreadsheet had a special feature: hidden columns that were easily revealed to show everyone's pay, bonuses, and stock options, including those of senior management. Fortunately, she had a new job lined up at the time.

Source: Luhn, Robert "D'oh! The Most Disastrous E-Mail Mistakes." *PC World.com.* April 29, 2002.
http://www.pcworld.com/features/article/0,aid,93283,00.asp

Peer to Peer (P2P) Networks

Use of networks of peer computers to share files, popularized by music services such as Napster, is an extremely dangerous practice from a cyber security standpoint. These networks are becoming the second most effective way, after email, for malware authors to distribute their destructive payload to unsuspecting victims. Again, larger firms should, and generally do, block all such activity through their Internet gateways. Individuals and smaller businesses that cannot enforce this automatically need to rely on education to avoid exposure.

Software Downloads

Just about every PC user takes advantage of the vast number of useful software applications that are available for free over the Internet. Some, like Adobe Acrobat Reader, are almost essential. There are also many dangers associated with the use of free downloads. Trojan horses hidden within legitimate programs are common. The most benign of these will simply compromise privacy by sending information about your computer to the software author. This is known as **spyware.** More malicious programs will destroy programs and data.

Unauthorized Users

PCs and PDAs issued by a business for professional use should never be shared by anyone other than the person to whom it was assigned. This is generally a primary stipulation in an AUP. Beyond the fact that unauthorized users do not have the necessary training and skills for acceptable use, any breakdown in cyber security resulting from such use could expose the company to additional legal liability or invalidate the firm's insurance coverage.

Public Networks and Wireless Networks

Public networks, particularly wireless networks, are becoming an increasingly popular amenity at hotels, networks, trade shows, and cafes. Connecting a PC or handheld to wireless networks exposes it to anyone who is monitoring that network. Extra precaution is needed to shield sensitive information on wireless networks and VPNs. Those PCs must have a personal firewall, password protection, and encryption.

Chapter Summary

There are numerous risks and dangers that need to be controlled by secure-use practices. Those practices involve policies and technology. There are best practices to follow and worst practices that must be avoided. These practices need to become part of the company's culture and integrated with other human resource and security policies.

The effectiveness of security practices requires uncompromising diligence. Policies and technology help harden the electronic wall around the enterprise. Through the institution of secure-use practices, organizations can strike the appropriate balance between security and capability, while getting the most from their investments in protective technology.

Effective information security, like any other process, originates *inside* the organization. It requires informed leadership, investment, and attention to detail and innovation. A secure, productive environment can only be achieved when the appropriate set of secure-use practices governs every aspect of online activity.

Key Terms

- spoofing
- directory protocol
- lightweight directory access protocol (LDAP)
- incident response policy
- port
- permissions
- roles
- regression
- security audit
- auto reply or auto responders
- spammer
- spyware

Discussion Questions

1. Why have organizations been slow to implement training in secure-use practices?
2. How might companies effectively reinforce training?
3. Should compliance with policies be rewarded? Why, or why not?
4. What should a person do who witnesses obvious dangerous behavior? What should a person do who witnesses potentially dangerous behavior?
5. What are the characteristics of strong passwords? What are characteristics of weak passwords?
6. Why is a majority of cyber-security intrusion unreported?
7. Why might administrators be reluctant to apply security patches to applications or software as soon as those patches become available?
8. What are the risks of wireless networks? What policy rules can improve wireless security?

Endnotes

1. McCafferty, Joseph. "The Phantom Menace." *CFO Magazine.* Vol. 15. No. 6. June 1, 1999. P. 89.
2. Cavallini, Silvia. "The E-Mail Read 'Round the World.'" *The Industry Standard.* May 22 2001.
3. See *2002 CSI/FBI Security Survey* at http://www.gocsi.com
4. Mimoso, Michael S. "SQL Worm Slows Internet: Some Root DNS Servers Down." *SearchSecurity.com.* January 2003.

5. Rothke, Ben. "Put it in Writing." *Access Control and Security Systems Integration.* May 2001.

6. Burkitt, Mike. "Security Strategy Must Go Beyond Technology." *Computing.* March 28, 2002. P. 35.

7. Salgado, Richard P. "Forensics and Incident Response." *Framework and Best Practices: Managerial and Legal Issues.* (8.5) SANS Institute. March 2003.

8. Konrad, Rachel "Duped by Worm Hoax, Victims Seek File Fix." *CNET news.com* May 31, 2001.

9. *2002 CSI/FBI Computer Crime and Security Survey.* http://www.gocsi.com

10. Ibid. Veta, July 2002/August 2002.

11. Ernst and Young's *2001 Information Security Survey.* http://www.ey.com

CHAPTER 8

TECHNOLOGY AND AUDITING SYSTEMS: HARDWARE AND SOFTWARE DEFENSES

Learning Objectives

◆ Defining defense-in-depth.

◆ Creating a layered-technology approach.

◆ Using multiple and diverse layers of security technology.

◆ Understanding the functions and limitations of security technology.

◆ Reviewing security audits and logs.

INTRODUCTION

Computer crimes and threats are increasing in number and severity, and so are fears about them. Hackers have been a threat for decades, but the attacks on the World Trade Center and the Pentagon have raised fears that terrorist groups might wreak havoc on the Internet.[1] While cyber terror attacks are not considered weapons of mass destruction, they are *weapons of mass disruption*. Companies feeling the pressure from these concerns are primarily in telecommunications, transportation, financial services, and the chemical, water, energy, and power grid industries. These services comprise the **critical infrastructures** that the national economy depends on. Companies in these sectors and their business partners must guard against cyber terrorism now that critical infrastructure protection is a national priority.[2]

Interdependencies—where one computer system may be secure but threatened because it is tied to another that is not secure—make it necessary for all companies to implement multiple and diverse layers of technology security. Perfect security is impossible, but organizations need a level of security appropriate to their business and their operational needs and as required by national security mandates.

In this chapter, essential defensive technologies and reconnaissance tools, including those used by hackers, are discussed. These technologies include firewalls, port scanners, intrusion detection systems, virus detectors, authentication mechanisms, public key infrastructure, virtual private networks, and encryption. Multiple and diverse layers of security software, hardware, and auditing systems are needed for several reasons. First, they validate and enforce compliance with AUPs, secure-use practices, and other legal requirements. Second, multilayered defenses are necessary countermeasures to stop the spread of malware, to monitor for illegal activity, and to filter **inbound**

> **CASE ON POINT**

WIRELESS VULNERABILITY DISCOVERY

During a vulnerability audit, the IT security analyst at a food processing plant discovered serious network security gaps despite his company's multimillion dollar investment in IT security.[3] In particular, he had discovered the presence of wireless access points, which were direct violations of the company's security policy. The analyst discovered these violations by simply walking through headquarters scanning for wireless connections with a self-made detection tool. His tool for detecting wireless LAN connections consisted of a notebook computer with an antenna.

One of the violators was the director of marketing. He was using a laptop computer with a wireless card and an unencrypted connection to the company network. This single connection exposed the company's communication and file transfers to anyone with a PC or PDA, a $100 wireless card, and free detection software downloaded off the Web. Corporate network traffic could have been monitored from as far away as several hundred yards.

> **CASE ON POINT**

FUTURE BATTLEFIELD

During the May 8, 2002 Senate hearing on securing the infrastructure, Senator Robert F. Bennett referred to the following statement by Osama bin Laden that came out on December 27, 2001: "It is very important to concentrate on hitting the U.S. economy through all possible means. Look for the key pillars of the U.S. economy. The key pillars of the enemy should be struck." According to Senator Bennett, this makes it clear that

He wants to go after the economy. And obviously critical infrastructure represents,

by definition, those parts of the economy that he would attack. . . . 85 percent of the critical infrastructure in this country is owned by the private sector, so this represents a vulnerability different than any we've ever faced in warfare before. Always before an enemy would concentrate on military targets. . . . In this case, as Osama bin Laden's quote indicates, they're going to go after any aspect of the economy that would shut us down . . . and 85 percent of the future battlefield is in private, not public hands.[4]

TABLE 8.1	DLM Defense Infrastructure
Tier 1	Senior management commitment and support
Tier 2	Acceptable-use policies and other statements of practice
Tier 3	Secure-use procedures
Tier 4	**Hardware, software, and network security tools**

⬡ **CYBERBRIEF** ⬡

WHEN TO FIX THE FLAW

According to security expert and SANS Fellow Stephen Northcutt: "How do you know if something is a priority countermeasure in a world where everything is the number one priority? If an attacker can exploit a vulnerability from the Internet as easily as a hot knife slicing through butter, you have to decide whether you want to fix the problem before or after the system is compromised."

Source: Northcutt, Stephen. *Network Intrusion Detection: An Analyst's Handbook.* Indianapolis, IN: New Riders Publishing, 1999, P. 195.

packets received from the Internet or by email and **outbound packets** sent from the company network. Inbound and outbound packets are filtered to deny transfer of dangerous packets.

FACTORS DRIVING THE NEED FOR DIVERSE TECHNOLOGY LAYERS

GROWTH IN COMPUTER CRIME

Growth in the number of users, online services, and devices connected to the Internet has made more computer crimes possible, profitable, and low-risk. The first half of 2002 saw a 28% increase in Internet attacks, and almost 200,000 of them were successful.[5]

Fifty or more new computer viruses are created each week.[6] Using evidence from sophisticated malware and hacker attacks, the FBI estimated that losses by U.S. businesses had exceeded $7 billion in 2001.[7] This estimate does not include the costs of fraud or damages by disgruntled or corrupted employees, which will be discussed in Chapter 10.

However, estimates cannot reflect all damages because security specialists and others worry that sharing sensitive data about intrusions exposes them to job loss, embarrassment, or lawsuits. With the government, customers, and shareholders' low tolerance for security breaches, companies and their officers most likely will be held responsible for losses caused by failing to apply security technology correctly. Furthermore, because of ever-new hacker/criminal activity, technology plans must be updated regularly and network activity must be monitored frequently for suspicious behavior. The harsh alternatives are to learn about an intrusion from a system crash, a call from an angry system administrator, by reading it in the daily news, or worse.

GROWTH IN SOFTWARE COMPLEXITY AND FLAWS

Due to complexity or design flaws, operating systems and software have become even more vulnerable to malicious code and crime. New ecommerce services, such as digital cash and digital certificates, and interorganizational online collaboration have created greater opportunities for fraud. Companies have made themselves easy prey by not

⟨ **CYBERBRIEF** ⟩

SHARING ATTACK DATA COULD THWART HACKERS

According to a model developed by two Harvard University security researchers, organizations that share their sensitive data about network attacks and security breaches are less attractive targets. This decreases their chances of being attacked. Hackers who invest their time and money searching for and exploiting vulnerabilities in common applications want to keep that information confidential. Once the information is revealed, it reduces their chances of successfully compromising other potential targets.

Source: Fisher, Dennis. "How Sharing Thwarts Hacks." *eWeek.* January 13, 2003. http://www.eweek.com/article2/0,3959,825430,00.asp

implementing technologies needed to secure their new ways of doing business. They introduce wireless networks or IM without encryption *and* firewalls. Or they run their internal networks, called **intranets,** on the Internet without adequate security checkpoints.

Vendors issue security patches to fix security holes in their software or applications. This leads to another closely related factor driving the need for a layered technology—the rate of release of security patches.

GROWTH IN THE RELEASE RATE OF SECURITY PATCHES AND SERVICE PACKS

The Cases on Point in Chapters 2 and 3 emphasized the importance of keeping software patches up-to-date. Software patches, which Microsoft refers to as **service packs,** could have protected companies against Slammer and Code Red, other malware infections, and hackers. This seems like an obvious and easy solution, but the rate at which hackers or experts find new software vulnerabilities has reached nearly 50 per week.

The patch problem stems from vendors releasing software that has not been adequately tested with serious security holes that are subsequently fixed with software patches. Typically, patches must first be downloaded from a commercial or government Website and then installed. IT managers may spend an average of two hours per server to test and deploy a patch. Research company Gartner estimates that the total cost to a company with 1,000 servers is roughly $300,000 per patch.

There are tools available for managing or automating the server and desktop patches that cut the time and cost involved. However, patching is "a problem that's reached ridiculous proportions" says Lloyd Hession, chief information security officer (CISO) at Radianz, a financial services network provider.[8] "In most instances, the tech people are [just] worried about keeping the network up and applications running," according to Ron Baklarz, CISO for the American Red Cross in Falls Church, Virginia.[9] When the IT staff must also deal with the complex security component, it has an adverse impact on their ability to support users.

SECURITY TECHNOLOGY

NO "OUT-OF-THE-BOX" SOLUTIONS

Without correct installation and monitoring of security mechanisms, no set of defenses will be resistant to attack. There are no tools that are usable "out of the box." Furthermore, security tools have widely varying

- Deployment costs.
- Installation or implementation complexity.
- Operational and maintenance costs.
- Potential to be effective.

Many people falsely believe that technology solutions, such as firewalls, once installed, offer continuous automatic protection. They must be maintained if they are to serve any purpose. Without maintenance, they will cease to function.

TOOLS AND TARGETS

Technology tools can be very expensive to purchase and maintain. Regardless of cost, they will be useless if they are applied indiscriminately, used improperly, or installed using default settings, as was discussed in Chapter 7.

Servers may be unprotected either because they were installed improperly or because patches were never installed, explains Fred Rica, a PricewaterhouseCoopers partner and national leader for its National Threat and Vulnerability Assessment Practice in New Jersey. Another problem is that in the rush to keep up with the demand of electronic business systems, organizations have often turned to off-the-shelf software, much of which is released without thorough security testing, thus making entire systems vulnerable. Ultimately, the corporate consumer must determine where the holes are and fix them.[10]

Technology tools often are targets for hackers who want to infiltrate networks, or simply prove they can defeat the latest defenses. With each reported security breach, defenders try to harden vulnerable technologies—and the cycle begins again. This cyclical process leads to the development and marketing of new or upgraded hardware and software tools, whose effective life span continues to shorten.

@LERT
Thousands of viruses get released weekly. The availability of Windows-based programs, such as Worm Generator 2000 and Sub7even's Trojan virus creator, encourages script kiddies to create viruses. The ICQ Chat Kicker can be used to launch attacks against ICQ users.

MULTILAYERED, DIVERSE TECHNOLOGY INFRASTRUCTURE

Multiple layers of various types of technology are needed at various checkpoints in the network—from **host computers** to personal computing devices—to compensate for

<CYBERBRIEF>

PRELIMINARY SCANNING, OR INFORMATION GATHERING, LEAVES AN ELECTRONIC TRAIL INDICATING A CYBER TERRORIST ATTACK

Mark Fabro, president and chief scientist at Terrasec Corp., a Canadian information security firm, says that since 1998 there have been no less than three global scanning projects sponsored by rogue nations. When the intrusion detection logs of large multinational corporations are "closely and correctly cross-referenced, they show precise data-gathering operations in which outsiders are looking at network structure, points of weakness, and infrastructure locations of weak security."

Source: Shein, Esther. "Are Companies Prepared for Cyber-Terrorism? Security Experts Say Attacks on Corporate Networks May Already be Under Way." *CFO Magazine.* December 1, 2001. http://www.cfo.com/article/1,5309,5988,00.html

software weak in quality and users weak in judgment. A host is a computer system on a network that has full two-way access to other computers on that network. The effectiveness of technology protection against hacker attacks and lawsuits increases with vigilant auditing of networks, applications, and employees for signs of vulnerability or unauthorized use.

CHARACTERISTICS OF A DEFENSIVE TECHNOLOGY INFRASTRUCTURE

Security hardware and software are countermeasures to the threats and vulnerabilities outlined in the TTV so they must be expertly implemented, maintained, and documented. A defensive technology infrastructure depends on appropriate security technologies

- Properly installed and configured at correct checkpoints.
- Placed on each device connected to the network.
- Continuously maintained, patched, and audited.
- With incident response and disaster recovery plans in place.
- Routinely tested by people with technology expertise.

Clearly, no amount of senior management commitment or policy statements eliminates the need for IT security people who know what they are doing.[11] They must have resources to provide for an educated staff and to learn about developments in hardware/software vulnerabilities. Experts at the security company Foundstone predict that the success of security is directly related to the location of the security officer in the organizational chart. Without power (and money), servers may not get set up correctly or documented. And difficult decisions may be swayed by concerns that compromise security.

One of their tasks is making difficult technology decisions. Technology decisions are difficult because they require trade-offs between utility and security, between user convenience and controlled access, and between privacy and the need to monitor activity and content. These difficulties increase when the primary directive is to get systems up and running.

UNDERLYING TECHNICAL ISSUES

FUNCTIONAL REQUIREMENTS OF HARDWARE AND SOFTWARE

Before implementing technical solutions, the critical requirements of security hardware and software need to be identified. Those requirements include

- *Confidentiality:*   The information (or file or message) must be protected from unauthorized disclosure.
- *Integrity:*   The information must be protected from unauthorized, unanticipated, or unintentional modification.
- *Authenticity:*   The content must not have been altered.
- *Nonrepudiation:*   The origin or the receipt of a specific message is verifiable by a third party and cannot be denied.
- *Accountability:*   The actions of an entity can be traced uniquely to that entity.
- *Availability:*   The IT resources, both systems and data, are available on a timely basis to meet mission requirements or to avoid substantial losses. Availability also includes ensuring that resources are used only for intended purposes.[12]

Technology decisions have to take each of these requirements into consideration. A system that is made highly secure by restricting access to only a few individuals or requiring time-consuming log-on procedures rates low on the *availability* requirement, and vice versa.

As discussed in Chapter 3, data are transferred over networks in units called *packets*. IP does not include mechanisms to ensure the integrity or authenticity of data transmissions. A variety of tools are needed to compensate for IP vulnerabilities.

TCP/IP

TCP/IP (transmission control protocol/Internet protocol) is *the* protocol of the Internet. A system must run TCP/IP to connect to the Internet. TCP/IP works by assigning an IP number, or address, to each computer that wants to communicate via the network. An **IP address** uses a four-part scheme to uniquely identify every computer that is connected to the Internet. The IP address is made up of four parts called an *octet*. An example of an IP address is 128.4.8.43.

Individuals and organizations are assigned IP addresses, or ranges of IP addresses, by their Internet service providers (ISPs). Each ISP receives its set of IP addresses from a central governing body called **ARIN,** or the American Registry for Internet Numbers. ARIN controls the allocation of IP addresses to ensure that there are no duplicates.[13]

PORTS

TCP/IP uses IP addressing to route data packets to a destination computer. Every IP address is broken down further into smaller components called **TCP/IP ports.** A port is a number that tells IP what application is trying to communicate. To ensure that packets get delivered to their intended application, port numbers are assigned to each application on a network.[14]

For example, the main uses of the Internet are Web pages, email, and file downloads. These services use protocols that are subsets of TCP/IP. The **HTTP (hypertext transfer protocol)** is for Web pages. **SMTP (simple mail transfer protocol)** is for email. **FTP (file transfer protocol)** is for file transfer. These protocols are assigned specific ports.

@LERT

For a complete listing of all of the well-known port numbers, see http://www.iana.org/assignments/port-numbers/

Ports are set to **listen** for incoming requests for a connection and accept them. For example, port 80 listens for requests for connections to the Website to accept the connection. The port identifies the application that is speaking or listening. The combination of IP addresses and ports is one way to differentiate between expected and unexpected or illicit traffic on a network.

FILE INTEGRITY CHECKER

A checksum (discussed in Chapter 3) is a numeric value used to verify that a file has not been tampered with. It is calculated based on the contents of the file. It is a fast way to check if anything in a file had been changed. If there has been a change in the file's contents—even a single character or space—the checksum would be radically different. Thus, an infected file can be detected because of the change in its checksum. However, when an existing file is modified, you have to create a new checksum. This is often too inconvenient for users to do whenever they modify any file. Tripwire software can be used to create an MD5 (message digest) checksum snapshot of a system.

ROUTERS

Routers are devices that transfer packets between two or more networks. A router contains continuously updated directories of Internet addresses called *routing tables*. The router takes each packet from the original document and sends it to the next available router in the direction of the destination Website. Because each router is connected to many other routers, and because the connection between any two given routers may be congested with traffic at a given moment, packets from the same document are typically sent to different routers. Each of these routers, in turn, repeats this process, forwarding each packet it receives to the next available router in the direction of the destination Website. Collectively, this process is called **dynamic routing.** Some routers incorporate technology that allows for filtering at the application level, which can prevent viruses from infecting Web servers.

PERIMETER AND FILE PROTECTION

MAINTAINING CONFIDENTIALITY AND INTEGRITY

There are several tools to protect against or to monitor intrusion. They help ensure that inbound or outbound traffic, or both, are safe. These tools are

1. Firewalls
2. Intrusion detection systems (IDS)
3. Access control and virtual private networks (VPN)
4. Biometrics and tokens
5. Antivirus software
6. Cryptography/encryption
7. Public key infrastructure (PKI) and certificates

FIREWALLS

Most people have only a rudimentary understanding of what a **firewall** does, protects a company from the Internet. Few understand how a firewall provides that protection. The basic definition of a firewall is that it protects one computer network from another. In most cases, the firewall not only protects a company's network from the Internet, it also protects one part of a company's network—for example, payroll—from the rest of the network. It does this by permitting or denying certain types of traffic to pass through based on the source address in the IP packet, as shown in Figure 8.1.

The combination of IP addresses and ports is the only way for a firewall to identify "good" traffic that should be let into and out of the network, and "bad" traffic that should be blocked. The firewall looks at the individual IP packets and decides what to allow or deny based on the rules configured on the firewall.

Correct Location for a Firewall

Figure 8.2 shows the correct physical location of a firewall to protect a network from the Internet. A firewall located off in a remote part of the private network won't be effective in providing Internet protection. In order to provide protection from the Internet, the firewall needs to be the first device the Internet connection encounters once it enters the company.

FIGURE 8.1 Basic Function of a Firewall

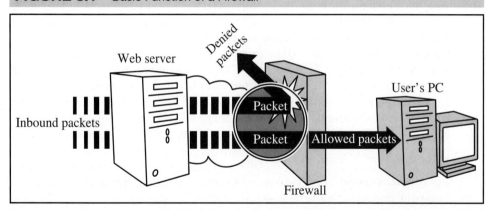

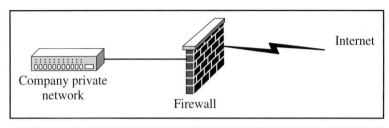

FIGURE 8.2   Correct Location of a Firewall

Block or Allow Functions of Firewalls
Depending on the firewall, it can be configured to

- Block all access to specific devices on a network from certain sources, which are identified by the source IP address.
- Selectively block access depending on the content of the message as identified by key words or other text in the data area of the IP packet.
- Block devices from accessing specific external services.
- Block any response that is not consistent with the request that triggered it.

Firewall applications can be implemented in hardware, software, or a combination of the two. Since they are usually rule based, they are flexible. The rules must be programmed correctly and thoroughly to allow legitimate communication and deny unauthorized attempts. They should also block outbound traffic (originating from within the network) from access to external services that violate the AUP.

Firewalls can be stand-alone devices but often are combined with other technologies, such as IDS, to better secure the perimeter between the company network and the Internet. Firewall logs collect valuable data for analysis and learning about the traffic allowed and denied by source, destination, or service.

There are several types of firewalls in terms of their components. Two main types of firewalls are *packet filters* and *proxy servers*.

Packet Filter Firewalls
Packet filters control the flow of data into and out of a network. A packet filter examines header information in the packet—specifically, source and destination addresses and the type of service being initiated. Port numbers indicate the type of service. Web pages are transmitted using the HTTP service, which is usually assigned to port 80. File transfers often use the FTP service, which is routed through ports 20 or 21.

These pieces of information are compared to a set of rules called an **access control list (ACL)** that is configured and maintained by the system administrator. Based on rules defined in the ACL, the packet filter decides whether to accept or deny packets traveling to or from a particular IP address; or whether to allow access to/from network applications and services based on port number. For example, a packet filtering rule can be defined to allow users inside the company's LAN (local area network) to use FTP (port 20) to access the Internet but block access to port 20 from users outside the LAN.

Weaknesses of Packet Filtering

They Are Based on Historical Events   Packet filtering does a good job of enforcing policy and protecting against known threats coming from specific places. The nature of rule-based systems, however, is that the rules are based on experience. They cannot anticipate new threats very well. If a packet does not violate a filtering rule, it is allowed to pass through to the network.

They Do Minimum Filtering, Allowing for Buffer Overflows Another weakness is that packet filters only examine the header information, but not the payload. Hackers make use of this weakness by using tools freely available on the Internet to create malicious packets that appear to the filter as a normal packet. These are normal packets in that their header information is valid. However, malicious packets have payloads that can overload the computer's buffer, causing a **buffer overflow,** and disrupt the network. To protect against this type of attack, other defensive techniques are required.

STATEFUL INSPECTION FIREWALLS

A more robust firewall performs **stateful inspection.** With stateful inspection, the fields in the inbound IP packet are compared to fields in the outbound messages that had preceded it. This information is used to build a database of characteristics of legitimate traffic. An example is the permission of a file transfer connection to a specific PC following a request for a file coming from that same PC, which is known by its IP address.

PROXY SERVER FIREWALLS

If outbound packets are sent from the corporate server to the Internet, those packets contain the corporate server's IP address. By revealing this IP address, extremely confidential information is exposed. An IP address is needed to attack a network device. To prevent packets from revealing any critical IP addresses, a **proxy server,** or, simply, *proxy,* is used to intercept and relay all inbound/outbound requests. In this way, the identity of internal network is hidden.

The proxy server makes requests to the Internet using the proxy's IP address instead of the actual source network address and evaluates the data returned. This is important because the proxy not only looks at header information, it also examines the data portion of the IP packet. If the data or commands in the packet are suspicious, the proxy server discards the packet. Proxy servers can also be used to block access from within a private network to Websites and services considered off-limits by the AUP.

MULTIPLE-DEFENSE FIREWALLS

Proxy servers should be used with packet filters. As stated, unless they are configured correctly and tested thoroughly, however, they will fail to protect against intrusions and may block legitimate traffic. Certain Internet services, like automatic updates to AV software from the publisher, require special adjustments to operate through a proxy server. If no one at the company is experienced with firewalls or proxy servers, this job should be outsourced to an expert.

Firewalls, routers, and proxies can be used to create a barrier between the local (private) and public (Internet) networks. Those barriers are called *demilitarized zones,* or DMZs.

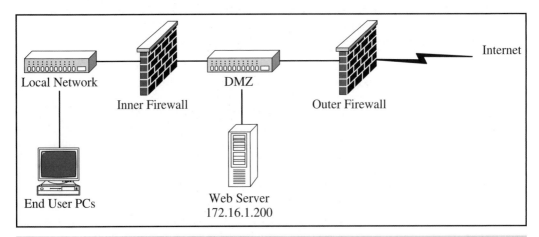

FIGURE 8.3 Multilayered, Diverse Technology Architecture of Firewalls and a DMZ

DMZ

Web servers, FTP sites, and other servers that are intended to be visible and directly accessible on the Internet are the most vulnerable servers on a private network. To protect the rest of the network, there should be a buffer zone that separates the public server(s) from the rest of the private domain. This is referred to as a **DMZ.** Traffic that flows to servers within the DMZ is never allowed to reach the private domain directly. Figure 8.3 illustrates a multilayered architecture of firewalls and a DMZ.

This protection can be accomplished in a number of ways. One is to simply put the public server(s) between an interior firewall and the main Internet gateway, or "outer" firewall. Another is to configure a router to create a DMZ by dedicating a single local port to handle all Web server traffic. This is a popular performance option in some of the higher-end routers and many cable/DSL router products for personal and small business applications.

PERSONAL FIREWALLS

When home-based or laptop computers have remote access to a secure private company network, they need personal firewall protection. Remote access can become a backdoor through which an attack can be launched. Intruders are constantly scanning the Internet for unprotected systems that offer such opportunities.

These personal firewalls are also very effective for small, home-based businesses and come in both hardware and software implementations. The hardware versions might be combined with other network devices such as DSL/cable modems or routers to form a secure Internet gateway.

One technique often used in this type of firewall is **network address translation,** or **NAT.** This effectively disguises the home network by assigning a hidden IP address to each protected device. Since the true address is not exposed to the Internet, hackers cannot attack what they cannot find. This provides much of the protection of a proxy server, without most of the expense or configuration burden.

Personal firewalls are also available as software applications. Many AV vendors bundle personal firewalls with AV software. Once installed, they are initiated at start-up time and run in the background, monitoring all network activity for suspicious inbound or outbound traffic from an untrusted address or application.

WHAT FIREWALLS CANNOT DEFEND AGAINST

Firewalls are often mistaken as something of a cure-all defense against external attack. This is certainly not the case. According to CSI's *2002 Computer Crime and Security Survey,* a majority of firewalls have been breached.

Certainly, firewalls are necessary, but alone they are an incomplete defense for several reasons. They don't prevent the introduction of viruses sent via email or IM. Nor can they prevent the theft of data that is physically carried out on a CD. They can be circumvented by the installation of a modem on the protected network. For these reasons, several other technologies are used to compensate.

PORT SCANNING AND SCANNERS

Port Scanning

Port scanning is the process of connecting to TCP or UDP (user datagram protocol) ports on a target system to identify services that are active, or running, and ports that are listening to traffic.[15] Not only can port scanning be used to determine listening ports, some of these tools are capable of identifying

1. The **operating system (OS),** which is a low-level control program that runs the computer, e.g., OS/2, Linux, Windows XP, Unix, Mac OS X.
2. The specific applications or versions of a specific service.

From the security administrator's perspective, listening ports are potential access points into a network that need to be secured. The same is true about any insecure service that is running, since it can be exploited to gain access to the system. From the hacker's perspective, port scanning gathers valuable information to learn about a target system's or application's vulnerabilities and how best to attack it.

@LERT

A simple port scan test is available from the Gibson Research Website at http://grc.com. The port scan runs a test on a system to identify vulnerabilities that need to hardened.

Port Scanners

Port scanners are tools or techniques for inspecting computers connected to the Internet for accessible open ports. Several of these tools are Foundstone's SuperScan,[16] Fyodor's nmap,[17] NetScanTools Pro 2000 (NSTP2K),[18] Legion Network's port scanner, and X-Scan.

> **@LERT**
> The Legion scanner looks for network-shared folders and opens them on the hacker's computer as a folder. The X-Scan network port scanner scans individual IP addresses looking for open ports to find shared folders or files.

Port scanners are critical for remote users that access the company network using always-on Internet connections, such as an **asymmetric digital subscriber line (ADSL).** ADSL is a high-speed digital service providing fast file downloads from the Web. A computer with an ADSL connection has a **fixed IP address,** or **static IP address,** which is the IP address that is permanently assigned to it. Fixed IP addresses are easy to identify and attack because every email sent from that PC would contain that IP address.

In contrast, slower-speed dial-up connections are less exposed because they are assigned an IP address, called a **dynamic IP address,** every time a new connection to the Internet is made. However, they are not immune from the dangers of port scanning by hackers or their automated scripts.

It is important to check for open or unguarded ports that can be used by unauthorized people. It is safer to have the port undetectable instead of blocked because hackers cannot crack what they cannot see.

INTRUSION DETECTION SYSTEMS (IDS)

An IDS can play a significant role in an overall security architecture. Before deploying an IDS, a company should consider the **total cost of ownership (TCO),** which is the sum of the purchase, installation, operation, and maintenance costs. The TCO of an IDS is high because of its ongoing operational and maintenance costs.

IDS products monitor activity within a network and can alert security administrators of suspicious activity. It is important to point out that an IDS must know that an intrusion has occurred. That is, there must be an overt activity by an attacker and a manifestation of that activity that is observable by the IDS and that the IDS knows it signifies an intrusion.

Slow Sweeps and Recons

An IDS depends on people paying attention and understanding what the information means. Careful inspection of the frequency, type, and source of attacks can lead to insights that the intrusion detection software cannot provide. This is particularly important for **slow sweeps** during **reconnaissance probes,** or **recons,** which are scans performed to identify information in preparation for an attack. Slow sweeps are scanning probes that are deliberately intermittent to avoid detection.

False Positives

Identifying an intrusion is not trivial. If an IDS is configured to be highly suspicious, it will generate a huge number of **false positives,** or false alarms, incorrectly indicating an intrusion. False positives waste time and cause transmission delays. The IDS could create a bottleneck of data traffic and require additional equipment to store the

<CYBERBRIEF>

SHARING INTRUSION DETECTION INFORMATION

Ronald L. Dick, director of the FBI's NIPC, explained the importance of sharing intrusion detection information. Because of information sharing in May 2002, damage from Klez was mitigated. NIPC had received calls from the private sector about the Klez worm. According to Dick,

> The worm had spread quickly and had the potential to affect a number of vulnerable systems by destroying critical operating system files. After consulting with our private sector partners and within a few hours of the initial notification, we released an alert,

which was immediately disseminated via email and teletype to a host of government, civilian and international agencies.

Information sharing is promoted through NIPC's InfraGard, the largest government–private sector partnership for infrastructure protection. InfraGard has direct contact with the private sector infrastructure owners and operators and shares information about cyber intrusions and other critical infrastructure vulnerabilities through the formation of local InfraGard chapters within the jurisdiction of the FBI field offices.[19]

Source: Hearing of the Senate Governmental Affairs Committee. Senator Joseph Lieberman, Chair. "Securing Our Infrastructure: Private/Public Information Sharing." Washington, DC. *Federal News Service.* May 8, 2002.

suspicious data packets. Conversely, if the IDS is made less sensitive, the risk of failing to identify real attacks increases. In which case, the investment in the IDS is wasted.

Because of false alarms, the decision as to how to react to an IDS alert is not easy. Even though alerts tend to be in real time, it might be impossible to determine the best reaction. Damage from intrusions can occur within seconds so reactions must be pre-planned, but an IDS can't be 100% sure that a suspicious activity is a genuine hostile intrusion. If an IDS alert is generated, who should have the authority to shut down the company's network or Website during business hours in response? This is where the expertise and the experience of the administrator come into play. Despite these limitations, IDS warnings have a secondary benefit. They can help administrators confirm the proper configuration and operation of other security mechanisms, such as firewalls. In this manner, an IDS can function as a useful diagnostic tool.

Intrusion detection products can be implemented as dedicated hardware or software designed to run on host servers. They come in several varieties, each with certain advantages and drawbacks. If an organization chooses to deploy an IDS, there is a range of products to choose from, with varying degrees of effectiveness and deployment costs. The two major types are network IDS and host/application IDS.

Network IDS

A network IDS usually is a dedicated device that plugs into the network and monitors all network traffic that passes through it for suspicious activity. As with all perimeter defenses, it can only monitor what passes through it.

Suspicious activity is based on a database of known "attack signatures." The advantage of an IDS is that it is very efficient and can work invisibly in real time spotting

⟨ **CYBERBRIEF** ⟩

OPEN-SOURCE GROUP NAMES TOP 10 WEB VULNERABILITIES

The Open Web Application Security Project (OWASP) released a list of top 10 vulnerabilities in Web applications and services. OWASP is a volunteer open-source community project created to bring attention to security for online apps (applications). The group wants government and the private sector to fix weaknesses immediately and remediate and improve their security project planning. "Ultimately, Web application developers must achieve a culture shift that integrates security into every aspect of their projects." The well known OWASP vulnerabilities cause significant risk because they are widespread. They can be exploited by code in HTTP requests that are not detected by IDS and pass through firewalls and into servers despite hardening. The complete report and list of vulnerabilities is available at http://www.owasp.org.

Source: Government Computer News, January 13, 2003. http://www.gcn.com/vol1_no1/daily-updates/20862-1.html

attackers before they can complete their attacks. The drawback is that it is not very intelligent; it cannot understand encrypted transmissions and can be fooled by attackers that devise new ways to conceal their activity.

Host IDS

Host-based IDS technology can be implemented in software or hardware on the host server and within an application running on that host. This type of IDS typically uses transaction logs to monitor activity. It can be tailored to the device or application that it is designed to protect, so far more intelligence can be built in to precisely identify and anticipate suspicious activity specific to that application. These rules might also adapt themselves automatically in response to changes in legitimate usage patterns.

Host-based IDS can be very useful in spotting questionable events originating inside a network, possibly the work of a saboteur in the act. Another advantage is that it can be programmed to automate the response to certain types of events. For example, it can forcibly log off or disconnect a suspicious user. These tools are not as fast or efficient as their network-based counterparts. As such, they do not react instantaneously and can degrade application performance in some instances.

An IDS can provide warnings indicating that a system is under attack, even if the system is not vulnerable to that specific attack. These warnings are often used to analyze and document the frequency of attempted attacks, which can justify changes or enhancements to the defensive infrastructure.

HONEYPOTS

Vulnerability assessment tools work well with IDS. One common tool is called a **honeypot.** This is a specially configured server that serves as a decoy. It is purposely left exposed with known vulnerabilities but stripped of any valuable data and placed in a safe area as bait for potential attackers to test any defenses placed around it. To test for hacking activity, an anonymous test server, or honeypot, was set up and left unprotected by *PSINet* in Europe. The honeypot was attacked maliciously 467 times within 24 hours of its installation even though it had no data.[20]

CRYPTOGRAPHY AND ENCRYPTION KEYS

Cryptography is used as a security measure to keep information secure while it is being transmitted or in storage. If encrypted information is intercepted or stolen, it is useless because it cannot be read by anyone except the intended recipient or owner. This security is accomplished with special codes called *keys* that are used by the sender/owner to encrypt messages and keep them secret. Keys also allow the intended recipient to decrypt the message so that it can be read.

Successful cryptography not only provides confidentiality but also ensures the integrity of the information in the original message since attempts to decrypt an altered message will fail, even with a key. In some applications, it can also provide *authentication* and *nonrepudiation* in the form of a digital signature.

Some hackers have been able to crack weak encryption schemes using high-performance computers and sophisticated mathematics. But there are commonly available encryption tools that are practically impossible to crack when used properly. Hackers have far more success stealing keys using social engineering than cracking codes.

Symmetric and Asymmetric Encryption

There are two basic forms of encryption: symmetric and asymmetric, which are illustrated in Figures 8.4 and 8.5, respectively. Asymmetric methods use separate, but

FIGURE 8.4   Symmetric Encryption

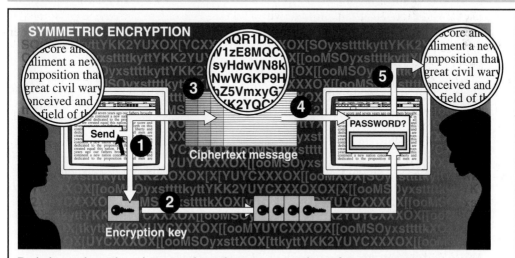

Both the sender and receiver must have the same encryption software program.
1. The sender creates a file and then encrypts it with the software, which creates an encryption key.
2. The key, which can be a password or file, is sent to the receiver.
3. The key is used to encrypt the file.
4. The encrypted file is sent via a route that differs from the key.
5. The receiver's encryption software decrypts the file using the key.

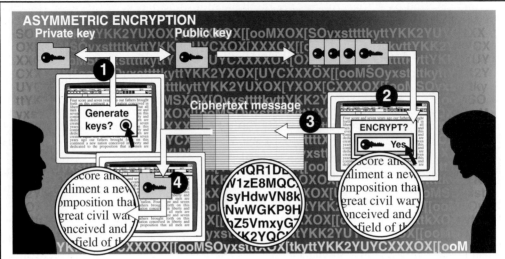

Both the sender and receiver must have the same encryption software program.
1. In order for someone to send an encrypted file to a receiver, the receiver must generate a public key and a private key, which is done by the software. The receiver sends the sender the public key.
2. Using the public key, the sender encrypts the file.
3. The sender sends the encrpypted file.
4. The receiver's private key is used to encrypt the file.

FIGURE 8.5   Public Key Infrastructure Using Asymmetric Encryption

associated, key *pairs*—one key for each party, a private key and a public key. One example of asymmetric encryption is the **PGP (pretty good privacy)** standard. Using PGP, anyone can send secure encrypted email to anyone else who has a registered PGP key pair using the unique public key. Only the intended recipient is able to open the email using the associated private key. If the message opens successfully, it is further assured that the message has not been tampered with. The advantage of asymmetric methods is that they avoid the need to share the secret key between parties, thereby risking exposure.

Encryption is the technology that enables the Internet to be used for trusted ecommerce and secure global communication. Without it, actually conducting business over the Internet would be impractical. Two examples of its use in this context are public key infrastructures and virtual private networks.

PUBLIC KEY INFRASTRUCTURE (PKI)

The two questions that prompted the PKI industry were

1. How do you know the person with whom you are dealing on the network is who they say they are?
2. How do you know that the public key you wish to use to open a secure message from me really came from me?

In the physical world, people looking to enter into business relationships can meet face to face. They can present credentials issued by trusted third parties, like governments and banks, that certify the identity and integrity of the presenter. PKI fills a similar role in ecommerce and can be applied to any commercial contact made over the Internet.

PKI Certificates

A PKI is a service that is designed to establish trust between parties conducting business or simply communicating across private or public networks. PKIs use *certificates* that are issued as guarantees of identity and integrity by a vendor or by trusted third parties. These are exchanged as credentials by unfamiliar parties who wish to conduct a secure interaction. They contain the unique public key that is to be used when opening messages or files from the certified entity.

Think of a PKI in the same context as an individual's signature that is verified by a seal from a notary. PKI standards call this role the **certification authority, or CA.** An example of this is often seen when one downloads software from a Website. The publisher will display a certificate issued by a CA to attest to the integrity of the software as well as the publisher. Figure 8.6 shows an example of a certificate. Your browser keeps a record of the certificate.

In this case, Microsoft is acting as its own CA. Several private firms, such as banks and cyber security firms like VeriSign, as well as public agencies, such as the U.S. Postal Service, are active as third-party certification authorities. Some of these firms also provide the infrastructure, the software, and consulting/outsourcing services to implement PKI. Browsers such as Internet Explorer ship with a library of certificates that apply to commonly used CAs. See Figure 8.7.

It had been predicted that the development and nearly universal adoption of PKI standards would be a vital precursor to the growth of ecommerce. That prediction was wrong. While PKI is certainly necessary to enable the commercial use of asymmetric cryptography, it has been very slow to catch on as an ecommerce standard. There are several reasons for this. One has been the slow development of technology standards for PKI itself. This has resulted, predictably, in the marketing of several incompatible technologies by competing vendors. Many of these technologies involve multiple encryption and decryption cycles that are slow to perform, thus limiting their use on a very large scale. Finally, the technology can be complex and expensive to implement, leaving many to question its worth when simpler, less expensive (although less effective) encryption technologies are available for simple forms of ecommerce, like Internet retail.

VIRTUAL PRIVATE NETWORKS (VPNS)

For multinational companies that need to connect many global sites or mobile employees, or small business owners who want to connect to their networks from home, the Internet is normally not safe enough. Remote access to networks exposes data communication to electronic eavesdropping and potential hijacking of data. One solution is to buy or lease a private network connection, which would be prohibitively expensive. Using a VPN, firms communicate over shared Internet connections securely for a

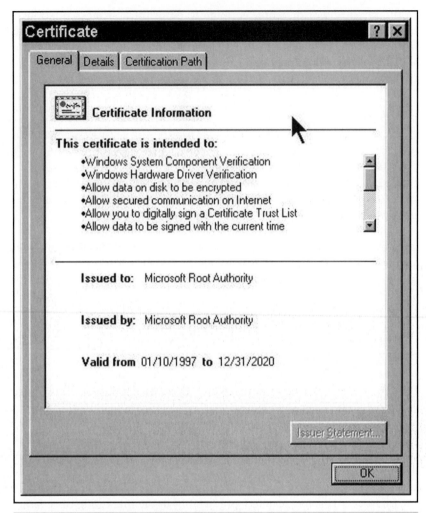

FIGURE 8.6 Microsoft-Issued Certificate

fraction of the cost of private networking. VPN technology, called a **gateway,** is placed between the originating device or network and the Internet. Figure 8.8 illustrates how VPN can be used to create a private tunnel through the Internet to connect remote locations.

VPNs use encryption to shield both the message and information about the sender from intruders. Once the message reaches the gateway of its intended destination, both the intended recipient's address and contents of the message are decrypted and readable to devices on the protected private network. VPNs are used in conjunction with firewalls to allow only filtered and anonymous traffic between the private network and the public Internet. This technique of privileged access from an authenticated source through a firewall is called **tunneling.**

FIGURE 8.7   Microsoft Certificate Manager

Securing the Ends of the VPN

VPNs should never be used by computers without active firewalls installed. For home or remote users with broadband connections that are always on, network access without a firewall via the VPN must be prohibited.

As effective and cost-efficient as VPNs are, they are not a perfect solution. The technology is still evolving, and technologies from different vendors are often proprietary and incompatible. An emerging standard, called IPSec, for secure IP, may resolve this issue in the future. Another potential weakness involves the potential for a PC with VPN-enabled client software to be used by someone other than the owner to penetrate a protected network. To guard against this, special authentication technologies are used to verify the identity of the user operating the VPN client.

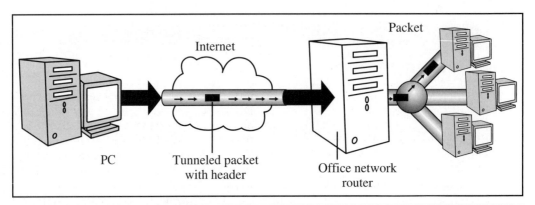

FIGURE 8.8 Virtual Private Network

ACCESS CONTROL: TOKENS AND BIOMETRICS

A **token** is a physical device, analogous to an ID card, designed to be used by only one person to prove his/her identity. Tokens are better than ordinary passwords, which are effective only as long as it is secret. A token, which you must physically possess, used in conjunction with a password offers far better authentication.

One example is a smart card that is activated with the user's password. Once activated, it returns a temporary password granting access to the private network that expires after a set time period, typically one minute or less. In this fashion, both the token (the card) and the password are required to gain restricted access to the network through the firewall.

A **biometric device** uses a personal characteristic to confirm identity. Fingerprints, voice prints, and retinal scans are examples of characteristics that can be read by biometric devices. These are also used in conjunction with revocable passwords to ensure that only the intended user of any computer can use it to connect to a secure network.

ANTIVIRUS (AV) SOFTWARE

As we discussed in Chapter 3, viruses have become pervasive. As a result, all defensive technology plans for individuals or businesses must include AV software protecting both the network itself and the individual computers on the network as well. Currently, the majority of virus transmission is via email simply because this is the easiest way to do it if the attacker's goal is large-scale replication and widespread distribution. There are, however, as many ways to introduce a virus to a target site as there are ways of transferring data.

Originally, viruses were spread via infected floppy disks. Although floppies are largely obsolete, replacement media such as CDs and any connected device with built-in memory—for example, digital cameras, MP3 players, PDAs, and other computers—can be used to carry a virus. All of these must be monitored at all times for malicious code. This is most effective when AV capability is installed on both individual PCs and network gateways, including email and Web servers, to form a complete defense against all means of entry.

CYBERBRIEF

PDA AND WEB PHONE MALWARE

Affordable and feature-rich PDAs and Web phones are often indispensable mobile communications devices for businesses. Their multifunctionality and increased Internet accessibility also have made them targets for hackers and virus writers.

In September 2000, AV researchers discovered two PDA malwares. The Liberty Crack Trojan horse program and the Phage virus deleted application files from the PDA. The Phage wireless virus spread by transmission via the infrared beam link when the PDA's data were backed up to a PC or when it exchanged data with another device. In Japan, the 911 Trojan targeted the i-mode device. When users of NTT DoCoMo's i-mode participated in an online love quiz, answering *yes* to a certain question caused their phone to dial 110—emergency assistance. Throughout Japan, police switchboards were swamped with bogus calls that prevented authorities from responding to true emergencies.

More serious risks are viruses that do not affect handhelds, but that transmit infections from them to desktops and networks. Viruses loaded onto PDAs or Web phones through wireless modems or synchronization can spread viruses faster and more covertly than Internet-borne malware.

Sources: Dejesus, Edmund X. "Airborne Viruses." *Information Security.* April 2001. P. 80. Chidi, Jr., George A. "Finjan Builds Defense Against PDA Attack." *InfoWorld Daily* News. October 31, 2000.

TECHNOLOGY FOR ENFORCING POLICY

In this section, the focus is on *internal* threats and abuses of network resources by employees. These are the tools that enforce an AUP by automatically detecting violations and blocking the transmission of prohibited content. The last example in the following list—the use of portable disk drives—makes it possible to avoid Internet connections entirely while facilitating backup of critical data.

1. Email and IM filters
2. Content monitors
3. Pattern recognition
4. Sniffers and scanners
5. Auditing tools
6. Portable drives and backups

EMAIL AND INSTANT MESSAGING (IM) FILTERS

These are programs whose sole purpose is to detect the presence of material deemed unacceptable in an AUP and remove it from the network. Examples of this might be incoming traffic consisting of explicit materials from a porn site or outgoing trade secrets in email, IM, or file transfers. At the extreme, they can also be used to enforce stricter rules, such as a prohibition on all HTML mail, attachments, or external forwards.

Many commercial firms ban IM outside the firewall altogether, as the commonly used IM services are totally insecure. These products act in a manner similar to AV software in that they constantly monitor all network gateways for indications that prohibited content is being transmitted. Although methods vary by product, this determination is generally made based on rules that target specific key words or phrases in the header or body of the message. "XXX images" might be such a key phrase.

An important caution is that filters can be defeated by encrypted messages. Encrypted content can be blocked arbitrarily, but that would prohibit the use of secure email, which might be necessary.

CONTENT MONITORS

Content monitoring applications are similar to filters in that they are also rule-based technologies that seek out the presence of restricted material. They apply to Websites that are accessed by employees or attempts to access sites that are expressly forbidden. They can also be used to block downloading of certain types of files, including program files. Customization ability is also important here. For example, access to a site for would-be bomb makers may be out-of-bounds for most users but perfectly acceptable for law enforcement. Some of the more sophisticated products can analyze images for signs of illicit content. These products can be installed on an individual PC, where they work with the Web browser. But most firms implement them on their networks in conjunction with their firewalls and proxy servers.

Many leading vendors sell integrated suites of products that include all of these capabilities. This has several advantages, including a single source of support and the ability to administrate and maintain all three tools simultaneously in response to improvements in the technology or changes in policy. Another advantage is the ability to generate logs and reports that can show use (or abuse) patterns by individual, department, application, etc.

SNIFFERS AND SCANNERS

These tools are important ways to enforce policies against unsanctioned connections to a network, particularly if they involve rogue connections via public ISP dial-in modems or other public resource.

@LERT
Broadband networks, such as the DSL services found in hotels, are notoriously insecure. It is possible for sales executives, while preparing for a bid presentation the following day, to check the Windows Network Neighborhood while connected to the DSL line. They can look for access to information from PCs of competitors staying in the hotel.

Recently, the focus has shifted to the use of wireless access points to create instant network connections for laptops and PDAs equipped with transmitters. These networks, in effect, broadcast your private network over the radio. Anyone within range equipped with a scanner cannot only monitor your traffic but also establish a connection of their own with the same rights and privileges as the exposed device.

Chapter Summary

Recent events have created a mandate for the globally networked economy to secure its critical infrastructure. Every networked organization needs to deploy a diverse, multilayered security architecture.

Decisions regarding technology components begin with an assessment of the unique needs, priorities, and threat profile of the organization. No single type of protection can be effective against all threats. A secure design calls for overlapping layers of technology components that enforce the documented policies discussed in previous chapters. Technology decisions require trade-offs between performance and effectiveness and cost and functionality.

Detection technology methods are based on signatures, historical attack data, or behavioral rules designed to detect suspicious behavior that indicates attacks. Several tools, such as firewalls and proxy servers, focus on perimeter defense against external intrusion. Others, such as content monitors, examine traffic inside the protected network for signs of activity in violation of policies and procedures.

There are no out-of-the box solutions. All technology components must be configured and maintained properly by knowledgeable staff to be effective. Since the factors that drive technology selection are dynamic, sustained protection depends on incorporating new technologies in response to changing threats and business requirements.

Key Terms

- critical infrastructure
- inbound packet
- outbound packet
- intranet
- service pack
- host computer
- confidentiality
- integrity
- authenticity
- nonrepudiation
- accountability
- availability
- transmission control protocol/Internet protocol (TCP/IP)
- IP address
- American registry for Internet numbers (ARIN)
- TCP/IP ports

- hyper text transfer protocol (HTTP)
- simple mail transfer protocol (SMPT)
- file transfer protocol (FTP)
- listen
- router
- dynamic routing
- firewall
- packet filters
- access control list (ACL)
- buffer overflow
- stateful inspection
- proxy server
- demilitarized zones (DMZ)
- network address translation (NAT)
- port scanning
- operating system (OS)

- port scanner
- asymmetric digital subscriber line (ADSL)
- fixed IP address
- static IP address
- dynamic IP address
- slow sweep
- reconnaissance probes
- recons
- false positive
- honeypot
- pretty good privacy (PGP)
- certification authority (CA)
- gateway
- tunneling
- token
- biometrics

Discussion Questions

1. Why have critical infrastructures become a national priority?
2. What is a weakness of a rule-based technology?
3. What are the advantages and disadvantages of hardware-based defenses?

4. Identify the different types of firewalls. How do they function? What are their limitations or weaknesses?

5. Explain the differences between a firewall and an IDS.

6. Why is port scanning dangerous? Why is it necessary?

7. Why should firewalls be used with AV? What other defenses should be used in combination with firewalls?

8. Why has the adoption of PKI and certificate technology been so slow?

9. What are the limitations of firewalls and IDS?

10. Why should technology be the final tier to be fully implemented in a security program?

Endnotes

1. Shein, Esther. "Are Companies Prepared for Cyber-Terrorism? Security Experts Say Attacks on Corporate Networks May Already be Under Way." *CFO Magazine.* December 1, 2001. http://www.cfo.com/article/1,5309,5988,00.html

2. See President George W. Bush's *CyberSecurity* Report. February 2003. http://www.whitehouse.gov/

3. Hulme, George V. "Networks Without A Safety Net: Wireless LANs Present Security Challenges for Businesses." *InformationWeek.* June 21, 2002. http://www.informationweek.com/story/IWK20020621S0001

4. Hearing of the Senate Governmental Affairs Committee. Senator Joseph Lieberman, Chair. "Securing our Infrastructure: Private/Public Information Sharing." Washington, DC. *Federal News Service.* May 8, 2002.

5. Barbaro, Michael. "Internet Attacks On Companies Up 28 Percent, Report Says." *The Washington Post.* July 8, 2002. P. E5.

6. Vise David A., and Daniel Eggen. "FBI Warns of Cyber-Attack Threat: U.S. 'Very Concerned' About Vulnerability of Infrastructure." *The Washington Post.* March 21, 2001. P. A16.

7. Fonseca, Brian. "IT Security Under the Gun." *ITWorld.* March 12, 2001. http://www.itworld.com/Sec/3832/itwnws010312security/

8. Hulme, George V. "Intrusion-Prevention Tools Prove Themselves by Stopping Worms Like Slammer in their Tracks." *InformationWeek.* February 3, 2003.

http://www.informationweek.com/story/IWK20030202S0002

9. Shein, Esther. "Are Companies Prepared for Cyber-Terrorism? Security Experts Say Attacks on Corporate Networks May Already be Under Way." *CFO Magazine.* December 1, 2001. http://www.cfo.com/article/1,5309,5988,00.html

10. Ibid. Shein, Esther.

11. "Business IT Strategy—Calculating Risks." *Accountancy.* December 27, 2001. P. 56.

12. Swanson, Marianne. "Security Self-Assessment Guide for Information Technology Systems." *National Institute of Standards and Technology Report,* August 2001.

13. See http://www.arin.net for more information.

14. Shinder, Debra Littlejohn. *Computer Networking Essentials.* Indianapolis, IN: Cisco Press, 2001, P. 92.

15. McClure, Stuart, Joel Scambray, and George Kurtz. *Hacking Exposed.* 3d ed. New York: Osborne/McGraw-Hill, 2001, P. 38.

16. SuperScan is available from http://www.foundstone.com/rdlabs/termsofuse.php?filename=superscan.exe

17. Nmap is available from http://www.insecure.org/nmap

18. NSTP2K is available from http://www.nwpsw.com

19. See National Infrastructure Protection Center at http://www.nipc.gov/ or the InfraGard at http://www.infragard.met/

20. Silicon.com. January 29, 2003. http://zdnet.com.com/2100-1105-982554.html

CHAPTER 9
ELECTRONIC EVIDENCE, ELECTRONIC RECORDS MANAGEMENT, AND COMPUTER FORENSICS

Learning Objectives

◆ Electronic evidence and its role in legal actions.

◆ Liability exposure of electronic evidence and email-evidence.

◆ Minimizing risk through electronic records management.

◆ Computer forensics and the discovery of electronic evidence.

INTRODUCTION

In addition to the information security challenges discussed in prior chapters, companies' information assets can be exposed as a result of **legal actions.** Legal actions include civil disputes, criminal cases, class-action lawsuits, employment grievances, and government or homeland security investigations. In a legal action, if the opposing party submits a **discovery request** (an official request for access to information that may be considered as evidence) for the company's emails and other electronic data, the company is required by law to retrieve and produce that evidence. The cost of responding to a discovery request can be huge if the company has to sort through several years' worth of email and files to remove confidential material. And courts now impose severe sanctions, including criminal penalties, for improper destruction of electronic documents.

To avoid the risk of indiscriminately retaining or destroying information that may be requested as evidence, companies need to implement and enforce electronic records management (ERM) practices. ERM's two main components are electronic record retention and destruction.

When electronic documents are used as evidence, they are referred to as electronic evidence, or **e-evidence.** Broadly defined, e-evidence is information stored electronically on any type of computer device that can be used as evidence in a legal action. By 2000, email had become the most common type of e-evidence. In 2003, email evidence had become so prevalent it became known as **evidence-mail.** According to Garry Mathiason, whose law firm defends major corporations in employment cases, almost every case they handle has a "smoking email" component to it.[1] In legal actions where evidence-mail or other e-evidence is used, it is as powerful as a smoking gun or DNA

> ⟨ **CASE ON POINT** ⟩
>
> ## COMPLYING WITH A DISCOVERY REQUEST LEADS TO INCRIMINATING EMAIL EVIDENCE AND $92.5 MILLION FINE
>
> In October 1997, Boeing, the world's largest aircraft manufacturer, announced a $1.6 billion write-off because of production problems earlier that year. When this news was released to the public, the value of the company's shares dropped so sharply that a class-action lawsuit for securities fraud was filed against Boeing.[4]
>
> During the pretrial investigation, the attorney for the plaintiffs (the party that is suing) learned that Boeing had 14,000 email backup tapes stored in a warehouse in Washington, DC. The attorney filed a discovery request for all Boeing's email related to their production problems. Company officials had to produce those tapes for use as evidence in the case. Boeing faced serious problems because it could not figure out whose emails were on which tapes without restoring and searching all 14,000
>
> of them. They did not have an ERM system in place.
>
> Tapes are rarely configured so that they can be easily searched. Tapes are the most common backup media, but they are designed primarily for disaster recovery, in which the entire tape is simply reloaded. However, regardless of how difficult or expensive it is to retrieve files from backup tapes, companies must comply with discovery requests and produce the emails or records that are requested.[5] Boeing had no choice. It had to restore all tapes, which took thousands of hours of employee time. In addition to the huge cost of responding to the discovery request, the emails that Boeing produced for the plaintiffs' attorney contained so much damaging evidence that the company paid $92.5 million to settle the class-action case.

evidence and as hard to deny or refute. A closely related issue to e-evidence and ERM is computer forensics. Computer forensics is the discovery, recovery, preservation, and control of electronic documents for use as evidence.

In 2002, President George W. Bush pledged that the Justice Department would "hold people accountable" for mismanaging their companies through "deceit and corruption."[2] With the government's efforts to reassure the public, it is beyond question that company emails and other electronic documents will be sources of evidence for all sides of a dispute.[3]

ELECTRONIC EVIDENCE

Every computer-based activity—whether it is sending email, invoices, viruses, or hacker attacks—leaves an electronic trace. (More discussion of cyber criminals hiding or deleting their traces will be discussed in Chapter 10.) These traces may be the actual content of emails or files, as was required at the companies discussed in the Cases on Point. Or the traces may consist of audit trails of the activity or attack, which are contained in log files or **meta-data.** Meta-data are descriptions or properties of data files or email, examples of which are dates/times an email or file was created or accessed. When these electronic documents or logs are requested or subpoenaed in a legal

⟨CASE ON POINT⟩

ENRON BECOMES THE LARGEST COMPUTER FORENSICS CASE IN HISTORY

Like most investigations of suspected corporate crime, the outcomes of the Enron case and Enron-related cases were determined by computer forensics examinations. The enormous scope of the Enron financial fraud case alone made it the largest computer forensics investigation in history.[6] Government investigators had to search through more than 400 computers and handheld devices plus over 10,000 computer backup tapes. Eric Thompson, chairman of Access Data Inc., who provided forensic software for the Enron investigation, said even encrypted or password-protected email and documents that had been erased would be recovered.[7]

The House Energy and Commerce Committee had asked Enron's accounting firm, Arthur Andersen, to turn over hundreds of documents from the firm's audits of Enron. The Senate's Permanent Subcommittee on Investigations went beyond "asking" for documents and issued 51 subpoenas to Enron and Andersen demanding the documents. Within the mountain of records that investigators looked at were *hot documents*—spreadsheets, invoices, contracts, and memos—that showed a pattern of wrongdoing.[8]

In the billion-dollar insurance investigation of J.P. Morgan Chase & Co.'s financing of Enron,[9] the determining factor was Judge Jed S. Rakoff's ruling to allow "explosive" email into evidence. Eleven insurance companies were suing Chase claiming the bank knew Enron's futures contracts for oil and gas were really loans. On December 23, 2002, the judge ruled that internal bank emails written over nine months be admitted as evidence.[10] In one of the emails, a senior Chase official allegedly called the transaction a "disguised loan." J.P. Morgan tried to refute the evidence-mail unsuccessfully by claiming that the emails did not refer to the Enron transactions in question. Other internal emails suggest J.P. Morgan Chase officials were shocked to learn in October 2001 just how much Enron had outstanding. "$5B in prepays!!!!!!!!!" wrote one employee. The response was: "shutup and delete this email."[11]

Before the Enron cases, electronic records retention and destruction were not a main concern. But after watching members of Congress on CNN or C-SPAN asking accountants and oil executives about their document-retention practices, that has changed.[12] The Enron and Andersen cases have clearly focused attention on e-evidence, the risks associated with a poorly structured or implemented document-retention management, and computer forensics.

action, they become e-evidence. This issue reinforces the need for AUPs, enforcement, and user training to ensure compliance.

Discovery of email in federal civil litigation cases is becoming broader and more common.[13] Email is specifically targeted for evidence because highly placed executives and employees discuss issues candidly, even if they are discussing confidential, incriminating, or criminal issues.

DISCOVERY OF ELECTRONIC BUSINESS RECORDS FOR USE AS EVIDENCE

With very few exceptions, all email communication and business documents are **business records.** Business records include computer records or printouts created as

◁ LEGALBRIEF ▷

EMAIL DEFINED AS A BUSINESS RECORD BY FEDERAL RULES

Email is not simply communication, but may also be considered a business record under Federal Rule of Evidence 803(6). Email qualifies as a business record if all five conditions are met. Those five conditions as stated in Federal Rule of Evidence 803(6) are:

1. The record must be kept in the course of a regularly conducted business activity.

2. The particular record at issue must be one that is regularly kept.

3. The record must be made by, or from, information transmitted by a person with knowledge of the source.

4. The record must be made contemporaneously. (That is, the document or file must be created at the same time as the business activity.)

5. The record must be accompanied by foundation testimony. (Someone must be able to validate that the record was made at the time of the activity.)

Source: U.S. Federal Rule of Evidence 803(6).

part of an organization's operations or transactions. Examples of business records are purchase orders, human resource files, vendor reports, sales reports, and inventory/production schedules. According to the Federal Rules of Evidence, business records are subject to **discovery.**[14] Discovery is the process whereby each party learns (or collects) as much information as possible about an opponent prior to a trial.

Any party in a legal action against a company or its employees can request discovery of information stored on computers, PDAs, iPAQs, cell phones, fax machines, voicemail, or other electronic devices or communication systems. In 1995, a U.S. District Court stated that "the law is clear that data in computerized form is discoverable even if paper 'hard copies' of the information have been produced."[15] Inarguably, a company's electronic records and communication are discoverable for use as evidence.

CONSEQUENCES OF FAILING TO COMPLY WITH DISCOVERY REQUESTS

Every day hundreds of U.S. companies face electronic discovery requests that they must comply with or face additional legal problems.[16] As a standard practice, lawyers and investigators are adding email to the list of records and documents they demand during the discovery process of cases. Companies had better be able to respond to a discovery request by the required date—or risk even more serious legal problems. One risk is a charge of obstruction of justice, a crime punishable by prison time.[17] A related risk is **spoliation,** which is the intentional destruction of evidence. Spoliation is such a serious offense that most lawyers would rather face a smoking gun than spoliation.

⟨ **LEGALBRIEF** ⟩

LOCATIONS FOR
E-EVIDENCE EXTENDS TO PDAS

BlackBerrys, PalmPilots, and iPAQs are commonplace. Users treat their PDAs as a day planner, email and file center, and Rolodex in one. Like a wallet, if the device is lost or stolen, users risk losing the "currency of modern life"—credit card and Social Security numbers, ATM passwords, and phone numbers.

Professionals in several industries, such as law and health care, face the even greater risk of loss of confidential client or patient information.

"If you wouldn't want to see something blown up 10-by-10 in a courtroom, don't put it on your computer, your laptop or your PDA," said Kristin M. Nimsger, attorney for Ontrack Data International, a computer recovery and forensic data recovery company. "PDAs, in general, are becoming accepted locations to find evidence in any litigation."

Source: Dratch, Dana. "Protect Your PDA." Special to the *Fulton County Daily Report.* May 20, 2002.

@LERT
Failure to comply with a subpoena or discovery request may lead to an obstruction of justice charge. Arthur Andersen was charged with obstruction of justice for destroying Enron-related electronic records, which triggered a chain of events that eventually destroyed the company.

According to the law, companies cannot destroy what they can reasonably expect will be subpoenaed. That is, they must retain all relevant documents and edocuments when they know, or should have reason to know, that they might become necessary as evidence in the future. Not surprisingly, this is a major dilemma for companies. They are required to retain records, including emails, that might get destroyed when backup tapes get reused.

PRESERVING AND DISCLOSING E-EVIDENCE

When a company has received an electronic discovery request, one of the first issues is to preserve potential evidence. As explained in the prior section, evidence that may be useful in a legal action (even if a company does not know that it would become useful) must be preserved, or the company may be charged with obstruction of justice. Once a company is instructed to preserve e-evidence, it must do whatever is necessary to make sure that the information does not get written over, lost, or altered.

The next step is disclosure, which requires locating all sources and locations of electronic data—and getting it into readable format. That is, locating data on desktops, laptops, PDAs, network hard disks, and removable media (e.g., tapes, CDs, and zip

> ### CYBERBRIEF
>
> ## 1.4 TRILLION
> ## EVIDENCE-MAILS
>
> E-evidence, especially email, has taken over business litigation. It is not just because email is the primary means of communication in the workplace. In 2001, U.S. businesses generated over 1.4 trillion emails. Email is very difficult to get rid of and can be recovered about 90% of the time.
>
> Kristin M. Nimsger, a legal consultant at the electronic data recovery firm Ontrack Data International Inc., was involved in a case in which an employee who knew his laptop was about to be searched jumped up and down on it then threw it out the window into a swimming pool. His emails were still recovered. Even obliterating the hard drive by shooting the computer, as happened in another case, was not enough. Because emails are sent over a network system, they live on in several other servers and backup systems.
>
> *Source:* Loomis, Tamara. "Electronic Mail: A Smoking Gun for Litigators." *New York Law Journal.* Vol. 227. May 16, 2002. P. 5.

drives). Data also may be in the possession of third parties, such as ISPs, or on the computer systems of business partners or employees at their homes.[18] Figure 9.1 lists the common locations from which edocuments or email are recovered.

After identifying the physical locations of devices, the sources of information in those devices are identified. These are the data files created by software applications and communication systems—email, word processing documents, reports generated by databases, and spreadsheets. They can be any memorandum, report, record, or data compilation in any form if it is created as a result of a business activity. And they may include meta-data.

FIGURE 9.1   Locations for the Recovery of E-Documents or Email

- Computer files and their meta-data or properties lists.
- Recycle bins, including the dates of the deletions.
- Backup tapes and other archives.
- Logs and cache files.
- Slack and unallocated space.
- Email, copies to self, forwarded messages, and deleted messages folders.
- SWAP files: This is a memory-extending feature that downloads data from main memory to a temporary storage area on the PC. These temporary files can hold many megabytes of information, including passwords or encryption keys.
- "Off-the-end data": This is information stored on a tape, but not overwritten when reused.

> ⟨ **CYBERBRIEF** ⟩
>
> ## META-DATA REVEALS
> ## HIDDEN FACTS
>
> Meta-data is invisible information that programs like Microsoft Word, Excel, and Outlook attach to each file or email. For example, Outlook meta-data might include who was bcc'd (blind copied) on an email and when and to whom an email was forwarded. "Obviously, this can be very important in setting up a who knew what and when type of scenario," according to Mark Kroese, vice president of marketing at Applied Discovery.
>
> ---
>
> *Source:* Jones, Ashby. "Discovery Becomes Electric." *New York Law Journal.* March 11, 2002.

FEDERAL RULES OF CIVIL PROCEDURE— "THE RULES"

RULE 34 AMENDED TO INCLUDE ELECTRONIC RECORDS

In 1970, Rule 34 of the Federal Rules of Civil Procedure was amended to address changing technology and communication. The amendment to Rule 34 made electronically stored information subject to "subpoena and discovery" for use in legal proceedings.[19] This amendment and other Federal Rules, discussed in the next section, have had enormous implications for the management of electronic records and communications.

UNSETTLED LEGAL ISSUES ADD COMPLEXITY AND RISK

Federal Rule of Civil Procedure 34 states that a party shall produce documents for inspection "as they are kept in the usual course of business or shall organize and label them to correspond with the categories in the request."[20] Rule 34, which refers to business records or documents, contains two components.

1. "as they are kept in the usual course of business"
2. "shall organize and label them to correspond with the categories in the request"

It is not clear how a company meets either of these two requirements with respect to email, which is often unstructured and unorganized. The law has not been explained or settled on these issues.[21]

There are several other unsettled issues. For example, Federal Rule 26(c) allows a court to protect against oppressive or harassing discovery. And Federal Rule 26(b)(2) directs the court to prevent overly burdensome or expensive discovery requests. But neither of these rules gives clear guidance as to the meaning of the phrases "oppressive or harassing" or "burdensome." Thus, the Federal Rules provide general ideas, but they do not give precise guidance about how to manage electronic records. As such, companies must define their own electronic records retention and destruction policies so they have some defense in the case of a legal action.

⟨ **LEGALBRIEF** ⟩

EMPLOYEES' RIGHT TO USE COMPANY EMAIL TO COMMUNICATE ABOUT WORK CONDITIONS IS PROTECTED BY FEDERAL LAW

An employee of Timekeeping Systems, Inc. had used company email to harshly criticize the change in vacation policy. Management found out about the criticism and asked the employee to apologize. When he refused, he was fired. Then the employee filed a complaint with the National Labor Relations Board (NLRB) that led to a suit against the company. In 1997, in the case of *Timekeeping Systems, Inc. vs Lawrence Leinweber,* the NLRB found that the employee was engaging in protected activity under Section 7 of the National Labor Relations Act. By law, the company had to reinstate the employee with back pay.

Anna DeMarco had been fired in June 2002 for using Symantec's email system to criticize and build employee opposition to Symantec's plan to outsource its customer service department. Even though Symantec was not unionized, DeMarco filed a complaint with the NLRB. As part of the settlement, Symantec paid DeMarco $5,000 for lost wages and benefits. In addition, the company posted a 17" × 17" poster at the office where DeMarco worked stating that employees had the right to use company email to discuss issues affecting the workplace. It also stated that Symantec would not interfere with employees' right, under federal law, to communicate about the terms and conditions under which they work.

Sources: Leibowitz, Wendy. "As I Was Saying: Imposing Order on EChaos." *Law Practice Management.* November/December 2002. Vol. 28, No. 8. P. 8. National Labor Relations Board, 323 NLRB No. 30.

OTHER LEGAL ISSUES WITH SIGNIFICANT CONSEQUENCES

There are two other important legal issues for employers and employees to consider, especially those who never expect to be confronted with electronic discovery or evidentiary issues:

- In the courts, it is widely accepted that email will be used on occasion for personal purposes, as is the telephone. If an employee is fired for using email for personal purposes, that employee can subpoena the email records of the company president or the person who did the firing. Those emails may reveal that they often had used company email for personal purposes. Besides losing the case, the company or its managers' email messages might reveal extremely sensitive or embarrassing content.
- U.S. Companies cannot fire anyone for communicating about a work-related issue on company email even if it contains content that is objectionable to the company or its policies. This is the law even if the company is a nonunion shop. See the *LegalBrief* above for instances of this type of legal case.

ELECTRONIC RECORDS MANAGEMENT (ERM)

ERM is a "systemic review, retention, and destruction of documents received or created in the course of business."[22] It consists of a broad range of policies, procedures, classification schemes, and retention and destruction schedules for electronic records.

Electronic record retention and destruction policies can reduce costs and disruptions significantly. ERM reduces costs when requested information can be promptly found, preserved, and protected against accidental deletion. Disruptions are avoided because normal backup and overwriting procedures can continue to go on without bringing company information systems to a halt.[23] A policy that requires separate servers for business documents will expedite the identification of privileged material in case of a discovery request.[24]

A study of record retention at DuPont revealed that more than 50% of documents the company had collected for discovery requests between 1992 and 1994 should never have been retained.[25] DuPont estimated that it cost the company between $10 million and $12 million over those three years in unnecessary retention and production costs.

SARBANES–OXLEY ACT OF 2002

Congress passed an investor protection bill, known as the Sarbanes–Oxley Act of 2002, after financial scandals at Enron, WorldCom, and other companies sent stocks plummeting.[26] The Sarbanes–Oxley Act orders the SEC to issue rules requiring disclosure of financial transactions. Companies will no longer be able to hide their debt. Lynn Turner, former chief accountant at the SEC, commented that "for the first time ever, we are going to find out about how much people are really hiding, and I think the world is going to be shocked when they see that."[27]

The Sarbanes–Oxley Act of 2002 is having an impact on corporate document preservation, filtering, and production obligations. It is also setting expectations for lawyers and managers with respect to official corporate records keeping. While this act specifically refers to accounting records and audit work papers, the SEC rules will likely apply to all official corporate disclosures. That will include certain categories of business records. Although the precise impact of Sarbannes–Oxley on corporate ERM policy is not yet known, it is expected to be serious. According to Michael Prounis, "expect more companies to stumble or possibly self-destruct when unexpectedly drawn into some high-profile situation where their actions or lack thereof detonate a discovery time bomb with respect to information disclosure."[28]

ERM GUIDE FOR EMPLOYEES

To ensure understanding and compliance, users need an ERM guide. The guide describes employees as "record custodians" and states the rules they must follow. Those rules need to include

- Retention periods and locations for each type of document needed to comply with business and legal obligations.
- Retention periods for email messages that are sent, received, or saved. For example, email that is either unread, read but left in the in-box folder, or put into a deleted-email folder is automatically deleted after 30 days.
- Coding systems for email or electronic records that are retained.
- Locations for the long-term storage of email or electronic records that are retained.

- Assign an ERM team to audit the ERM process on a regular basis.
- Get senior management to support of the ERM process and policies.
- Identify and classify e-record types according to business considerations and legal restrictions.
- Set time limits for each e-record type, including email messages that are created, sent, and stored in folders.
- Put the ERM policies in writing. Document all company data retention and destruction polices. Keep paper copies in addition to digital copies.
- Require employees to sign off on the policies.
- Use IT to manage the ERM process and compliance with its rules.
- Keep records of the locations of all mobile devices, hardware, and software.
- Create document retention and destruction policies that specify each of the following:
  - Backup and archival procedures
  - Disaster recovery plans
  - Onsite and offsite and storage area networks
  - Names of record custodians
  - A log of destroyed documents.
  - A log of backup tapes and indexes of files on those tapes.
- Implement a discovery response team of IT and HR staff and corporate counsel that have authority to stop document destruction activities at first notice of a possible legal action.
- Provide employees with an ERM guide and train them on email and data retention and destruction policies.

FIGURE 9.2 ERM Essentials

ERM AND AUP

Despite their importance, few firms have documented and enforced ERM practices. And as discussed in this chapter, unmanaged business records are dangerous. They expose companies to legal risks that are as equally damaging financially as a virus or a security breach. Just as an AUP is necessary to help protect against litigation and confidentiality breaches, so are ERM policies for retaining and destroying records. In fact, ERM shares several characteristics with AUPs, including the need for senior management support and user training. The essential requirements for ERM are listed in Figure 9.2.

COMPUTER FORENSICS

Computer forensics is the discovery, recovery, preservation, and analysis of digital documents, electronic media, or audit logs of computer/online activities. Computer forensics is used to gather e-evidence for human resource and employment proceedings, trade secret and antitrust violations, fraud, harassment cases, discrimination suits, and other civil lawsuits. It is also used for identifying network intrusions and hacker attacks, which will be discussed in Chapter 10.

<CYBERBRIEF>

COMPUTER FORENSICS
RECOVER EVIDENCE OF A CON BY
EMPLOYEES

An employee of a leading multinational company had confidential boardroom-level documents stored on his computer that he had planned to sell. When he was tipped off that management had found out about his plan, he deleted the files. He assumed that deleting the files from his hard drive would get rid of the evidence of his crime.

The company brought in a team of computer forensic specialists to investigate. They recovered evidence from the employee's computer showing that he had conspired with two other employees to steal sensitive intellectual property from the company. The three employees were dismissed and later charged with both civil and criminal actions.

Source: Guider, Ian. "Computer Conmen." *Business and Finance.* November 21, 2002. P. 22.

WHAT CAN BE REVEALED

Computer forensics can reveal what users have done on the company network, including

- Theft of intellectual property, trade secrets, confidential data.
- Defamatory or revealing statements in chat rooms, usenet groups, or IM.
- Sending of harassing, hateful, or other objectionable email.
- Downloading of criminally pornographic material.
- Downloading or installation of unlicensed software.
- Online gambling, insider trading, solicitation, drug trafficking.
- Files accessed, altered, or saved.

WHAT CAN BE RECOVERED

Computer forensics also offers important benefits. It can reveal what users have done on the company network, including

- Recovery of lost client records that were deleted by an employee who had been stealing funds from the company.
- Proof that an ex-employee stole company trade secrets for use at a competitor.
- Proof of violations of noncompete agreements.
- Proof that a supplier's information security negligence caused costly mistakes.
- Proof of a safer design for an item named in a product liability suit.
- Recovery of an earlier draft of a sensitive document or altered spreadsheets to prove intent in a fraud claim.

HANDLING E-EVIDENCE: THE 3 C'S

The use of computer forensics by law enforcement is increasing for criminal cases and by lawyers in civil cases. In the Computer Security Institute's *Alert* newsletter, Michael J. Zuckerman stated, "There is going to come a time when there isn't a single criminal

⟨ **LEGALBRIEF** ⟩

KILLING THE VAMPIRE

Experienced trial lawyers know that electronic discovery is like the plot of a vampire movie. There's always something unexpected lurking out of sight and it cannot be destroyed.

Source: Withers, Kenneth J. "Killing the Vampire: Computer Users, Facing Discovery, Attempt to Make the 'Delete' Key Stick. Part I." *Federal Discovery News.* February 15, 2000.

case that doesn't involve some electronic evidence."[29] And in order for e-evidence to be admissible, it must be recovered and handled in a way that complies with the rules of evidence.

Organizations may be able to easily find and retrieve computer-data. However, retrieving and preserving e-evidence for use in a civil case are more complex than simply finding the e-evidence. For example, in order to use e-evidence in court, it might be necessary to have created an exact duplicate copy of the files for proof that the e-evidence had not been altered. Thus, an expert may be needed for computer forensics investigations. Also, it may be wise to hire an objective, outside investigator to prevent accusations that the company is deliberately trying to malign an employee.

There are legal protocols to be followed to ensure that the e-evidence is admissible. The operations used to collect, analyze, control, and present e-evidence cannot modify the original item in any manner. Any alteration to the primary source of evidence could contaminate it and render it inadmissible in court.

Like all other types of evidence, the handling of e-evidence must follow the 3 C's of evidence:

1. Care
2. Control
3. Chain of custody

Care and Control

The first steps that are taken in collecting evidence are the most important. Everyone who touches the e-evidence can contaminate it. To ensure that care and control of the e-evidence are maintained, the investigators must know what they are doing before they do it. Also, the files and digital audit trails must be kept safe and secured.

Chain of Custody

Chain of custody is a legal guideline to ensure that the material presented in court as evidence is the same as the evidence that was seized. It requires documentation that the evidence is still in its original state. Maintaining the chain of custody of e-evidence is more difficult than for physical evidence because it is more easily altered.

ELIMINATING ELECTRONIC RECORDS

To eliminate data, there are software tools that "wipe" files from storage disks by writing random strings of 1's and 0's over the space where the files were stored. There are programs that defragment disks by moving information around on the surface of the disk so data can be retrieved more efficiently, and can also write over old data. Hard disk drives can also be reformatted entirely. Reformatting may not eliminate the files. It is possible to take a disk apart and use an electron microscope to read information from the individual magnetic spots on the surface of a disk that may have been intentionally erased. Those magnetic spots are not eliminated by a reformat of the drive.

HIGH-PROFILE LEGAL CASES

The outcomes of high-profile legal cases have been determined by the discovery and introduction into evidence of defendants' email or digital files, including those that users were wrong in believing were private, secure, or gone. Several of those cases are described in the following sections.

Cyber Trial of the Century

During the cyber trial of the century, investigators discovered damaging internal email from a Microsoft executive in which he wrote that Windows "must be a killer on OEM shipments so that Netscape never gets a chance on these systems." The majority of evidence used by the DOJ came from subpoenaed internal Microsoft email, which prosecutors used to refute Bill Gates's testimony.

Discrimination Case

Morgan Stanley was sued by employees for racial discrimination because of racial jokes distributed via the company's email system. The suit was dismissed, but the court indicated that a significant basis for dismissal was that only one email message had been discovered. This case made a legal rule very clear: Employers will be held liable for their employees' behavior, including what they say in email messages sent on company networks, with only narrow exceptions.

Antitrust Case

In an antitrust case, Bristol Technology, Inc. sued Microsoft for $263 million in damages. The eight-member jury handed Microsoft a victory on July 16, 1999 with a $1 award to Bristol. The most damaging evidence was a single email sent in May 1998 from a Bristol director to CEO Keith Blackwell that referred to the upcoming lawsuit as the "We 'sue Microsoft for money' business plan." After the trial, the plaintiff's lawyer complained that the jury focused on the email message and disregarded relevant evidence.

Illegal Sickout Case

In a lawsuit in which Northwest Airlines alleged that employees had used email or message boards to promote an illegal sickout on January 1, 2000, a federal court order required 22 Northwest flight attendants to turn over their personal hard drives and laptops for inspection by the company's investigators. Hard drives at flight attendants' homes and union offices were searched for evidence revealing the identity of those responsible for that job action. A union member's reaction to the court's subpoena was "How can the company take on the Constitution?"[30] Privacy advocates condemned the court order, complaining that if Northwest had tried to get permission to allow its lawyers to enter employees' homes to search through their file cabinets, the airline's request would have been refused.

Wrongful Termination Case—and Its Reversal

In 1997, Adelyn Lee, the administrative assistant who Oracle CEO Larry Ellison had been dating, filed a wrongful termination case against Oracle. During electronic discovery, damaging email sent to Ellison by Lee's supervisor stating, "I have terminated Adelyn per your request" was recovered. Oracle paid $100,000 to settle the lawsuit. On further investigation, computer forensics helped prove that the damaging email had been written by Lee and sent from her supervisor's PC. A cellular phone bill that indicated that he was in his car at the time the email was sent substantiated her supervisor's alibi.

Chapter Summary

The escalating role of e-evidence has made the discoverability of email and electronic records an information security issue. Given today's technology and legal forces, companies face potentially serious risks if a court subpoenas their electronic records. The risk and costs increase if the company lacks enforced ERM practices.

As with AUP, ERM requires senior management support, user training, and enforcement procedures. A significant investment in ERM systems can ensure compliance with industry regulations and prevent much more costly problems in the event of a legal action or government investigation. Many companies have paid multimillion dollar fines because they paid too little attention to the pervasiveness of e-evidence, the power of computer forensics, and the protection provided by ERM.

Computer forensics is the discovery, recovery, preservation, and control of digital data or documents for use as evidence—and the analysis, verification, and presentation of that evidence in court or investigations. It has been used to gather evidence for human resource and employment proceedings, trade secret and antitrust violations, fraud, sexual and racial harassment cases, discrimination suits, and civil lawsuits. Deleted or not, there is a good probability that email, drafts and revisions of documents, spreadsheets, voicemail messages can be retrieved. Computer forensics will play a major role in legal cases as new legislation is passed to combat fraud, such as the Sarbanes–Oxley Act of 2002.

In the next chapter, the role of computer forensics in discovering computer crimes and perpetrators will be discussed.

Key Terms

- legal action
- discovery request
- e-evidence (electronic evidence)
- evidence-mail
- meta-data
- business records
- discovery
- spoliation
- chain of custody

Discussion Questions

1. What is a discovery request? What types of legal actions might involve discovery requests?
2. Explain why the total costs of responding to a discovery request can exceed a million dollars. Why might the IT staff not be able to respond in time?
3. What is the difference between e-evidence and evidence-mail? Why is evidence-mail referred to as a smoking gun?

4. Why is evidence-mail commonly requested in a legal action? Name a legal case that involved evidence-mail.

5. In 2002, why did President George W. Bush pledge that the Justice Department would "hold people accountable"?

6. What cases have focused attention of managers and lawyers on document-retention policies? Briefly explain the evidence in those cases.

7. What is meta-data? List five examples of meta-data and what each can reveal.

8. What is ERM? What policies are part of the ERM practice?

9. What did DuPont's study of its record-retention policy reveal? What was the impact of its lack of effective ERM between 1992 and 1994?

10. Will the Sarbanes–Oxley Act of 2002 increase or decrease the amount of electronic records that are retained? Explain your answer.

11. What can computer forensics reveal? What can it recover?

12. Explain the three C's of handling e-evidence. Why might it become more difficult to handle e-evidence?

13. Describe how electronic records might be eliminated so that they are not recoverable.

Endnotes

1. Varchaver, Nicholas. "The Perils of E-Mail." *Fortune.* February 3, 2003.

2. Gordon, Marcy. "WorldCom Stock Drops to 6 Cents." *AP Wire Story.* July 1, 2002. 12:58 PM.

3. Tambe, Jayant W., and Jonathan M. Redgrave. "Electronic Discovery Emerges as Key Corporate Compliance Issue." *The Metropolitan Corporate Counsel.* October 2002. P. 6.

4. Melnitzer, Julius. "Keeping Track of the Invisible Paper Trail: What Legal Departments Can Learn From Boeing's Experience." *Corporate Legal Times.* February 2003. P. 15.

5. Varchaver, Nicholas. "The Perils of E-Mail." *Fortune.* February 3, 2003.

6. Iwata, Edward. "Enron Case Could Be Largest Corporate Investigation." *USA Today.* February 18, 2002. http://www.usatoday.com/life/cyber/tech/2002/02/19/detectives.htm

7. Harrington, Mark. "Computer Experts to Root Out Missing Files." *Newsday.* February 5, 2002. http://www.newsday.com/business/local/newyork/ny-bzenro052576192feb05.story

8. Iwata, Edward. "Enron Case Could Be Largest Corporate Investigation." *USA Today.* Feb. 18, 2002.

http://www.usatoday.com/life/cyber/tech/2002/02/19/detectives.htm

9. *J.P. Morgan Chase Bank vs Liberty Mutual Insurance Co.,* 01 Civ. 11523 (http://www.law.com)

10. "'Explosive' E-Mails Allowed into Evidence in Enron Loan Trial." *Digital Discovery and e-Evidence.* Vol. 3, No. 1. January 2003. P. 14.

11. Reason, Tim. "Reporting: See-Through Finance?" *CFO Magazine.* October 2002.

12. Doerner, Saunders, and James C. Milton. "Document Retention after Enron: When Should I Press 'Delete'?" *Oklahoma Employment Law Letter.* Vol. 10, Issue 6. May 2002.

13. Burke, Patrick J. "Learning from Wall Street's E-Mail Nightmare: Discovery and Admissibility of E-Mail." *The Metropolitan Corporate Counsel.* September 2002. P. 48.

14. The Federal Rules of Evidence require the party offering a computerized record to prove it was created "at or near the time" of the transaction, act, or event recorded in order to qualify as a business record exception to hearsay. [Nimsger, Kristin M. "Same Game, New Rule: E-discovery Adds Complexity to Protecting Clients and Disadvantaging Opponents." *Legal Times.* March 11, 2002. P. 28.]

15. Rasin, Gregory I., and Joseph P. Moan. "Fitting a Square Peg into a Round Hole: The Application of Traditional Rules of Law to Modern Technological Advancements in the Workplace." *Missouri Law Review* (66 Mo. L. Rev. 793). Fall, 2001.

16. Melnitzer, Julius. "Keeping Track of the Invisible Paper Trail: What Legal Departments Can Learn from Boeing's Experience." *Corporate Legal Times.* February 2003. P. 15.

17. Brown, Ken, Gregg Hitt, Steve Liesman, and Jonathan Weil. "Andersen Fires Partner It Says Led Shredding of Documents." *The Wall Street Journal.* January 16, 2002.

18. Schultz, David H., and J. Robert Keena. "Discovery Perils in E-information Age." *New Jersey Lawyer.* April 22, 2002. P. 7.

19. Rasin, Gregory I., and Joseph P. Moan. "Fitting a Square Peg into a Round Hole: The Application of Traditional Rules of Law to Modern Technological Advancements in the Workplace." *Missouri Law Review* (66 Mo. L. Rev. 793). Fall, 2001.

20. Federal Rule of Civil Procedures 34(b).

21. Burke, Patrick J. "Learning from Wall Street's E-Mail Nightmare: Discovery and Admissibility of E-Mail." *The Metropolitan Corporate Counsel.* September 2002. P. 48.

22. Scheindlin, Shira A., and Jeffrey Rabkin. "Outside Counsel Retaining, Destroying and Producing E-Data: Part 2." *New York Law Journal.* Vol. 227. May 9, 2002. P. 1.

23. Editor interview of Michael Prounis. "Plan For Electronic Discovery Now—And Avoid 'Bet The Company' Mistakes." *The Metropolitan Corporate Counsel.* August 2002. P. 24.

24. Scheindlin, Shira A., and Jeffrey Rabkin. "Outside Counsel Retaining, Destroying and Producing E-Data: Part 2." *New York Law Journal.* Vol. 227. May 9, 2002. P. 1.

25. Melnitzer, Julius. "Keeping Track of the Invisible Paper Trail: What Legal Departments Can Learn From Boeing's Experience." *Corporate Legal Times.* February 2003. P. 15.

26. Anderson Peter J., and Alana Rae Black. "Accountants' Liability After Enron." *S&P's The Review of Securities & Commodities Regulation.* Vol. 35, No. 18; October 23, 2002. P. 227.

27. Reason, Tim. "Reporting: See-Through Finance?" *CFO Magazine.* October 2002.

28. Prounis, Michael. "The Impact of The Sarbanes–Oxley Act: If You Can't Teach That Old Dog New Tricks, You May Have To Visit Him at the Pound." *The Metropolitan Corporate Counsel.* September 2002. P. 53.

29. Zuckerman, Michael J. "A Letter from Washington, *DC3.*" In *Alert. Computer Security Institute (CSI) Newsletter.* September 2002.

30. "Northwest Air Probes Union Computer Files." *The Wall Street Journal.* Feb. 10, 2000.

CHAPTER 10
COMPUTER CRIME, COMPUTER FRAUD, AND CYBER TERRORISM

———— ✑✑✑ ————

Learning Objectives

◆ Computer crimes and punishments.

◆ Federal statutes for prosecuting computer crimes.

◆ Computers as targets of crime.

◆ Computers as instruments of crime.

◆ Computer fraud and white-collar crime (WCC).

◆ Cyber terrorist threats.

◆ Incident response documentation and handling.

INTRODUCTION

In general, a crime is an offense against society as a whole (the state) punishable by law.[1] In order for an offense to be a crime, it must violate at least one criminal law. Criminal laws are statutory, which means that they must be clearly defined in rules that are called **statutes.** Prior to 1984, there were very few statutes that defined computer-related criminal offenses.

When the Morris worm paralyzed half the Internet in 1988, recovery costs were an estimated $186 million. Since there were no statutes against computer viruses or worms with which to prosecute Robert Morris, Jr., he was charged with violation of the Computer Fraud and Abuse Act (CFAA). At that time, the CFAA prohibited intentional unauthorized access to a federal computer that caused a loss of $1,000 or more. His sentence was three years probation, 400 hours of community service, and a $10,500 fine.[2] Since the mid-1980s, Congress has been actively passing new and amended cyber crime statutes with much stiffer penalties.

The terms *computer crime*, *cyber crime*, *information crime*, and *high-tech crime* are used interchangeably.[3] They all refer to two categories of offenses. In the first category, the computer is used as the *target* of a crime. In the second category, the computer is used as the *instrument* of a crime. When computer crime involves money, it is referred to as *computer fraud*. In addition to cyber crimes, there is heightened concern about cyber terrorist attacks against critical infrastructures. While not directly life threatening, these attacks are *weapons of mass disruption*. Tom Ridge, the Director of Homeland Security, said that his team monitors the Internet continuously for "state-sponsored information warfare."[4]

⟨ **CASE ON POINT** ⟩

ALLIED IRISH BANKS TRADER GETS 7½ YEARS FOR FOURTH-LARGEST BANK FRAUD SCANDAL IN THE WORLD

John M. Rusnak, 38, of Baltimore will receive 7½ years in prison as part of a plea agreement with federal prosecutors. The former currency trader for Allfirst Financial Inc., a U.S. banking subsidiary of Allied Irish Banks, pleaded guilty in Maryland federal court to bank fraud.[5]

According to court records, Rusnak entered fictitious options trades in Allfirst's computer system in the late 1990s, making it appear as if his $691 million in trading losses had been offset by the options positions and showing millions of dollars in bogus profits. The computer manipulation allowed Rusnak to illegally collect more than $850,000 in enhanced salary and performance bonuses.

The fraudulent activity was discovered by Allfirst and announced to the public on February 2, 2002. The bank later reported losses of more than $691 million, revealing that Rusnak had been able to circumvent the bank's oversight systems and to cover his tracks electronically from 1997 to 2001, according to court records.[6] It seems Rusnak's false verifications of fake trades had finally drawn the attention of his superiors, even though Rusnak had done his best to produce authentic-looking papers.

U.S. Attorney Thomas M. DiBiagio, the federal prosecutor who indicted Rusnak on seven counts of fraud, stated: "I think everything about this case surprised me—the magnitude of the loss, the extent of the fraud, the sophistication of the actual transactions, [and] the sophistication of the cover-up."[7]

This chapter provides an in-depth overview of federal statutes that pertain to computer crime, computer fraud, and acts of cyber terrorism. These federal laws criminalize computer-related offenses, which makes it possible to prosecute those who violate them. Of course, catching and convicting these criminals remains difficult. To improve the ability to catch and prosecute these crimes, this chapter also covers important methods for handling and documenting **incidents.** Incident refers to a harmful or threatening **event** in an information system or network. An event is something that is observable in an information system or network, such as a system crash or attempt to access a network.

U.S. FEDERAL STATUTES DEFINING COMPUTER CRIME, FRAUD, AND TERRORISM

NEW AND AMENDED LAWS ADDRESS INTERNET CRIMES

Over the past two decades, cyber crimes have ranged from Website defacements by juveniles to sophisticated intrusions sponsored by foreign powers. In response to changes in cyber crime and terrorism, Congress has passed laws making certain unlawful acts illegal when committed via the Internet.

Prior to new statutes, crimes did not escape prosecution if they were committed via the Internet. For example, a federal law that prohibits threatening the President's life had not been drafted with email in mind. In April 1994, Matthew Thomas sent an email

TRUSTED CONTROLLER COMMITS $2.5 MILLION FRAUD

A family-owned manufacturing firm was having a serious cash flow problem. The owners blamed inefficiencies in their manufacturing process as the cause of the cash problems although they could not identify any specific reason.

In an attempt to save their business from bankruptcy, the owners brought in a new chief financial officer (CFO), who implemented performance improvement measures. The CFO recognized that an inefficient manufacturing process was not the source of the company's financial problems.[8] His investigation showed that the company was purchasing 15 to 40% more raw materials than had been required based on its production output. Also, vendor purchases were overstated. Close examination of the checking account records disclosed that the payee names differed slightly from the actual company names. For example, "ABC Materials Co." might appear as "ABC Co." There were also presigned blank checks in the controller's desk that were drawn on local banks in names that were very similar to real company vendors. The controller had been with the company for 25 years.

A forensics accounting investigation revealed that the controller had been altering checks and depositing them into various bank accounts using slightly altered names of real companies. His fraud scheme had cost the firm $2.5 million over five years. He was stealing to pay his personal bills. Since fraud always involves trust and confidence, fraudsters are often long-time employees.

message to President Bill Clinton with the warning that he was going to "come to Washington and blow your little head off." The threat itself was a crime even though the statute did not specify that a threat sent via email was a crime. In June 1994, Thomas pled guilty to a felony.

THE COMPUTER FRAUD AND ABUSE ACT AND OTHER STATUTES

Most computer hacking in the U.S., is penalized under one or more federal statutes. The most commonly used federal statute for computer crime is the Computer Fraud and Abuse Act of 1986. This act is the name for Title 18 of U.S. Code section 1030, which is written 18 USC § 1030.

In 1986, Congress passed the first version of the Electronic Communications Privacy Act, (ECPA). This act updated the Federal Wiretap Act so that it would apply to the illegal interception of electronic communications or the intentional, unauthorized access of electronically stored data. On October 25, 1994, Congress amended the ECPA by enacting the Communications Assistance for Law Enforcement Act. In so doing, it noted that, "In the eight years since the enactment of ECPA, society's patterns of using electronic communications technology have changed dramatically. Millions of people now have electronic mail addresses. Business, nonprofit organizations and political groups conduct their work over the Internet."

KEY "COMPUTER FRAUD AND ABUSE" TERMS DEFINED

The DOJ broadly defines computer crime as "any violations of criminal law that involve a knowledge of computer technology for their perpetration, investigation, or

FIGURE 10.1 Specific Meanings of the Key Terms in the Computer Fraud and Abuse Act (Federal Statute 18 USC § 1030)

Key Terms	Specific Meanings of Key Terms in the Computer Fraud and Abuse Act
"Protected Computer"	A "protected computer" means a computer that • is used by a financial institution (broadly defined), or • is used by the U.S. government, or • affects domestic interstate commerce or communications of the United States, or • affects foreign commerce or communications of the United States In effect, every computer connected to the Internet is a "protected computer." "Protected computers" include computers located outside the United States. This allows U.S. prosecution of hackers who attack foreign computers.
"Authorized Access"	There are two references regarding "authorized access" specified in the statute: • **Without Authorization:** "Access without authority" applies to any outsider who breaks in and uses a computer for any purpose. (Since this only applies to outsiders, it does not apply to employees.) • **Exceeding Authorized Access:** "Access in excess of authority" applies to anyone who has authorized access to a computer and uses that access to obtain or alter information, which he or she is not allowed to obtain or alter.
"Damage"	"Damage" is defined as any impairment to the integrity or availability of data, a program, a system, or information. That impairment must cause: • a loss to one or more persons (or companies) during any one-year period totaling at least $5,000 in value, or • the modification or impairment of medical records, or • physical injury to any person, or • a threat to public health or safety, or • damage to a government computer system used for administering justice, national defense, or national security.
"Loss"	"Loss" is defined as any reasonable cost to any victim, including the cost of • responding to an offense • conducting a damage assessment • restoring the data, program, system, or information to its condition prior to the offense • lost revenue or other damages because of interruption of service
"Conduct"	If there has been "damage" to a "protected computer" that has caused "damage," the next issue is whether the conduct was intentional, reckless, or negligent. • "Intentional conduct" means conduct by anyone who knowingly transmits a "program, information, code, or command" that causes damage to a protected computer. This applies to both insiders and outsiders. • "Reckless conduct" means intentional access to a protected computer without authority that unintentionally, but recklessly causes damage. This only applies to outsiders.

Source: Information provided by Martin J. Littlefield, Assistant U.S. Attorney, U.S. Department of Justice, Western District of New York; Paul McCarthy, New York Assistant Attorney General; and Richard P. Salgado, Senior Counsel, Computer and Intellectual Property Section (CCIPS) of the U.S. Department of Justice.

FIGURE 10.2	Federal Statute 18 USC § 1020(a)(1)

> ### Access to a Computer for Government Secrets, 18 U.S.C. § 1030(a)(1)
> - Access without authority or in excess of authority of computer with government secrets
> - Includes data which could be used to injure the United States or benefit another nation
> - Delivers, attempts to deliver, or retains data

Source: Information provided by Martin J. Littlefield, Assistant U.S. Attorney, U.S. Department of Justice, Western District of New York; Paul McCarthy, New York Assistant Attorney General; and Richard P. Salgado, Senior Counsel, Computer and Intellectual Property Section (CCIPS) of the U.S. Department of Justice.

prosecution." To be effective, statutes must give details about their subject matter and define terms precisely. If the wording or terms were ambiguous, crimes would be extremely difficult to prosecute. Figure 10.1 lists the specific meanings of key terms in the Computer Fraud and Abuse Act statute. The definitions require lengthy and complex wording to ensure complete coverage of the issues. The complexity of federal statutes that deal with computer crime and fraud are evident in subsection 18 USC § 1030(a)(1), as shown in Figure 10.2

THE COMPUTER AS THE TARGET OF A CRIME: CRIMES AGAINST A COMPUTER

Federal statutes divide computer-related offenses into two categories; the computer as the target of a crime and the computer as the instrument of a crime. Crimes against a computer include attacks on network confidentiality, integrity, or availability. Unauthorized access to, or tampering with, information systems, programs, or data falls into this category. Figure 10.3 lists examples of "computers as targets of crime," as defined in 18 USC § 1030, and their penalties.

FIGURE 10.3	"Computers as Targets of Crime," According to U.S. Federal Statute 18 USC § 1030

Subsections of Federal Statute 18 U.S.C. § 1030	Description of the Federal Crimes	Type of Crime and Maximum Penalty
(a)(1)	Access without authority, or in excess of authority, of a government computer.	**Felony** • 10 years and $250,000 fine for 1st offense • 20 years and $250,000 for subsequent offenses
(a)(2)	Breach of the confidentiality of a protected computer's data. This includes mere access into a protected computer. It covers just reading the data, even if no download occurred.	Felony or Misdemeanor Felony if for: Commercial advantage or private financial gain; criminal or tortuous purpose; or value of information over $5,000. Penalties:

(Continued)

FIGURE 10.3 *(Continued)*

		• 5 years and $250,000 fine for 1st offense
		• 10 years and $250,000 for subsequent offenses
		Misdemeanor if intentional access without, or in excess of, authorization. Penalty: 1 year
(a)(3)	Access without authority of a government computer.	**Misdemeanor** 1 year
(a)(4)	Knowingly accessing a protected computer to commit fraud.	**Felony** • 5 years and $250,000 fine for 1st offense • 10 years and $250,000 for subsequent offenses
(a)(5)(A)(i)	Knowingly causing the transmission of a "program, information, code, or command" that intentionally causes damage to a protected computer.	**Felony** • 10 years and $250,000 fine for 1st offense • 20 years and $250,000 for subsequent offenses
(a)(5)(A)(ii)	Intentionally accessing a protected computer and recklessly causing damage.	**Felony** • 5 years and $250,000 fine for 1st offense • 10 years and $250,000 for subsequent offenses
(a)(5)(A)(iii)	Intentionally accessing a protected computer and causing damage. No *mens rea* or intent required. Causing any damage, either negligently or otherwise.	**Misdemeanor** • 1 year and $100,000 fine for 1st offense • 10 years and $250,000 for subsequent offenses
(a)(6)	Traffics in computer passwords with intent to defraud. Need not be for profit.	**Misdemeanor** • 1 year and $100,000 fine for 1st offense • 10 years and $250,000 for subsequent offenses
(a)(7)	Transmitting an extortion threat regarding a protected computer. Transmitting in interstate or foreign commerce. Any communication containing any threat to cause damage to a protected computer. With intent to extort money or anything of value from any person, firm, or entity	**Felony** • 5 years and $250,000 fine for 1st offense • 10 years and $250,000 for subsequent offenses

Source: Information provided by Martin J. Littlefield, Assistant U.S. Attorney, U.S. Department of Justice, Western District of New York; Paul McCarthy, New York Assistant Attorney General; and Richard P. Salgado, Senior Counsel, Computer and Intellectual Property Section (CCIPS) of the U.S. Department of Justice.

< **CYBERBRIEF** >

SPAMWARE

The Center for Democracy and Technology (CDT) investigated how junk-mail spammers get hold of email addresses. The CDT created hundreds of email addresses and used each of them only once. After six months, over 8,800 unsolicited emails arrived at these addresses.

Only when an address was obscured in some way, e.g., writing "at" instead of the @ symbol, did the **spamware**—software that automatically searches the Web to collect what it recognizes as email addresses—fail. Obscured addresses could not be detected by spamware.

Sources: The Center for Democracy and Technology Report, http://www.cdt.org. Rowan, David. "Tech Salvos." *The Times* (London). March 25, 2003. Pp. 2, 16.

THE COMPUTER AS THE INSTRUMENT OF A CRIME: *CRIMES USING A COMPUTER*

Crimes using a computer tend to be traditional offenses, such as theft, fraud, or forgery. The difference is that they are committed using a computer, computer network, or information or communications technology.

Federal statutes 18 and 47 address "computers as instruments of crime" as shown in Figure 10.4. These statutes include the Wire Fraud Act, Economic Espionage Act,

FIGURE 10.4   "Computers as Instruments of Crime" (Crime Using the Computer) According to U.S. Federal Statutes 18 and 47

Federal Statute	Description of the Federal Crimes	Type of Crime and Maximum Penalty
18 USC § 1343	**Wire Fraud Act** Schemes to defraud, or use interstate wire communication to defraud.	**Felony** 5 years
18 USC § 1831–§ 1839	**Economic Espionage Act** Theft of trade secrets. Two main provisions: • Foreign state sponsored • Commercial theft	**Felony** If the theft is sponsored by a foreign state, the penalty is 15 years. If it is theft for any commercial purpose, the penalty is 10 years.
18 USC § 2511	**Wiretap Act** • Intentionally attempting to intercept any wire, oral, or electronic communication. • Grabbing electronic signals as they pass; e.g., keystroke sniffers. • Intentionally attempting to disclose contents of a communication knowing (or having reason to know) that the information was obtained through an illegal wiretap.	**Felony** 5 years

(Continued)

FIGURE 10.4   *(Continued)*

18 USC § 2701	**Electronic Communications Privacy Act (ECPA)** Illegal access to stored electronic communications, including email and voice mail. This is also called snooping.	**Misdemeanor** 6 months, unless malicious or for commercial advantage or gain.
18 USC § 2252(A)	**Child Pornography Act** Criminalizes federally the transmission or possession of child pornography.	**Felony** 15 years 30 years if prior child-sex conviction, with 5 year minimum
18 USC § 875 (a)–(d)	**Email Threats and Harassment Act** Using email for threats or harassment. See also 18 USC 1030(a)(7).	
	(a) Prohibits the transmission of any communication demanding or requesting a ransom or reward for the release of any kidnapped person.	**Felony** 20 years
	(b) Prohibits the transmission of any communication that contains any threat to kidnap any person, or any threat to injure the person of another with intent to extort.	**Felony** 20 years
	(c) Prohibits the transmission of any communication that contains any threat to kidnap or injure any person.	**Felony** 5 years
	(d) Prohibits the transmission of any communication that contains any threat to injure anyone's property or reputation; or the reputation of a deceased person; or any threat to accuse anyone of a crime, with intent to extort.	**Felony** 2 years
47 USC § 223	**Email Threats and Harassment** Using email for threats or harassment. (a)(1)(C): Prohibits transmission of communication that is obscene with intent to annoy, abuse, threaten, or harass. Also prohibits anonymous use of telecommunication device with intent to annoy, abuse, threaten, or harass. (a)(1)(E): Prohibits repeated communications initiated solely to harass.	**Felony** 2 years

Source: Information provided by Martin J. Littlefield, Assistant U.S. Attorney, U.S. Department of Justice, Western District of New York; Paul McCarthy, New York Assistant Attorney General; and Richard P. Salgado, Senior Counsel, Computer and Intellectual Property Section (CCIPS) of the U.S. Department of Justice.

Wiretap Act, Electronic Communications Privacy Act, Child Pornography Act, and Email Threats and Harassment Act.

For more information, see the DOJ's Computer Crime Section at http://www.usdoj.gov, or CCIPS at http://www. cybercrime.gov.

COMPUTER FRAUD

DEFINING THE PROBLEM

According to *The Wells Report of* 2000, computer fraud and abuse cost U.S. companies over $400 billion a year.[9] Two years later, the Association of Certified Fraud Examiners (CFE), the largest antifraud organization, estimated that U.S. companies lost 6% of revenues, or $600 billion annually, to fraud in 2002.[10] Although there is no accurate way of determining how many companies are victims of computer crime or fraud, experts estimate that the victimization rate is 100%. According to forensics accountant Dr. W. Steven Albrecht, "if you think your company has not been the victim of fraud, it's only because you have not found it." The reason is simply that computers and the Internet have made crime easier. Tom Talleur, managing director in KPMG's Forensic and Litigation Services Practice and a retired federal investigator, stated that the Internet provides "a high-performance, low-cost-of-entry" way to commit fraud. The fact of the matter is, businesses are being taken to the cleaners across the Net, but most companies can't detect intrusions across networks, so they only tend to notice inside offenders."[11]

FACTORS CONTRIBUTING TO COMPUTER FRAUD

Computer fraud became a serious threat to organizations in the early 1990s, when business networks began connecting to the Internet. Fraud, as well as fraud detection, had increased during the booming dot-com economy because controls were loose or ignored. There was a lot of money available to divert.

But in today's economic downturn, organizations, dissatisfied investors, and the SEC are demanding accountability and control. Efforts to combat these crimes are increasing, aided in part by tougher laws. The private sector is also increasing its efforts. According to an *Accounting Today* survey, 37% of the top 100 accounting firms reported that they were expanding their computer forensics and fraud services in 2002.

Employees and others who commit fraud have long relied on management's inability to see what was going on, as shown in the opening Cases on Point. It is still very time-consuming and difficult to review logs of network activity or audit trails of business transactions to detect computer fraud.[12] Too often, the intensive record screening necessary to identify fraud slows down business processes or requires too much funding or staffing. At some point, the costs outweigh the benefits.

THE NATURE OF FRAUD—AND ITS WARNING SIGNS

According to the Association of Certified Fraud Examiners (ACFE) and John Warren, ACFE associate general counsel,

- Employees are the biggest threat to businesses.
- Small firms are at greatest risk.
- The most costly abuses occur in organizations with fewer than 100 employees.

- Losses caused by managers are four times higher than those caused by employees.
- The median losses caused by executives were 16 times those of their employees.
- The majority of large frauds succeed because the company lacks controls, someone has too much authority over the books, and there is inadequate supervision. There are several well-known warning signs: employees whose financial difficulties suddenly end, sudden upscale changes in an employee's life style, expenses that are way out of line with income, or an employee who never takes a vacation. Those occurrences combined with poor internal control mechanisms provide the perfect environment for the type of fraud referred to as *white-collar crime* **(WCC).** In general, WWC refers to nonviolent crimes. These crimes are committed using deception for purposes of economic gain.

ECONOMIC FRAUD AND WHITE-COLLAR CRIME

Securities fraud, tax fraud, and antitrust violations are all white-collar cases. WCC also includes bankruptcy fraud, bank fraud, health care fraud, and federal program fraud. One of the key reasons for the Health Insurance Portability and Accountability Act (HIPAA) was to stop Medicaid and Medicare fraud. See the HIPAA Appendix following Chapter 11 for more details about health care fraud and abuse control.

The harms inflicted by economic crime can be substantial. Theft and fraud are never victimless crimes.[13] According to Frank O. Bowman, III, Associate Professor of Law at Indiana University,

> Unlike, for example, narcotics offenses in which one can at least argue that the crime consists of a willing seller providing a willing buyer with a desired commodity, no one wants to be swindled. Moreover, the harm inflicted by economic offenses often extends far beyond monetary losses to loss of jobs, homes, solvency, access to health care, or financial security in retirement.[14]

THEORIES AND PRINCIPLES OF PUNISHMENT FOR WHITE-COLLAR CRIMES

Economic crime of the truly "white-collar" variety, i.e., fraud and swindles of substantial sums by educated members of the business and professional classes, are reprehensible. Such crimes are customarily crimes of greed rather than need.[15] There is a strong public sentiment against WCC. Recent data collected by the National White-Collar Crime Center demonstrated that Americans view this type of behavior as more costly and problematic than traditional or street crime. Research has demonstrated that the most effective deterrent to crime is not only to increase the severity of punishment but also to increase the certainty of punishment. This two-pronged approach to punishment is crucial.[16]

THE PROSECUTION AND COSTS OF WHITE-COLLAR CRIME

WCC is a significant problem of corruption in the private, as well as the public, sector. Private industries can be prey to bribery and kickbacks in exchange for contracts or other benefits.[17] The economic costs are difficult to quantify, but securities regulators and other prominent groups have estimated that securities fraud alone totals

FEDERAL EFFORTS TO STOP MONEY LAUNDERING AND TERRORIST FINANCING

Only weeks after the terrorist attacks of September 11, 2001, lawmakers passed the USA PATRIOT Act and new anti-money-laundering rules suddenly became reality. The Bank Secrecy Act of 1970 required banks to file "suspicious activity" reports on account holders whose transactions or other behavior seem odd. Banks had to try to detect money laundering and help the authorities stop it. These "know-your-customer" requirements forced financial companies to track customer transactions to detect unusual patterns that suggested criminal laundering activity.

However, banks had not really been at risk of losing their charters, paying million-dollar fines, or defending their top executives from criminal charges for failing to detect money-laundering activities. The USA PATRIOT Act has changed all of that—and bank officers can now be held criminally liable. "People at the very top of the elevator shaft are going to find themselves being held responsible," according to Charles Horn, a lawyer at global law firm Mayer, Brown, Rowe & Maw.

Source: Grebb, Michael. "Struggling with the Most Vital Information." *US Banker.* April 2003. http://www.us-banker.com/usb/index.shtml

$40 billion per year. This is compared to $10 billion in estimated annual economic loss from "street" crime, according to the FBI's *Uniform Crime Report.*[18]

Technological advances have made WCC more easy to commit on a widespread basis and more difficult to investigate and successfully prosecute. WCC is often expensive and time-consuming to discover and prosecute. When these crimes go to trial, and sometimes even if they do not, they consume disproportionate amounts of judicial resources.[19] Therefore, much stricter accountability rules for senior management and long jail time for violators are expected to deter WCC.

There is another potential risk to consider. There is a documented relationship between terrorism and white-collar criminal activities—directly impacting national security interests. Some groups have used illegally gained money from fraudulent schemes to fund the operation of their terrorist organizations.

MONEY LAUNDERING

Money laundering methods became more creative due to the expansion of products and services offered in trade, more complicated financial relationships, advances in technology, and the increased velocity of money flows worldwide. Terrorist financing, although only one aspect of money laundering, has become a critical concern.

The Office of the Comptroller of the Currency requires regulated institutions to develop and implement effective anti-money-laundering programs that encompass terrorist financing. This has included record searches against U.S. government lists of suspected terrorists and terrorist organizations. The USA PATRIOT Act contains provisions to combat international terrorism and block terrorist access to the U.S. financial system. Several international organizations have also issued measures to curb money laundering and terrorist financing.[20]

COMPUTER FORENSICS TECHNIQUES FOR CATCHING CYBER CRIMINALS

The computer forensics techniques discussed in Chapter 9 dealt primarily with the discovery and recovery of email messages and computer files. These investigations may involve searching through millions of business records for e-evidence of a crime, fraud, or intent to commit fraud. When files have been deleted or widely distributed across backup tapes, network drives, laptops, cell phones, or PDAs, the computer forensics investigation requires significant amounts of time, money, and expertise. Often the investigation is initiated and conducted by law enforcement agencies. And often the e-evidence contains source information, such as names and other incriminating identifiers.

There are often significant differences when the goal of a computer forensics investigation is to discover if an incident has occurred, what occurred, how it occurred, who did it, and who was the ultimate target.

A Computer Forensics Scenario

For example, if the network administrator notices a suspicious amount of traffic, the first step is to confirm that it is in fact an attack and not a false positive. Most likely, this will be an educated guess.

Next, a preliminary estimate needs to be made of which systems could have been affected and how. This preliminary inspection requires checking logs to see whether files had been accessed, modified, created, deleted, or moved. It also includes trying to identify the point of entry and determining whether that intrusion is a real threat to information system services.

Many factors can complicate a preliminary review. The intruder may have installed a Trojan to hide electronic traces. Or the company may not have been the targeted victim, but rather used as a **hop-through** (i.e., one node in the route to the intended victim used to camouflage the identity of the sender) to the ultimate victim. To determine whether the company's network is a hop-through requires looking for servers to or from which data was sent. Hackers may use hop-through points, which launder their IP addresses to disguise their activities. Even though a company whose network is used only as a hop-through does not face immediate threats, later it may face liability issues. Based on the company's incident response policy, people should know what they are authorized to do, and not do.

There are multiple logs containing potential information. These include logs of email servers, application servers, routers, IDS, and firewalls. For large companies, there may be gigabytes of data that might have to be profiled to get a clear picture of what has happened.[21] Currently, there is no quick and easy way to integrate disparate logs and correlate the network events to get that picture. Vendors who are introducing products to support integration and correlation of network events to identify an incident, which is referred to as **incident management,** are Symantec, Checkpoint, and Silicon Defense.

Using log information, the next steps are to determine

- The immediate origin of the attack.
- Whether data was sent out, and if so, the identity of the servers to which it was sent.
- The identity of other victims.

There are two critical actions to keep in mind throughout the investigation. First, know the impact of any action before taking that action. Second, keep detailed records of the investigation of the incident—and keep those records safe so that they cannot be altered or destroyed. Keeping records offline may be necessary. The following sections have samples of forms from the SANS Institute for documenting incidents and how incidents were handled during the investigation. These forms help ensure that the information is accurate, which is necessary for it to be admissible in a legal action.

DOCUMENTATION OF INCIDENTS AND INCIDENT HANDLING

Preparing for and documenting incidents of computer crime, fraud, or terrorism are critical activities. The company must be able to show that it took reasonable actions to minimize damage or disruption. Documentation also ensures that contact and other information that is needed during an incident are available so that attention can be focused on containing and documenting the incident.

Incident documentation minimizes waste and mistakes. There are five non-copyrighted incident and incident handling forms available from the SANS Institute.[22] The SANS Institute states that "these forms may be posted on your local Web server or you may use them in printed form as long as this notice is preserved." These five forms help keep people alert to suspicious events. If the incident becomes a legal action, such as a criminal case, documentation that was captured during the incident may prove proper care, control, and chain of custody of the evidence. The five forms are

1. Incident Contact List
2. Incident Contact List (part 2)
3. Incident Identification
4. Incident Survey
5. Incident Containment

The five forms are presented next in their entirety.

---

1. Incident Contact List Form

Date Updated: _____

Corporate Security Officer:
Name: _____
Work Phone: _____
Home Phone: _____
Pager: _____
Fax: _____
Email: _____

CIO or Information Systems Security Manager:
Name: _____
Work Phone: _____
Home Phone: _____
Pager: _____
Fax: _____
Email: _____

Corporate Incident Handling or Computer Incident Response Team (CIRT):
Name: _____
Work Phone: _____
Home Phone: _____
Pager: _____
Fax: _____
Email: _____

Corporate Public Affairs Officer:
Name: _____
Work Phone: _____
Home Phone: _____
Pager: _____
Fax: _____
Email: _____

---

2. Incident Contact List Form (part 2)

Date Updated: _____

Local Law Enforcement Computer Crime:
Name: _____
Phone: _____
Pager: _____
Fax: _____
Email: _____

Local FBI:
Name: _____
Phone: _____
Pager: _____
Fax: _____
Email: _____

Outside CIRT:
Name: _____
Work Phone: _____
Pager: _____
Fax: _____
Email: _____

3. Incident Containment Form

Date: _____
Page ___ of ____

Isolate affected systems:
Command Decision Team approved removal from network? (YES / NO)
If NO, what was the reason: _____
If YES, time systems were disconnected:_____

Backup affected systems:
System backup successful for all systems? (YES / NO)
Name of persons who did backup(s):

_____
_____

Time backups started: _____
Time backups complete: _____
Backup tapes sealed? (YES / NO)
Backup tapes turned over to: _____
Signature: _____
Location tapes will be stored: _____

---

4. Incident Identification Form

Date: _____
Page ___ of ____

Your contact information:
Name: _____
Phone: _____
Alternate Phone: _____
Pager: _____
Fax: _____
Alternate Fax: _____
Email: _____

Type of incident: (Denial of Service, Espionage, Hoax, Malicious code, Probe, Unauthorized access, Unauthorized use.)
Location of incident:
Address: _____

_____
_____

Building: _____
Room: _____

Additional Information:

_____

_____

_____

How was the incident detected:

_____

_____

_____

Who detected the incident: _____

Signature: _____

When was it detected: _____

---

5. Incident Survey Form

Date: _____

Page ___ of ____

Location(s) of affected system(s):

_____

_____

_____

Date/Time incident handlers arrived at site:

_____

_____

_____

Describe affected information systems: (one form per system is recommended)

Hardware Manufacturer: _____

Serial Number of CPU: _____

Corporate Property Number if applicable: _____

Operating System type/version: _____

Disk capacity (if known): _____

Is affected system connected to a network? (YES / NO)

System name: _____

System address: _____

MAC address: _____

Is affected system connected to a modem? (YES / NO)

Phone number: _____

Describe physical security of location of affected information system (locks, alarm systems, building access, etc.):

_____

_____

_____

FINDING E-EVIDENCE OF AN INTRUSION OR ATTACK

Major support for computer forensics analysis is provided by **sniffers.** Sniffers are software tools used to capture and filter information that has been transferred over a network. That traffic includes passwords, email, confidential documents, and any other unencrypted traffic. In essence, the sniffer acts as a primary logging program for all machines on a network. Like firewalls, there are different types of tools for filtering network traffic during an investigation. The type of tool used depends on many factors, including the size and configuration of the systems on the network. By capturing all packets, the sniffer also helps paint a picture of the network it is operating on. This provides a map of the network and the machines that are on them.

Several of the most common sniffers are Snort, Ethereal, and TCPdump. TCPdump is considered to be a more professional administrative tool and was the one used by Tsutomu Shimomura to capture Kevin Mitnick. Ethereal has become popular because of its relatively easy-to-use interface and excellent display features. Multiple sniffers can be used. For example, network traffic can be filtered with the Snort intrusion-detection tool and then the TCPDump network sniffer utility. See the Security Focus Website at http://www.securityfocus.com for an extensive collection of sniffers.

TRACKING DOWN CYBER CRIMINALS

It very difficult to track viruses back to their sources but not impossible. Officials at Cornell University were able to pin the Internet virus on Robert Morris, Jr. because of other evidence. They had found in Morris' files a list of passwords used to break into the system. In his files they also found an early version of the worm that later clogged the memory banks of computers on the network.[23]

David L. Smith was arrested for creating and releasing the Melissa virus. Like Morris, he was caught because of several pieces of evidence he left. He wrote the Melissa virus using Microsoft Office. The virus file contained a digital print, known as a global unique identifier, which was traceable to the computer on which it was created.[24] Even more useful, the virus's original posting on March 26, 1999 included an AOL return address. AOL's logs had a record of the telephone line used to post the Melissa virus, which linked to Smith. When Smith learned he might get caught, he allegedly tried to get rid of the e-evidence by throwing out his computer. But throwing his computer in the apartment complex's dumpster did not fool the FBI. And an investigation of Internet bulletin boards revealed email indicating interest in viruses that also referred to *DLSmith* and were sent from an email address containing the name *Smith*.

David Smith pled guilty to violating section 1030(a)(5) for releasing the Melissa virus that damaged thousands of computers across the Internet. Although Smith agreed, as part of his plea, that his conduct caused over $80,000,000 worth of loss (the maximum dollar figure contained in the sentencing guidelines), experts estimated that the real loss was as much as 10 times that amount. In addition, the law at that time set a mandatory sentencing guidelines minimum of six months in prison for any violation of 18 USC § 1030(a)(5) and for violations of section 1030(a)(4)—accessing a protected computer with the intent to defraud. As shown previously in Figure 10.3, the maximum penalty had been raised to 10 years for first offenders and 20 years for repeat offenders.

LEGALBRIEF

FIRST AMENDMENT RIGHTS

FBI Special Agent John Iannarelli said the First Amendment protects Websites that criticize U.S. policy, and the FBI is "not interested in quashing free speech. However, if you cross the line, calling for attacks on the U.S. or offering information on terrorist methods, that could be illegal."

Source: Shane, Scott. "Al-Qaida Expanding Its Web." *Desert News* (Salt Lake City, Utah). March 29, 2003. P. A08.

CYBER TERRORISM

Cyber terrorism is a worldwide fear—growing worse because of the war on Iraq. Cyber terrorism is the use of computers and the Internet to launch attacks and horrible acts that may directly or indirectly harm or kill people.[25] Computers control a wide range of operations that include power plants, telephone systems, and most manufacturing activities. Computer systems control airline traffic and transportation systems, water, oil pipelines, and energy. Therefore, disruptions in any one of these systems could cause loss of life or widespread chaos.

Most hacking or viruses involve people trying to steal passwords, disable individual computers, or get access to valuable information. These are rather isolated criminal activities. In contrast, cyber terrorism refers to a more sophisticated effort to attack and disrupt a critical information infrastructure[26] that would cause a breakdown in systems such as energy or transportation networks, health or emergency services, water or food networks, or telecommunications.

THE NATIONAL STRATEGY TO SECURE CYBERSPACE

Consistent with the National Strategy for Homeland Security, the strategic objectives of the National Strategy to Secure Cyberspace are to

- Prevent cyber attacks against America's infrastructures,
- Reduce national vulnerability to cyber attacks, and
- Minimize danger and recovery time from cyber attacks that do occur.

The full capability of IT to defend against cyber terrorism has been subject to scrutiny—"sometimes measured, sometimes nearly hysterical. . . . But what is difficult is the lack of a real barometer that gives us an easy way to distinguish the measured from the hysterical."[27] A study was conducted to test the feasibility of a digital Pearl Harbor.

DIGITAL PEARL HARBOR SIMULATION

In July 2002, the U.S. Naval War College and Gartner Group hosted a three-day seminar-style war game called **Digital Pearl Harbor (DPH).** Gartner analysts and national security strategists gathered in Newport, Rhode Island, with business and IT leaders

< **CYBERBRIEF** >

NIMDA RAISED CONCERNS ABOUT TERRORIST ACTIVITIES

Nimda, discovered on September 18, 2001, had no apparent political motive. Despite its destruction, it was still only a single act that was not associated with real-world terrorist acts. However, Nimda did raise concerns about the Internet being used to coordinate terrorist activities.

Source: McAfee Security Forum. "Cyber Crime, Cyber Terrorism, and Cyber War." *ESecurity News*. February 2002. http://dispatch.mcafee.com/esecuritynews/feb2002/firewallforum.asp?cid=2876

from enterprises that control parts of the national critical infrastructure. The objective of the test was to develop a scenario for a coordinated, cross-industry, cyber terrorism event.[28] The DPH simulation tested U.S. responses to attacks on telecommunications, the Internet, financial systems, and the power grid. This test demonstrated that assailants would need $200 million, intelligence information, and years of preparation time to accomplish significant disruptions.

The researchers also concluded that since the Internet would be crucial in attacking other national infrastructure systems, attacks on the Net would be left for last—so as to not interrupt ongoing attacks. According to the analysts, most scenarios also required coordinated physical attacks on systems. Industries in the United States may have a tough time recovering from an attack because "in contrast to defenses that are there to protect the territory and people and property of the U.S., for a digital Pearl Harbor we have no early warning systems" said a Gartner analyst.[29] The researchers believed that "following best practices for IT security will mitigate most of the risk."[30]

THE FREEDOM CYBER FORCE MILITIA HIJACKS AL-JAZEERA'S WEBSITES

On March 27, 2003, hackers calling themselves the Freedom Cyber Force Militia sabotaged the Websites of the Arab television network Al-Jazeera. Internet traffic directed towards Al-Jazeera's Website in English was hijacked—diverting the traffic to a Website located on servers operated by an ISP in Salt Lake City. On that Website was a Stars-and-Stripes U.S. logo with the messages, "Let freedom ring" and "God bless our troops," which were signed "Patriot." When someone clicked onto Al-Jazeera's Website in Arabic, a pornography Website displayed instead. Both the Arabic and English language sites were down for almost two days. The hackers had used free Websites.[31,32]

Hackers impersonating an Al-Jazeera employee had tricked a Web addressing company into making technical changes that gave them temporary control of the English and Arabic Al-Jazeera Websites. According to David Endler of iDefense, an Internet security company, "It probably didn't take a lot of effort, probably a fake phone call or fax. It's amazing how often the human element comes into play with security breaches. You can have levels of authentication, but obviously one person has the ability to circumvent all that." The FBI is investigating these hack attacks.[33,34]

ARMY TAPS DEFENSE MESSAGE SYSTEM (DMS) FOR WARTIME COMMUNICATION

The Army recently implemented the DMS to provide users with better-protected and faster communications than email over the Defense Department's Secret Internet Protocol Router Network (SIPRNET). DMS messages travel over the Defense Information Systems Network, which distributes voice, video, and data messages. This system is a $1.6 billion effort to secure DOD communications worldwide. It is designed to provide writer-to-reader service for classified and top-secret information, delivering messages to DOD users at their desktops.

Retired Air Force Master Sgt. Arthur Edgeson, a senior systems engineer, said DMS became active at Camp Doha in Kuwait at the end of February 2003 and has experienced a noticeable increase in traffic since Operation Iraqi Freedom began March 20. "Yes, SIPR email is classified, but it could be hacked into. Or if we're overrun by the enemy, they would have access to the computers and could send messages . . . to mislead or misdirect [coalition] forces," said Edgeson.

Source: Caterinicchia, Dan. "Army Taps DMS for Wartime Comm." *Federal Computer Week*. March 27, 2003. http://www.fcw.com/fcw/articles/2003/middle_east/web-dms-03-27-03.asp

Chapter Summary

Just as the Internet has improved organizations' ability to communicate and conduct business, it has made it easier for criminals to commit crimes that are difficult to detect. To deter computer crime and computer fraud, the federal government passed new and amended laws. Federal statutes divide computer-related offenses into two categories: the computer as the target of a crime and as the instrument of a crime.

These statutes are more comprehensive, impose longer prison terms, and have zero tolerance for intentional access to a "protected computer." Any computer attached to the Internet is now considered a "protected computer," which sends a clear message that the government will use prosecution, or threat of prosecution, to protect critical infrastructures.

Since the 1990s, computer fraud has become a widespread threat in all organizations. Several factors have intensified fraud and white-collar crime: business networks began connecting to the Internet, too many companies ignored financial and auditing controls during the economic upswing of the dot-com economy, and the economic downturn may have motivated financial crime. Americans view WCC as more costly and problematic than traditional or street crime.

During an incident or suspected attack, a sequence of steps should be followed to minimize waste and mistakes. Incident handling and documentation directly affect the ability to identify the source of the attack and prosecute the attacker. Computer forensics tools and techniques are used to discover whether an incident has occurred, what occurred, how it occurred, who did it, and who was the ultimate target.

Although there is some risk of cyber terrorism, cyber warfare simulations and research suggest that the risk is low.

Simulation demonstrated that assailants would need $200 million, intelligence information, and years of preparation time to accomplish significant disruptions to the Internet.

Key Terms

- statute
- incident
- event
- spamware
- white-collar crime (WCC)
- hop-through
- incident management
- sniffers
- Digital Pearl Harbor (DPH)

Discussion Questions

1. What are the two categories of computer-related offenses? Give an example of each type of crime.
2. Why were existing federal statutes amended throughout the 1980s and 1990s?
3. What are the key terms of the Computer Fraud and Abuse Act of 1986 (18 USC § 1030)? Why are those terms so precisely defined?
4. What is spamware and how does it function? Is there any defense against spamware?
5. Define white-collar crime. What factors may have increased the incidence of WCC? What factors may be decreasing it?
6. What is meant by a *hop-through*? Identify the risks a company faces if its network is used as a hop-through.
7. Explain the function of a sniffer.
8. Why is documentation of an incident important? What are necessary precautions to ensure the safety and completeness of documentation records?
9. Explain how well-planned incident response management can reduce cyber risks to a manageable level.
10. What are the three strategic objectives of the National Strategy to Secure Cyberspace?
11. Outline the Digital Pearl Harbor simulation. What were the conclusions regarding the risk of a successful cyber terrorist attack?

Endnotes

1. Gleim, Invin N., and Jordan B. Ray with Eugene P. O'Connor. *Business Law/Legal Studies*. Gainsville, FL: Gleim Publications, Inc., 1992.
2. *United States vs Morris,* 928 F. 2d 504 (2d Cir. 1991).
3. Goodman, Marc D., and Susan W. Brenner. "The Emerging Consensus on Criminal Conduct in Cyberspace." *UCLA Journal of Law and Technology*. Vol. 3. 2002.
4. Rowan, David. "Tech Salvos." *The Times* (London). March 25, 2003. Pp. 2, 16.
5. *United States vs Rusnak,* No. 02-CR-280, guilty plea entered (D. Md. October 24, 2002).
6. "Allfirst Bank Trader Pleads Guilty To $691 Million Derivatives Fraud." *White-Collar Crime Reporter*. Vol. 17. No. 1. December 2002. P. 25. "Fraud: *United States vs Rusnak:* Allfirst Bank Trader Pleads Guilty to $691 Million Derivatives Fraud." *Bank & Lender Liability Litigation Reporter*. Vol. 8. No. 12. November 14, 2002. P. 8.
7. Kercheval, Nancy. "What Led to the Allfirst Trading Scandal?" *The Daily Record* (Baltimore, MD). January 11, 2003.
8. Klein, Melissa. "Accounting Firms Mine Growing Niche in Forensics." *Accounting Today*. Vol. 15. No. 10. June 4, 2001. P. 1.
9. Ibid.

10. Rogers, Paul. "Enemies of a CEO?" *Chief Executive*. November 1, 2002. P. 32.

11. Klein, Melissa. "Accounting Firms Mine Growing Niche in Forensics." *Accounting Today*. Vol. 15. No. 10. June 4, 2001. P. 1.

12. Albrecht, W. Steve, and Conan C. Albrecht. "Root Out Financial Deception: Detect and Eliminate Fraud or Suffer the Consequences." *Journal of Accountancy*. Vol. 193. No. 4. April 1, 2002. P. 30.

13. Gainer, Glen B., III. *Statement of Glen B. Gainer, III, State Auditor of West Virginia; Chairman, Committee on Senate Judiciary Subcommittee on Crime and Drugs.* "Penalties for White Collar Offense: Are We Really Getting Tough on Crime?" June 19, 2002.

14. Bowman, Frank O., III. *Statement of Frank O. Bowman, Associate Professor of Law Indiana University School of Law, Committee on Senate Judiciary Subcommittee on Crime and Drugs.* "Penalties for White Collar Offense: Are We Really Getting Tough on Crime?" June 19, 2002.

15. Comey, James B., Jr. *Statement of James B. Comey, Jr., United States Attorney Southern District of New York, Committee on Senate Judiciary Subcommittee on Crime and Drugs.* "Penalties for White Collar Offense: Are We Really Getting Tough on Crime?" June 19, 2002.

16. *Statement of Glen B. Gainer, III.*

17. *Statement of James B. Comey, Jr.*

18. *Statement of Glen B. Gainer, III.*

19. Skolnik, Bradley, *Statement of Bradley Skolnik, Securities Commissioner of Indiana; Chairman, Enforcement Division North American Securities Administrators Association, Committee on Senate Judiciary Subcommittee on Crime and Drugs.* "Penalties for White Collar Offense: Are We Really Getting Tough on Crime?" June 19, 2002.

20. U.S. Department of the Treasury. January 17, 2003. http://www.occ.treas.gov/moneylaundering2002.pdf

21. Richardson, Robert. "Keeping Your Data Smart." *Alert*. October 2002. Pp. 1, 8.

22. The incident documentation forms may also be downloaded from http://www.incidents.org/Incident_forms/

23. Stover, Dawn. "Viruses, Worms, Trojans, and Bombs." *Popular Science*. Vol. 235. No. 3. September 1989. P. 59.

24. *Fundamentals of Computer Fraud*. No. 99-5403. ACFE. 1999. Pp. 35–36.

25. Dasgupta, Partha. "Cyber Terrorism." *The Statesman* (India). May 24, 2002.

26. Wasow, Omar. "Dangers of Cyber-Terrorism Now that the War with Iraq Has Begun." National Public Radio. March 20, 2003.

27. "The Stakes are Huge." *Government Computer News/Washington Technology*. March 2003.

28. Gartner Report. "Dealing with Cyberterrorism: A Primer for Financial Services." Reference Number: qa-1002-0104. October 2, 2002. https://www.gartnerg2.com/qa/qa-1002-0104.asp

29. NIPC (Infragard_unsecured) Daily Report. August 15, 2002. Daily Report.

30. Fraley, David, and Ron Cowles. "Could Terrorists Bring Down the Public Switched Telephone Network?" Gartner Group. September 3, 2002. http://www.gartnerg2.com/site/FileDownload.asp?file=qa-1002-0104-109349.pdf

31. "Protesters For and Against War Target Web Sites." *Newsday*. March 29, 2003.

32. Bridis, Ted. "Al-Jazeera Web Site Is Sabotaged by Hackers." Associated Press. March 28, 2003.

33. "Cyber Security: Hackers Replace Arab Web Site With Patriotic Messages." *National Journal's Technology Daily*. March 28, 2003.

34. Iqbal, Anwar. "FBI Investigates Al-Jazeera Hacking." United Press International. March 28, 2003.

USA PATRIOT ACT

Constitutional Amendments Expand Law Enforcement's Authority to Obtain Electronic Evidence and Investigate Computer Crimes

SECTION 202: GIVES AUTHORITY TO MONITOR VOICE COMMUNICATIONS IN COMPUTER HACKING INVESTIGATIONS

Previous Law

Under previous law, government investigators could not get a wiretap order to monitor voice (wire) communications to investigate violations of the Computer Fraud and Abuse Act (18 USC § 1030). This was a problem in cases when investigators needed to collect information about suspected hackers who had stolen services from a telephone company and used them to plan and execute hack attacks.

Amendment

Section 202 amends 18 USC § 2516(1), which is the subsection that lists crimes for which investigators may obtain a wiretap order for wire communications. The amendment also adds the felony violations of 18 USC § 1030 to the list of offenses. This provision will sunset December 31, 2005.

SECTION 209: GIVES AUTHORITY TO OBTAIN STORED VOICE COMMUNICATIONS, SUCH AS VOICEMAIL

Previous Law

Under previous law, the ECPA (18 USC § 2703 *et seq.*[1]), governed law enforcement's access to stored electronic communications, such as email. However, it did not allow access to stored wire communications, such as voicemail.

The wiretap statute governed such access because the definition of "wire communication" [18 USC § 2510(1)] included stored communications. This statute was a problem because law enforcement had to get a wiretap court order, rather than simply a search warrant, to obtain unopened voice communications. The need to get a court order created large and unnecessary burdens for criminal investigations.

Congress acknowledged that data and voice might co-exist in a single transaction, but it did not anticipate the convergence of these two kinds of communications, which is typical of today's telecommunications networks. With the arrival of MIME (multipurpose Internet mail extensions) and similar features, an email may include one or more "attachments" consisting of any type of data, including voice recordings. As a result, a law enforcement officer seeking to obtain a suspect's unopened email from an ISP by means of a search warrant [as required under 18 USC § 2703(a)] had no way of knowing whether the inbox messages include voice attachments, i.e., wire communications, which could not be compelled using a search warrant.

Amendment

Section 209 of the USA PATRIOT Act changes the way in which the wiretap statute and ECPA apply to stored voice communications. The amendment deletes "electronic storage" of wire communications from the definition of "wire communication" in section 2510. It also inserts language in section 2703 to ensure that stored wire communications are covered under the same rules as stored electronic communications. Thus, law enforcement can now obtain stored communications using the procedures set out in section 2703, such as a search warrant, rather than those in the wiretap statute, such as a wiretap order. This provision will sunset December 31, 2005.

SECTION 210: SCOPE OF SUBPOENAS FOR ELECTRONIC EVIDENCE

Previous Law

Subsection 2703(c) allows the government to use a subpoena to compel information, such as the customer's name, address, length of service, and means of payment. Prior to the amendments in section 210 of the USA PATRIOT Act, the list of records that investigators could obtain with a subpoena did not include certain records. For example, investigators could not get credit card numbers or other forms of payment for the communication service. This information was needed to determine a customer's true identity, since many users register with ISPs using false names. In order to hold individuals responsible for criminal acts committed online, the method of payment is essential in determining their true identities.

Also, many of the definitions in section 2703(c) were technology-specific—relating primarily to telephone communications. For example, the list included "local and long distance telephone toll billing records," but did not include terms for computer-based communications, such as "records of session times and durations."

Amendment

Amendments to section 2703(c) update and expand the list of records that law enforcement authorities may obtain with a subpoena. The new subsection 2703(c)(2) includes "records of session times and durations," and "any temporarily assigned network address." In the Internet context, such records include the IP address assigned by the ISP to the subscriber for a particular session and the remote IP address from which a subscriber connects to the ISP. Obtaining these records will make the process of identifying computer criminals and tracing their Internet communications faster and easier.

The amendments also state that investigators may use a subpoena to get the "means and source of payment" that a subscriber uses to pay for ISP service, "including any credit card or bank account number." [18 USC § 2703(c)(2)(F)].

This information is important in identifying the users of Internet services for which a company does not verify its users' biographical information. This section is not subject to the sunset provision in section 224 of the Act.

CHAPTER 11
PRIVACY AND DATA PROTECTION

Learning Objectives

◆ Recognizing the threats to privacy posed by the Internet and ecommerce.

◆ Using spam-avoidance procedures and tools.

◆ Tools and techniques for unauthorized data collection.

◆ Initiatives to protect privacy rights.

INTRODUCTION

The ease with which information can be collected directly from individuals or gathered secretly through technologies that track online activities presents new challenges to protecting individual privacy. Personal information can be used constructively, such as enabling retailers to customize their promotions to individual customer preferences. In the wrong hands, however, it may lead to invasion of privacy, cyber stalking, or identity theft. This chapter examines privacy issues and defenses.

SPAM

REASONS FOR THE INCREASE IN SPAM

Despite these legal roadblocks, the volume of spam has grown 16-fold within two years to the extent that it makes up over one third of all email sent.[1] There are several reasons for this.

- It is cheap. There is very little cost associated with mass emails beyond what is charged by the sender's ISP. Most of the cost gets paid by the victims.
- Addresses are still easy to get, particularly due to spamware. Despite recent restrictions imposed by the government and the marketplace, companies sell their customer email lists to spammers. Email addresses are confirmed when the recipient opts out, as stated in the instructions on the message. This sends a return receipt to the spammer.
- It is effective and profitable. The response rates to email campaigns are high enough to justify them as a business model. Profit margins are generally higher than for traditional direct mail campaigns.
- Spam is not prosecuted very often so the risk to spammers is low.

<CASE ON POINT>

ARE 30,000 EMAILS AGAINST AN EMPLOYER FREE SPEECH OR SPAM?

Ken Hamidi reportedly attempted to send mass emails to Intel employees several times. Messages alleged that Intel supported policies that were abusive and unfair to its employees, or claimed that the company would cut three times the number of jobs that had been previously announced. Using company email, he urged Intel employees to take a stand against the company, with messages such as: "Never trust Intel's HR representatives or attorneys." Most of his email messages were blocked by Intel's firewalls, but Hamidi was able to sneak his sixth transmission past Intel's shield by spoofing his return address.

Intel's legal team relied on a court order that was issued after it was determined that Hamidi had trespassed onto Intel property with his mass emails. They claimed that employee email addresses are "confidential and proprietary information." And that unsolicited bulk email "drains valuable resources by taxing Intel's internal systems."[2]

Hamidi's defense was that his messages were not commercial in nature. They were a form of a public protest and legally protected by the Constitution. Counsel for Intel responded: "Somebody can picket outside the facility and say the business is doing a bad thing, but it doesn't mean they can go inside and picket."[3]

A California appeals court, in a split decision, upheld the lower court's ruling against Hamidi, saying his email campaign amounted to trespassing. The court stated that "(Intel) showed he was disrupting its business by using its property and, therefore, is entitled to injunctive relief based on a theory of trespass to chattels."[4] This theory applies to the unauthorized use of someone else's private property. The judges stated that free speech does not include the use of someone else's private property for self-expression.

The ACLU of Northern California and the Electronic Frontier Foundation (EFF) had submitted briefs supporting Hamidi's rights to free speech, but the majority dismissed that argument as follows: "Strangely, EFF, purporting to laud the 'freedom' of the Internet, emphasizes Intel allows its employees reasonable personal use of Intel's equipment for sending and receiving personal email. Such tolerance by employers would vanish if they had no way to limit such personal usage of company equipment."[5]

There have been several other similar rulings in recent years pertaining to unsolicited email. Companies such as AOL Time Warner have used this legal doctrine to take spammers to court when their email clogs the AOL network.

THE ECONOMIC IMPACT OF SPAM

Spam is no longer just a minor nuisance; it is a significant drain on economic resources. According to industry analysts at Gartner Group, the average connected worker spends 49 minutes a day managing email accounts.[6] A lot of this time is spent sorting through and deleting spam. In addition, these hundreds of millions of messages, many of them including images and scripts, generate far more network traffic than standard text messages. They occupy an enormous amount of storage space on networks that could be used for productive purposes.

To make matters worse, the spam problem is now spreading to other messaging services and devices such as IM, cell phones, pagers, and PDAs that have wireless

⟨ **CASE ON POINT** ⟩

FTC ALLEGES COMPANIES' WEBSITES VIOLATED CHILDREN'S ONLINE PRIVACY PROTECTION ACT

Mrs. Fields Cookies and Hershey Foods Corporation each agreed to settle FTC charges that their Websites violated the Children's Online Privacy Protection Act (COPPA) by collecting personal information from children without first obtaining the proper parental consent. COPPA requires that Websites post adequate privacy policies, to provide direct notice to parents about the information they are collecting, how it will be used, and provide a reasonable means for parents to review the personal information collected from their children and a means to refuse to permit its use. Mrs. Fields had to pay civil penalties of $100,000; Hershey had to pay $85,000. These cases represent the biggest COPPA penalties awarded to date.[7]

COPPA applies to operators of commercial Websites and online services that are directed to children under the age of 13. It also applies to general-audience Websites and online services that collect personal information from children under 13. Among other things, COPPA requires that Website operators obtain verifiable consent from a parent or guardian *before* they collect personal information from children.

network capability. Since wireless bandwidth is often billed by usage, spam traffic can be a very expensive annoyance.

SPAM DEFENSES

In addition to the legislative and regulatory defenses, there are several ways individuals and businesses can defend themselves against unsolicited email.

Server-based Email Filters

Server-based email filters can be installed at the email gateway. There are several products on the market that can be used with an email server to block suspected spam on its way to the addressee's inbox.

Email filters function similarly to IDS. They are usually rule-based applications that detect suspicious messages based on keywords in the message or subject line. Examples of this might be "net casino," "get out of debt," or "you are a contest winner!" They can also contain rules to detect specific sender domains or IP addresses. As with all information security filters, these methods are not perfect. Specifically, they can mistakenly identify a legitimate message as spam.

Many ISPs are filtering out spam as a service for their customers' protection and to reduce their costs. The advantage of this method is that the spam never reaches the email client, which conserves bandwidth.

Client-based Email Filters

Client-based email filters are designed to enhance users' email clients, such as Outlook. Some of these filters work like AV programs in that they subscribe to a database of filtering rules that are constantly updated to adapt to new tactics of the spamming industry. Filters can be configured to automatically delete detected spam or

LEGALBRIEF

CRACKING DOWN ON SPAM

Within a year, interactive marketing company MonsterHut has bombarded consumers with more than 500 million commercial emails, according to a suit filed in May 2002 by New York State Attorney General Eliot Spitzer. These unsolicited messages advertised a wide variety of products and services. More than 750,000 people have asked MonsterHut to remove them from its lists.

Spitzer petitioned the court to prevent MonsterHut and two named executives from falsely representing their actions regarding unsolicited commercial email. Additionally, he wanted the court to force MonsterHut to reveal how it acquired the email addresses of private citizens on its lists. Finally, Spitzer asked that MonsterHut be made to pay civil penalties and court costs because it violated New York State's consumer protection laws.

This suit is another clear sign that U.S. authorities are attempting to get tough on spammers. Currently, 22 states have passed antispam laws, and the U.S. Congress is also considering several bills designed to crack down on spam.

Source: Robinson, Teri. "New York Sues Spammer." *E-Commerce Times.* May 2002.
http://www.ecommercetimes.com/perl/story/17978.html

divert it to a special folder for further review. The most sophisticated tools have a learning capability. They ask the user to review suspicious messages individually. They then use the results to refine the screening filters, thus improving their precision over time.

Unsubscribing from Unknown Internet Services

One very common spammer deception is to invite the addressee to click on a hyperlink within the message to unsubscribe. This is a deceptive promise to cut off all future unwanted messages. In fact, this serves as a return receipt to the spammer, who then sells the address to other spammers. These invitations should not be confused with the required opt-out disclosures that are included in email communications from legitimate senders. Privacy has become enough of an issue with customers that reputable merchants are not only making their privacy policies clear, they are enforcing them diligently.

PRIVACY

CHARACTERISTICS OF SECURITY

Privacy has many of the characteristics of security:

- It is a dangerous issue that should not be underestimated.
- It needs to be managed.
- If it is mismanaged, the consequences can be severe and expensive.
- It is an evolving and potentially explosive issue.
- It is of concern to employees and customers.

Privacy policies put consumers in charge of their information. To address consumers' concerns about this issue, companies should make their privacy policies easy to read, easy to understand, and easy to find on their Websites. It is also important to promote the policy internally in employee communications. Privacy policies need to be updated to stay current with the frequent changes in business and law.

LEAVING A DIGITAL TRAIL

The automation of personal and professional activities, such as automated toll payments, helps to make things more convenient and lower costs. But it also creates detailed and lasting records of people's identities and transaction histories. This information is intentionally shared with customers, partners, merchants, suppliers, or the government. Because commercial networks are linked together, personal information circulates digitally when businesses are bought and sold, partnerships are created, or government agencies pool their resources.

Advances in storage technology have made it possible to collect enormous amounts of detailed transactional data and retain it for an extended time. The data warehouses that store transaction data have capacities of 200 terabytes and could grow much larger.[8] The largest commercial data warehouses belong to mass retailers, like Wal-Mart, which retain data about every item that passes through their checkout scanners.

Data mining software is available to analyze data in a data warehouse to find general patterns in purchasing behavior or to profile individual customers. One example was the discovery of the tendency for fathers of young children to purchase beer and diapers simultaneously on Fridays. When these products were placed together near checkout lines, sales of both products improved dramatically. In addition to its use in marketing, data mining is also used to detect undesirable or illegal behaviors, such as drug prescription abuse, electronic fraud, or tax evasion.[9]

Information gathered about customers is valuable to businesses that generate it and to others who purchase it. Many Internet sites that have not been profitable have tried to increase revenues by selling information about their users without their consent. This information is collected in various ways, some more apparent than others.

METHODS OF INFORMATION COLLECTION

Cookies

The most common method of collecting data about Internet users started when Netscape introduced **cookies** in the second release of its Navigator browser. Cookies are now a standard feature in all Web browsers. A cookie is a block of text sent from the Website to the browser on the user's PC, where it is stored. Information that the cookie collects can be sent to the originating Website at a later time. Cookies enable customized interactions between a repeat visitor and Websites.

Data stored in cookies include:

- References to identify a specific account holder.
- Shopping cart information that can be held over for repeat visits to an ecommerce site.
- Stock portfolio information for personalized quotation service.
- Location information (e.g., zip codes) for personalized news and weather.

◁ **CYBERBRIEF** ▷

DOUBLECLICK SETTLES
CLASS ACTION SUIT

In August of 2002, DoubleClick settled with regulators in 10 U.S. states that had laws giving Web users the right to review information (records) that the company had collected with cookies. These records revealed categories of individuals, based on their surfing habits. DoubleClick used the category system to sell advertising targeted to specific interest groups.

In the settlement, DoubleClick admitted no wrongdoing, but agreed to pay state attorneys general $450,000 to cover "investigative costs and consumer education." The company also agreed to move data offline three months after its collection, to post its privacy policy prominently, and to inform users immediately of any changes. It also promised to hire an independent firm to oversee its compliance with terms of the settlement.

Source: Glasner, Joanna. "DoubleClick to Open Cookie Jar." *Wired.com*. August 2002.
http://www.wired.com/news/business/0,1367,54769,00.html

Site Profiles

Many general information Websites and Web storefronts either encourage or require that their visitors register by filling out a form. These profiles generally include contact information, demographic data, and credit card information to make purchases faster. For a frequent user, this is convenient. For the Website operator, profiles are a valuable source of marketing information, especially when combined with transaction histories built using cookies.

These profiles make it possible to match the history with information that identifies a specific individual, like a name, an email address, or a phone number. Of course, these profiles can be sold repeatedly to third parties. This leads to the legal problem of who owns the data—the collector or the individual? Even if the individual owns it, it means nothing if he or she has no control over it—or gave that control away by providing the information.

Most popular and reputable sites publish their policies regarding how they use or sell customer data. Customers may have the option to submit their preferences as to how their data may be used. Under current law, however, these preferences are subject to change without notice, as users of Yahoo found out in 2002. Their personal profiles were reset to allow their information to be used for solicitation by conventional mail, email, and telephone. These new settings would take effect in 60 days unless the "opt-out" settings were reset by the user.[10]

Web Bugs

Web bugs are links to small images that are often 1 pixel in size and thus not visible. They are placed within host Web pages specifically to eavesdrop. When a user requests a Web page from a known site, the bug is activated and the image is downloaded from its server (see Figure11.1.) That server, belonging to the unknown third party, can log valuable information about the user that downloaded it. The information

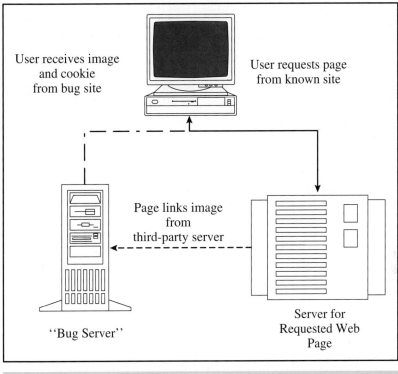

User receives image
and cookie
from bug site

User requests page
from known site

Page links image
from
third-party server

"Bug Server"

Server for
Requested Web
Page

FIGURE 11.1 Web Bugs

that is collected includes the Web page it was hidden on and other sites that were
recently visited. Web bugs might also be embedded in spam messages written in
HTML that activate to verify receipt of the message when the email is opened.

ISP Monitoring

ISPs log and retain the email traffic generated by their customers. Some have well-
documented privacy policies that are listed in the provider's AUP restricting what the
information can be used for and under what circumstances it will be released to a third
party. There are no legal guarantees that these policies will not change over time.

Current law places few restrictions on the use of ISP log data in the United States.
The USA PATRIOT Act makes it legal for an ISP to release log data on an individual
user to law enforcement without permission or a court order.[11] The European Union
has also issued guidelines requiring retention of ISP log data for use by law enforcement. However these have not been universally adopted by the individual states within
the EU.[12]

INTERNATIONAL PRIVACY LAW

United States law is quite explicit with regard to safeguarding the privacy rights of
individuals concerning data in the hands of the public sector. These laws—GLB,
HIPAA, and COPPA—and statutes have been described in earlier chapters. Other

countries, particularly in Europe, have taken a united and consistent stance on privacy issues. The **Organization for Economic Cooperation and Development (OECD),** of which the United States is a member, published a set of data privacy guidelines in 1980. Those guidelines have served as a basis for subsequent legislation both within the European Union and some states within the United States. In 1995, the EU passed Directive 95/46/EC: The Directive on Protection of Personal Datawhich specifies a set of guiding principles for the processing, retention, and disclosure of personal data. It goes on to require that such data not be transmitted across borders to any country that does not offer similar protections.[13] The OECD's principles and privacy guidelines are listed in the following sections.

OECD PRIVACY GUIDELINES[14]

Collection Limitation Principle: There should be limits to the collection of personal data and any such data should be obtained by lawful and fair means and, where appropriate, with the knowledge or consent of the data subject.

Data Quality Principle: Personal data should be relevant to the purposes for which they are to be used, and, to the extent necessary for those purposes, should be accurate, complete, and kept up-to-date.

Purpose Specification Principle: The purposes for which personal data are collected should be specified not later than at the time of data collection and the subsequent use limited to the fulfillment of those purposes or such others as are not incompatible with those purposes and as are specified on each occasion of change of purpose.

Use Limitation Principle: Personal data should not be disclosed, made available, or otherwise used for purposes other than those specified in accordance with the Purpose Specification Principle except:
- with the consent of the data subject; or
- by the authority of law.

Security Safeguards Principle: Personal data should be protected by reasonable security safeguards against such risks as loss or unauthorized access, destruction, use, modification, or disclosure of data.

Openness Principle: There should be a general policy of openness about developments, practices, and policies with respect to personal data. Means should be readily available of establishing the existence and nature of personal data, and the main purposes of their use, as well as the identity and usual residence of the data controller.

Individual Participation Principle: An individual should have the right:
- to obtain from a data controller, or otherwise, confirmation of whether or not the data controller has data relating to him;
- to have communicated to him, data relating to him
  (a) within a reasonable time;
  (b) at a charge, if any, that is not excessive;
  (c) in a reasonable manner; and
  (d) in a form that is readily intelligible to him;
- to be given reasons if a request is denied, and to be able to challenge such denial; and

- to challenge data relating to him and, if the challenge is successful to have the data erased, rectified, completed, or amended.

Accountability Principle: A data controller should be accountable for complying with measures that give effect to the principles stated above.

COMPLIANCE INITIATIVES

The public's concern for the safety of personal data on the Web has made it imperative for Web-based services and merchants to find ways to create trust and promote the use of strong privacy protection principles and practices. Several cooperative initiatives have been initiated to improve the public's trust.

P3P

The platform for Privacy Preferences Project (P3P) is a standard that allows Websites to communicate their data privacy policies automatically to a Web browser when that Website is visited. A P3P-compliant browser can be programmed to interact with a Website in specific ways, depending on the policies attributed to that Website. For example, it could reject any cookies from sites that do not have a policy that prohibits sharing of data with third parties. A P3P browser control is shown in Figure11.2. P3P client technology has been built into both Internet Explorer and Netscape Navigator.

FIGURE 11.2   P3P Implementation in Internet Explorer 6

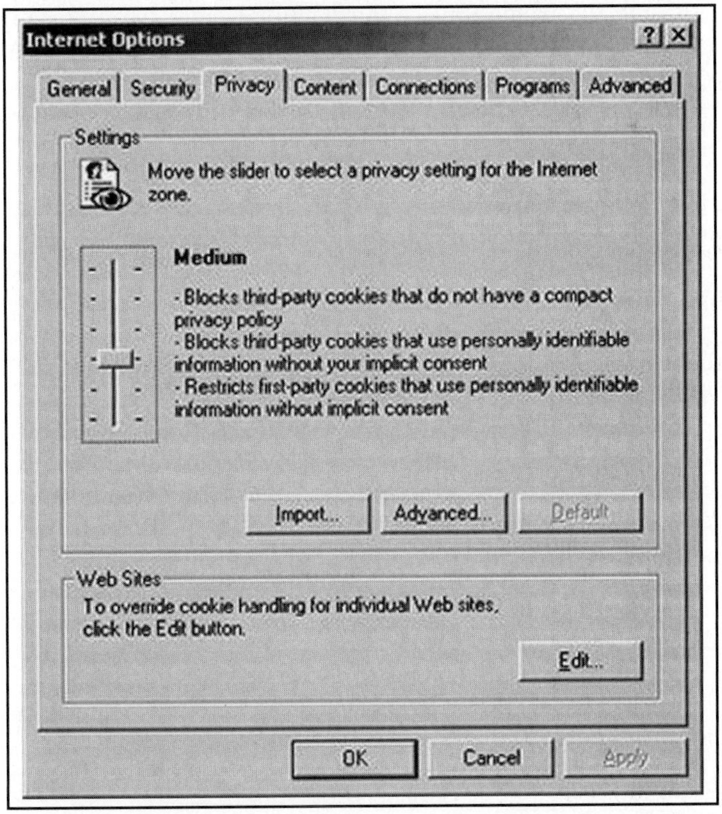

P3P compliance has been slow to build. According to Ernst & Young, as of January 2003 only 28% of the 100 most visited Websites and 18% of the 500 most visited Websites were P3P-compliant. That number was virtually unchanged from the previous study done in October, 2002.[15] It is also important to note that P3P is a system. There are no guarantees that P3P policies promised by the site will be followed, or that they will not be relaxed at a later date after information has been collected. This is left to the user and watchdog groups to verify.

Privacy Seal Programs

Several independent membership-based organizations promote and certify the integrity of data privacy policies on the Internet. Their mission is to follow a model of self-governance instead of government regulation. These organizations issue a seal of approval to their member organizations that certifies compliance with a set of policies. The policies require truth in advertising, transaction integrity, and privacy in accordance with OECD principles. The largest such organizations are TRUSTe, which is sponsored by the Electronic Frontier Foundation, and BBBOnline, which is owned by the Council of Better Business Bureaus.

Activist Organizations

Another response to public concerns over privacy issues has been the growth in membership of activist organizations dedicated to the protection of privacy rights. These organizations have been especially active in promoting public awareness about electronic data collection in the public and private sectors. Among the most prominent are EPIC, the Electronic Privacy Information Center (www.epic.org), the Center for Democracy and Technology (www.cdt.org), the Center for Media Education (www.cme.org), and the Online Privacy Alliance (www.privacyalliance.org).

Chapter Summary

Protecting privacy has emerged as a critical component of developing a trusted environment for communication and commerce online. Spam and the stealth collection of personal information are common practices that can be as intrusive and dangerous as viruses or hackers. Individual privacy is at risk when Websites do not provide full information about their data practices or fail to give individuals the ability to make informed decisions about the use and disclosure of their personal information.

Efforts by U.S. industry to self-regulate have been only partially successful. Globally, other governments have taken a proactive stance on privacy rights by legislating broader restrictions on the use of protected data. This includes barring the exchange of data across their borders to places without similar protections.

Regulation and the law will provide some protection, but those who choose to take advantage of the information economy must also assume the responsibility of defending themselves.

Key Terms

- spam
- data mining
- cookies
- Web bugs
- Organization for Economic Cooperation and Development (OECD)
- privacy preferences project (P3P)

Discussion Questions

1. On what legal theories did the California Appeals Court base its decision that Intel could block emails sent by an employee to protest company policies?
2. Why is spam so prevalent? Why is it so difficult to contain or regulate?
3. What are some of the ways that individuals and organizations can protect themselves against spam?
4. Identify several activities that create personal transaction histories.
5. Under what circumstances can Internet transaction histories be associated with individual identities?
6. How can data mining be used to violate privacy? How might data mining be used beneficially?
7. What is the purpose of Web bugs? How do they violate personal privacy?
8. What is the significance of the OECD Privacy Guidelines?
9. What is the goal of the P3P project? What are its weaknesses?

Endnotes

1. Gelles, Jeff. "Email Headed for a Spam Jam." *The Philadelphia Inquirer.* Sept. 7, 2002. http://www.philly.com/mld/philly/business/4020758.htm
2. Hu, Jim. "Intel Scores in Email Suit." *CNET News.com.* Dec. 1998. http://news.com.com/2100-1023-218747.html?legacy=cnet
3. McCullagh, Declan. "Axed Intel Man Loses E-Mail Case." *Wired.com.* Dec. 2001. http://www.wired.com/news/politics/0,1283,49031,00.html
4. *Ibid.* McCullagh, Declan.
5. *Ibid.* McCullagh, Declan.
6. Behr, Mary E. "Vacation To-Do List: Relax, Check E-Mail." *PC Week.* July 2001. http://www.pcmag.com/article2/0,4149,391797,00.asp
7. FTC Press Release, "COPPA Civil Penalties to Date in Settlements with Mrs. Fields Cookies and Hershey Foods." Feb. 27, 2003. http://www.ftc.gov/opa/2003/02/hersheyfield.htm
8. Hicks, Matt. "Scaling toward the Petabyte." *Eweek.* June 2002. http://www.eweek.com/article2/0,3959,1670,00.asp
9. NCR Corporation Press Release. *Teradata Takes Data Mining Beyond Beer and Diapers.* July 31, 2002. http://www.ncr.com/media_information/2002/jul/pr073102b.htm
10. Delio, Michelle. "Yahoo's Opt-out Angers Users." *Wired News.* April 2002. http://www.wired.com/news/privacy/0,1848,51461,00.html
11. Chidi, George A. "Patriot Act Opens ISPs to Monitoring." *PCWorld.com.* Nov. 2001. http://www.pcworld.com/news/article/0,aid,69662,00.asp
12. Leyden, John. "Germany, Austria Take Stand Against EU ISP Data Retention Laws." *The Register.* Nov. 2002. http://www.theregister.co.uk/content/6/28228.html
13. *Directive 95/46/EC of the European Parliament* Article 56. http://www.europa.eu.int/smartapi/cgi/sga_doc?smartapi!celexapi!prod!CELEXnumdoc&lg=EN&numdoc=31995L0046&model=guichett
14. *OECD Guidelines on the Protection of Privacy and Transborder Flows of Personal Data.* Sept. 23. 1980. Part Two http://www.oecd.org/oecd/pages/home/displaygeneral/0,3380,EN-document-43-1-no-no-10255-0,00.html
15. *Ernst & Young P3P Dashboard Report.* Jan. 2003 http://www.ey.com/global/download.nsf/US/P3P_Dashboard_-_January_2003/$file/E&YP3PDashboardJan2003.pdf

HIPAA APPENDIX AND GLOSSARY

OVERVIEW OF HIPAA

The Health Insurance Portability and Accountability Act of 1996 (HIPAA) was signed into law on August 21, 1996. This act applies to health care providers, which it defines as "a provider of medical or other health services or supplies, limited to those entities that furnish, or bill and are paid for, health care services. The proposed definition of a provider would not include workers who do not provide health services, such as admissions and billing personnel, housekeeping staff and orderlies."

HIPAA outlines medical security and privacy rules and procedures to simplify the administration of health care billing. The security regulations, which will be issued by the Centers for Medicare and Medicaid Services (CMS), would impose safeguards for implementing the privacy regulations. The *proposed* rules for patient privacy and confidentiality were published in November 1998. The *final* rule was published in December 2000 with a compliance date of April 14, 2003. However, small health plans have until April 14, 2004 to comply.

The Administrative Simplification provisions of HIPAA direct the Secretary of Health and Human Services (HHS) to adopt national electronic standards for automated transfer of certain health care data between health care payers, plans, and providers. HIPAA seeks to simplify and encourage the electronic transfer of data by replacing numerous nonstandard formats with a single set of electronic standards that would be used throughout the health care industry. This is called the National Standard Format (NSF).

Health Care Fraud and Abuse Control Program

HIPAA established a national Health Care Fraud and Abuse Control Program, under the joint direction of the Attorney General and the Secretary of Health and Human Services. Coordinated efforts of federal, state, and local law enforcement have helped prevent health care fraud and abuse. Since the program began, more than $3 billion has been returned to the federal government.[1]

PROTECTIONS AND STANDARDS PROVIDED BY HIPAA

HIPAA attempts to provide the following protections and standards—insurance portability, fraud enforcement, and administrative simplification.

Insurance Portability

Insurance portability ensures that individuals who move from one health care plan to another will have continuity of coverage. They could not be denied coverage under the preexisting condition clauses.

Fraud Enforcement

HIPAA increases the federal government's fraud enforcement authorities in many different areas of health care. It is intended to combat Medicare and Medicaid fraud. Health care providers are held accountable for charges.

Administrative Simplification

The U.S. Department of Health and Human Services must develop standards and requirements for maintenance and transmission of health information that identifies individual patients by

- Improving the efficiency and effectiveness of the health care system by standardizing the interchange of electronic data for specified administrative and financial transactions; and

- Protecting the security and confidentiality of electronic health information by all health care organizations that maintain or transmit electronic health information.

CMS announced the adoption of a unique identifier for employers in the filing and processing of health care claims and other transactions. The standard identifier, mandated by HIPAA, seeks to eliminate paperwork, save money, and simplify various administrative duties.

HIPAA COMPLIANCE REQUIREMENTS

Applicability
All health plans and clearinghouses, and any provider electronically transmitting any HIPAA transactions, must comply with this standard.

The following must occur if a standard transaction is transmitted to a health plan:

- Health plan must conduct the transaction.
- Health plan must not delay the transaction.
- Transmitted and received information must be standardized data elements.
- Health plans that utilize agents (i.e., clearinghouses) for transactions must ensure the agent meets all requirements.

In order to meet requirements, a person or entity may either

- Transmit and receive stated standard data elements, or
- Utilize a clearinghouse to process its nonstandard data elements into standardized transactions.

Privacy Regulations, Effective April 14, 2003
Privacy issues that are regulated by HIPAA are

- Development and enforcement of personal health information disclosure policies and procedures.
- Right of patients to access and amend their health information records.
- Creation of fair information practices to inform people how their health information is used and disclosed.
- Audit trail of health information disclosures.
- Designation of a Privacy Compliance Officer.
- Limit on the disclosure of health information to the minimum necessary to achieve a relevant purpose.
- De-identification of health information used for purposes such as research.

Security Standards, Final Regulations not yet Released
The proposed security requirements are divided into four categories.[2]

Administrative Procedures   This category addresses an organization's need for formalized, documented practices. It applies to the implementation and execution of security measures that protect data and the behaviors of personnel in regard to data protection. Included in the standard are requirements for: certification, chain of trust partner agreement, contingency plan, formal mechanism for processing records, information access control, internal audit, personnel security, security configuration management, security incident procedures, security management process, termination procedures, and training.

Physical Safeguards   Physical safeguards address the implementation of procedures to ensure assigned security responsibility, media controls, physical access controls, policy guidelines on workstation use, secure workstation location, and security awareness training.

Technical Security Safeguards   The Technical Security Services category addresses the following requirements: access control, audit controls, authorization control, data authentication, and entity authentication.

Technical Security Mechanisms   This category addresses protection against unauthorized access to data through the use of integrity controls, message authentication, access controls, encryption, alarms, audit trails, entity authentication, and event reporting.

PENALTIES FOR FAILURE TO COMPLY WITH HIPAA REGULATIONS

General Penalty

- Each violation: $100.
- Maximum penalty for each violation of an identical requirement may not exceed $25,000.

Wrongful Disclosure of PIHI

- Wrongful Disclosure: $50,000 and/or 1-year imprisonment.

- Offenses under false pretenses: $100 and/or 5-year imprisonment.
- Offenses with intent to sell information: $250,000 and/or 10-year imprisonment.

CONSENT AND AUTHORIZATION

Of greatest importance are consent and authorization, which the federal government defined in very specific terms.

Consent

Consent is defined as a written general agreement given by an individual to a covered entity (health care provider, health plan, or clearinghouse) to permit his or her personally identifiable health information (PIHI) to be used or disclosed for normal health care activities. Consent is general in that it is a blanket permission for the protected health information to be used or disclosed in the course of these activities permitted under that definition.

Authorization

Authorization is a specific permission granted in writing by an individual for the covered entity to use PIHI for a purpose that goes beyond the activities outlined previously.

The key to both the consent and authorization concepts is that the covered entity only uses or discloses the minimum information necessary for the purpose at hand.

HIPAA GLOSSARY

Biometric Identifier: An identifier based on some physical characteristic, such as a fingerprint.

Business Associate (BA): Under HIPAA, this is "... a person who performs a function or activity regulated by this subchapter on behalf of a covered entity ..." (45 CFR 160.103). A business associate can be a covered entity in its own right but cannot be part of the original covered entity's workforce.

Chain of Trust (COT): Agreements that extend protection of health care data by requiring that each covered entity, which shares health care data with another entity, require that that entity provide protections

comparable to those provided by the original covered entity. That entity, in turn, must require that any other entities with which it shares the data satisfy the same requirements.

Compliance Date: Under HIPAA, this is "... the date by which a covered entity must comply with a standard, implementation specification, or modification adopted under this subchapter" (45 CFR 160.103). This is usually 24 months after the effective date of the associated final regulation for most entities, but 36 months after the effective date for small health plans. For future changes in the standards, the compliance date would usually be at least 180 days after the effective date but can be longer for small health plans or for complex changes.

Covered Entity (CE): Includes health care providers, health plans, or clearinghouses. It is any provider of medical or other health services or supplies, limited to those entities that furnish, or bill and are paid for, health care services.

Data Dictionary (DD): A document or system that characterizes the data content of a system.

Data Element: Under HIPAA, this is "... the smallest named unit of information in a transaction" (45 CFR 162.103).

Data Model: A conceptual model of the information needed to support a business function or process.

Direct Data Entry (DDE): Under HIPAA, this is "... the direct entry of data (for example, using dumb terminals or Web browsers) that is immediately transmitted into a health plan's computer."

Electronic Media: Under HIPAA, this is "... the mode of electronic transmission. It includes the Internet, extranet, leased lines, dial-up lines, private networks, and those transmissions that are physically moved from one location to another using magnetic tape, disk, or compact disk media" (45 CFR 162.103).

Health care provider: A "provider of medical or other health services or supplies, limited to those entities that furnish, or bill and are paid for, health care services. The proposed definition of a provider would not include workers who do not provide health services, such as admissions and billing personnel, housekeeping staff and orderlies."

Health Information: Under HIPAA, this is "... any information, whether oral or recorded in any form or medium, that (1) Is created or received by a health care provider, health plan, public health authority, employer, life insurer, school or university, or health care clearinghouse; and (2) Relates to the past, present, or future physical or mental health or condition of an individual; the provision of health care to an individual; or the past, present, or future payment for the provision of health care to an individual" (45 CFR 160.103).

Health Insurance Portability and Accountability Act of 1996 (HIPAA): A federal law that makes a number of changes that have the goal of allowing persons to qualify immediately for comparable health insurance coverage when they change their employment relationships. Title II, Subtitle F, of HIPAA gives HHS the authority to mandate the use of standards for the electronic exchange of health care data; to specify what medical and administrative code sets should be used within those standards; to require the use of national identification systems for health care patients, providers, payers (or plans), and employers (or sponsors); and to specify the types of measures required to protect the security and privacy of PIHI.

National Standard Format (NSF): Generically, this applies to any national standard format, but it is often used in a more limited way to designate the file record format used to submit professional claims.

Transaction: Under HIPAA, this is "... the exchange of information between two parties to carry out financial or administrative activities related to health care" (45 CFR 160-103).

Endnotes

1. "2001 Healthcare Fraud Investigations Net $1.3 Billion." *Healthcare Financial Management.* Vol. 56, No. 6. June 1, 2002. P. 20.

2. Information provided by the Cerner Corporation.

GLOSSARY

Access control list (ACL) A set of rules that determine what parts of a network users can access and what packets can enter or exit a network.

Accountability A functional requirement of hardware and software that requires that the actions of an entity can be traced uniquely to that entity.

Address A data field in an IP packet header that specifies either the sender (source address) or the intended receiver (destination address) of the packet.

Allow With regard to packets, *allow* is an action that permits, or allows, the packet to be sent or received by a network. The opposite is *block*. See **Block.**

Anna Kournikova A virus that arrives as an email attachment. Opening this attachment infects a machine. Once infected, the virus mails itself to all recipients found in the Windows address book.

Asymmetric cryptography Electronic signature technology eliminates the need for manual signatures on contracts. Digital signature technology utilizing asymmetric cryptography is a form of electronic signature particularly appropriate for electronic contracting, because it replaces manual signatures with digital codes that ensure the identity of the sender.

ADSL (asymmetric digital subscriber line) Technically, ADSL allows large data transfers over copper telephone lines. Operationally, ADSL is a high-speed digital service providing fast file downloads from the Web. Its upload speeds are much slower. Because of lack of symmetry in speeds for downloading and uploading with DSL service, it is referred to as *asymmetric DSL* or ADSL. A computer with an ADSL connection has a *fixed* or *static* IP address that is permanently assigned to it. These connections have fixed IP addresses that are easy to identify and attack. See **DSL.**

Antivirus (AV) software Software programs that filter incoming email and computer files to detect and deter viruses.

Application gateway A type of firewall that applies security mechanisms to specific applications, such as FTP and Telnet. They can be highly effective but tend to degrade performance.

Application virus These are viruses that attack software programs or database management systems.

Application level Programs that support business functions like accounting or marketing applications.

ARIN (American Registry for Internet Numbers) Companies are assigned their IP addresses by their Internet service providers (ISPs), who have been assigned their IP addresses by a central governing body called ARIN. ARIN controls the allocation of IP addresses so that there are no duplicates. See www.arin.net.

ASP (application service provider) A company that develops and hosts software applications on its own servers within its own facilities for other companies. In effect, companies outsource their applications to an ASP rather than manage the application in-house.

Asynchronous *Asynchronous* means that the data transfer rate is not the same in both directions.

ATM (asynchronous transfer mode) In an asynchronous transfer mode, the data transfer rate for uploading is slower than for downloading. For example, cable modems download files or Websites from a network (e.g., the Internet) at a much faster rate than they upload files to the network. This method is used to transmit data, voice, and video over high-speed local area networks at up to 2.2 Gbps.

AUP (acceptable-use policy) A company policy that defines (or should define) acceptable and unacceptable use of all components of the company's information, computer networks, and communication systems. An AUP should clearly specify the company's standards for onsite access and remote access to corporate networks and secure use of company usernames, passwords, and computer accounts.

Authentication A method by which a computer system attempts to validate or verify (authenticate) that a user is really who he or she claims to be. The process is usually based on a username and password. In security systems, authentication is not the same as authorization, which gives individuals access to a system based on their identity.

Authenticity A functional requirement of hardware and software that the content must not have been altered.

Autoreply or Autoresponse An email feature that allows the system to send a prepared message automatically to every email message it receives. This is often considered a courtesy to inform senders that the recipient is unavailable to read messages at the current time.

Availability A functional requirement of hardware and software that the IT systems and data are available for operations or to avoid substantial losses. Availability also includes ensuring that resources are used only for intended purposes.

Backdoors Hidden and typically undetectable ways left by the programmer, hacker, or malware, such as a **blended threat,** to get back into a system.

Back Orifice One of many backdoor programs that attackers have used to access a computer system without anyone's knowledge or consent. Back Orifice 2000 allows complete remote administrative control of infected Windows 95/98/NT computers.

Bandwidth A measure of the throughput, transfer, or access speed for telecommunications. It is the amount of data a network can transport in a given period of time (1 second). Higher bandwidth means more data per second can be transferred. Bandwidth is measured in kilobits per second (e.g., a 56K modem) and megabits per second.

Best practices An industry standard that is determined or based on what is commonly accepted as the most effective or efficient methods. Best practices are not necessarily recognized by the courts as the standard providing a sufficient defense. That is, best computer security practices for an industry may not be an effective defense for a company if those practices can be shown to be substandard or outdated.

Biometric device A device that uses something a person was born with to positively identify that person in lieu of a token. Fingerprints, voiceprints, and retinal scans are examples of such unique properties that can be read by special devices attached to a computer.

Biometrics An identification process that involves a human or biological feature, such as eyes (retinal scan), voiceprint, handprint, fingerprint, face print, or handwriting.

Black hat hackers or Black hats Black hat hackers commit illegal hacks for personal gain or notoriety. They are malicious individuals who try to break into computers and networks. The number of hackers and systems available for them to attack is growing, which means many attacks on Internet-connected resources can be expected. See also **White hat hackers.**

Blended threats A malicious application that spreads like a computer virus or worm but blends the capabilities of viruses and worms to attack security vulnerabilities in applications and operating systems. Viruses are destructive code, which have to be a script or macro or attach to an executable file to spread. Worms can spread through memory and disk space. A blended threat may attempt to infect by having the properties of an email virus and attempting to find an insecure operating system or application to infect/attack. Once the PC or server is infected, there is no limit to the destruction or manipulation of files. These threats can install backdoors, Trojan horses, or zombies. Blended threats are a continuation of the evolution of malicious code. Also called *hybrid threats.*

Block With regard to packets, *block* is an action that denies, or blocks, the packet from being sent or received by a network. See **Allow.**

Broadband A network that provides very high (that is, broad) bandwidth. It is the short way of saying "broad bandwidth."

Brute force attack A cracker term that means continuously hurling passwords at a system until it is compromised.

Bug A problem in software or hardware, which have been referred to jokingly as "undocumented features." Bugs can adversely affect computers or networks or make them vulnerable to security breaches.

Bugbear This dangerous virus spreads by mailing itself using the addresses found in the victim's address book. It also changes the email FROM: field. Thus, it may appear that this virus has been received from a known person, when it was actually sent from a different user. The worm opens remote access and searches for various running programs and stops them. The remote access allows a hacker to steal files, run, terminate, and delete programs on the victim's computer.

Bugtraq An email mailing list for computer security issues. SecurityFocus is host of the BugTraq newsgroups. It is used to alert everyone, including hackers, about vulnerabilities. For example, Jeffrey Baker, who discovered the password vulnerability in E-Trade, wrote an alert to the BugTraq mailing list. Baker said that he had notified E-Trade about its problem, but since nothing had been done, he alerted E-Trade customers to the potential risk via BugTraq.

Buffer overflow This occurs when the capacity of the memory buffer is exceeded. During a buffer overflow, the network is vulnerable to attack. Many of the vulnerabilities that exist in the Internet software systems today are buffer overflow vulnerabilities. Buffer overflows are the most significant security problem that exists. All of the buffer overflow attacks in IIS could pass through a firewall and not show up in log files either.

Business records Documents, communication, and printouts created as part of an organization's operations or transactions.

Cache Temporary file copies to enhance system performance.

CERT® Coordination Center A federally funded research and development center operated by Carnegie Mellon University dedicated to information security monitoring and alerts.

Certification authority (CA) A CA authenticates or attests to the integrity of an entity. CAs are part of PKI standards.

Chain of custody This is a legal term referring to a showing of how evidence was handled from the time of collection to the time it was admitted as evidence in a judicial proceeding.

Chatroom Real-time, text-based teleconferences that can be private (entered by invitation only) or public (anyone can enter).

Checksum A numeric value used to verify that a file has not been tampered with. It is calculated based on the contents of the file. It is a fast way to check if anything in a file had been changed. If there is any change in the file's contents—even a single character or space—the checksum would be radically different. Thus, an infected file can be detected because of the change in its checksum. However, when an existing file is modified, a new checksum has to be created. This is often too inconvenient for users to do whenever they modify any file. The software Tripwire can be used to take an MD5 (message digest) checksum snapshot of a system. See **File Integrity Checker.**

Children's Online Privacy Protection Act (COPPA) This act, effective since April 21, 2000, applies to the online collection of personal information from children under 13. The new rules spell out what a Website operator must include in a privacy policy, when and how to seek verifiable consent from a parent, and what responsibilities an operator has to protect children's privacy and safety online.

Circuit-level gateway A firewall technique that applies security mechanisms at the time when an Internet connection is originally made. After the connection is made, packets can flow between the hosts without checking.

Civil Rights Act of 1964 This act prohibits any type of discrimination based on gender, race, national origin, or age. The act also requires employers to provide nonhostile, nonharassing workplaces and holds them legally responsible for failure to maintain such workplaces.

Clear text Unencrypted text.

Code Red virus On July 19, 2001, over 359,000 computers were infected with the Code Red worm in less than 14 hours. It spread at up to 2,000 new infections per minute. Code Red and Nimda cost businesses worldwide $3 billion in lost productivity, disinfection, follow-up testing, and deployment of patches to computer systems. Each of these worms was a sophisticated blended threat that infected hundreds of thousands of systems worldwide. See **Blended threats.** Mercifully, hackers had not written hybrid (blended) threats Code Red, Code Red 2, and Nimda to do damage to critical data. Nimda and Code Red infected IT systems but did not attack data.

Computer crime Any violation of criminal law that involves a knowledge of computer technology for its perpetration, investigation, or prosecution.

Computer Emergency Response Team (CERT) CERT is a federally funded computer security research center operated by Carnegie Melon University.

Computer forensics The discovery, recovery, preservation, and control of electronic documents for use as evidence. This imposes unique risks on companies and impacts litigation strategies.

Computer Security Institute and FBI (CSI/FBI) *Computer Crime and Security Survey* The *Computer Crime and Security Survey* is conducted by CSI with the participation of the San Francisco Federal Bureau of Investigation's (FBI) Computer Intrusion Squad. The aim of this effort is to raise the level of security awareness, as well as help determine the scope of computer crime in the United States.

Confidentiality A functional requirement of hardware and software that information (or file or message) must be protected from unauthorized disclosure.

Counterfeit Access Device and Computer Fraud and Abuse Law This law addresses computer crimes in which the computer is the subject of the crime.

Contributory negligence Legally, failure by the injured party to exercise reasonable care (due care) for his/her/its own safety.

Convention on Cybercrime An international treaty designed to improve international cyber crime prevention. Among its provisions, the Cybercrime Convention seeks to ensure that when a corporation fails to properly supervise employees in leading positions, and that failure makes certain computer crimes possible, the corporation itself will be held liable for the cyber crimes committed for its benefit, even if such crimes were committed without its knowledge, consent, or approval.

Convergence The integration of different technologies or capabilities into one device. Examples are accessing the Internet over a cell phone or making phone calls through a PC.

Cookies A block of reference data sent from a Website to the browser of a specific user and stored on the PC for later use. Cookies enable the Website to deliver customized content to that user and can be a convenience, invasion of privacy, or malicious.

Cracker A person with malicious intent who breaks into a computer system without authorization. The term refers to a bad hacker, but since the term *hacker* has acquired malicious connotations, *cracker* has become synonymous with *hacker*. Crackers are also utility programs or tools, such as password crackers, used to identify holes or weaknesses in networks and systems. Of course, these tools can be used illegally for spying or gaining access to unauthorized resources. Such tools are not *network aware*, so they do not run autonomously and transmit their findings back to a remote server— as do RATs. See **RAT.**

Critical infrastructure An infrastructure made up of service companies that the national economy depends on. These companies are primarily in telecommunications, transportation, financial services, chemical, water, and energy and power grids.

Cryptography A form of encryption; the study of mathematical codes for making or breaking encryption algorithms. See **Asymmetric cryptography.**

Customer relationship management (CRM) A popular business strategy that requires collecting extensive amounts of customer information.

Cyber law Any law dealing with computers, computer networks, the Internet, email, or digital information.

Daemon In computer systems, daemons perform specific operations at predefined times, such as email handling, or perform administrative tasks for the operating system.

Datagram A datagram, often called a *packet*, is a small piece of data. Datagrams are completely self-contained. They have a source and a destination. Datagrams have no relationship to any others that came before or after them.

Data mining A class of software applications that automatically seek out previously undetected patterns within a set of historical data. These patterns can be used to predict future purchasing behavior or profile individual customers.

Data warehouse An application designed to provide integrated access to information about customers, finances, and operations.

DDOS (distributed denial of service) A type of denial of service attack that takes over thousands of computer systems to orchestrate a simultaneous attack on a Website— forcing that Website to crash or become unavailable to legitimate users. Sometimes simply referred to as "denial of service" (DOS). DOS or DDOS attacks prevent any part of a system or network from functioning properly. These incidents have become common due to increased hacker activity. See also **Zombie.**

Decryption Decoding encrypted data to return it to its original form.

Default The configuration and behavior of software or hardware on installation before any changes are made to it.

Demilitarized zone (DMZ) A subnet that contains a firewall and proxy server. It serves as a barrier or buffer zone between a company's private intranet and the public Internet.

Department of Justice (DOJ) A department of the U.S. federal government that is responsible for the prosecution of federal crimes.

Detection avoidance The method by which a virus attempts to hide itself.

Digital certificates See **Digital signatures.**

Digital liability All the ways the information on computer devices and networks can hurt a company or an individual.

Digital liability management (DLM) A model that explains how people, process, and technology all play a key role in implementing an effective cyber security program.

Digital Pearl Harbor In July 2002, the U.S. Naval War College and Gartner Group simulated a distributed digital attack on U.S. critical infrastructures, which was called Digital Pearl Harbor.

Digital signatures The equivalent of a physical signature on a document or message. It verifies that the encrypted message or document originated from the person whose signature is attached to it. Digital signatures issued by a company are referred to as *digital certificates*. They are also referred to as *dig sigs*.

Directory The Unix equivalent of a Mac or Windows file folder. All UNIX files are stored in directories.

Directory protocol Standards that make it possible to edit a user's set of access privileges. The edits are made in one centralized location and apply across all systems.

Discovery In preparation for trial, each party has the right to learn as much as possible about an opponent or the opponent's case. The process of collecting information is called *discovery*. The purpose of discovery is to help the parties determine what the evidence may consist of, who the potential witnesses are, and what might be relevant. Discovery also helps preserve relevant evidence so that it is not destroyed. Information is discoverable if it is relevant to the facts that lead to the lawsuit or litigation and does not violate the confidentiality of communication between an attorney and client.

Discovery request In a legal action, if the opposing party submits a discovery request for the company's emails and other electronic information, the company is required by law to retrieve and produce that evidence.

Distributed Coordinated Attacks (DCAs) See **DDOS.**

DNS (domain name server) An Internet service that translates domain names (easy to remember words) into IP addresses (long set of numbers).

Domain A subsection of the Internet that ends with .com, .net, .edu, .gov, or .org.

DOS (denial of service) attack This term refers to an attack on a network or server that causes it to receive more hits (requests for service) than it can respond to—so the server "denies service." This happens when a Website or server is deliberately overwhelmed (usually by a hacker) with so many requests for service that it cannot respond to normal requests for information or access. If the attack is set up so that the requests for service come from more than one computer, it's referred to as a **DDOS (distributed denial of service) attack.** Since most attacks come from more than one computer, DDOS and DOS are used interchangeably.

DSL (digital subscriber line) Transmits data over existing copper wire telephone lines at a much greater speed than regular phone wires. DSL works only when the user is close to one of the telephone company's central offices. It is faster than dial-up and cheaper than leased lines. DSL can be sold in a variety of bandwidths.

Duty A legal obligation not to interfere with a protected interest. See also **Right.**

Duty of care Refers to a very high degree of responsibility. It is a defense needed for business and legal reasons and means that a company or person cannot create unreasonable risk of harm to others.

Dynamic IP address When dialing up to access the Internet, a user gets a different IP address for each Internet session, referred to as a dynamic IP address. During a single Internet session, every email message sent by the user will have the same IP address, but new sessions get different dynamic IP addresses. This is in contrast to a fixed IP, or static IP, address that is permanently assigned. See **ADSL** and **Internet protocol (IP) address.**

Dynamic routing Routing that adjusts automatically to changes in network traffic. See **Router.**

ebusiness Using Internet technologies to conduct business, serve customers, and streamline processes.

ECHO A situation in which a user's computer sends back a copy of the data that it received to the originating computer—comparable to a sound echo. This lets the sender visually inspect what the recipient has received.

ecommerce Buying and selling goods and services on the Internet.

Economic model of marginal cost–benefit analysis According to marginal analysis, the firm is not negligent if and only if the marginal costs of safeguards are greater than the marginal benefits of those safeguards.

Electronic document retention policy An effective document retention policy ensures that electronic documents are efficiently handled and neither retained too long nor destroyed too soon. In the event of a subpoena or lawsuit, a document retention policy can protect the firm against a claim of spoliation. Courts do not approve of companies that fail to preserve electronic evidence. Sanctions for the destruction of electronic evidence include monetary fines, adverse jury instructions, and possibly entry of a default judgment.

Electronic evidence (e-evidence) Refers to any electronically stored data or information that can be used as evidence in a legal action.

Electronic fraud (efraud) Electronic records are amenable to fraudulent use because they are susceptible to illegal interception and manipulation. There has been a migration of traditional crimes—including threats, fraud, and extortion—to electronic records because online perpetrators can reach victims easily and anonymously.

Electronic record The **Uniform Electronic Transaction Act (UETA)** broadly defines an electronic record, or electronic document, as a record "created, generated, sent, communicated, received or stored by electronic means."

Electronic records management (ERM) The systemic review, retention, and destruction of documents received or created in the course of doing business. It is the policy for managing the retention, destruction, and storage of electronic records. See **Electronic document retention policy.**

Email-borne viruses Viruses spread via email.

Email header Every email message contains a header that shows the path that the email traveled from its point of origin to its ultimate destination. Depending on the software, sometimes the header will appear at the bottom of an email message.

Encryption The process of encoding data to protect it from being understood by unauthorized users.

Ethernet One of the most widely used LAN (local area network) standards for transferring data.

Ethical hacking To exercise reasonable care, many corporations hire outside security firms to test their firewall security. Called *ethical hacking*, the process is intended to help system administrators pinpoint weaknesses in networks. In addition, ethical hacking enables IT managers to gauge response time to an attack—crucial in the fight against cyber crime.

Event An event is something observable that happened in an information system or network; for instance, a system crash or an attempt to access a network.

Evidence-mail Email used as evidence.

Execution The carrying out of a plan.

Expected loss A quantitative model that provides an important benchmark against which to assess and justify investments in digital security. Expected loss equals the amount of the loss multiplied by the probability of its occurrence.

Expected value (EV) The expected average value of a loss.

Exploit A tool (software program) or technique designed to take advantage of a weakness or vulnerability in a program or computer system to exceed the user's authorized level of access.

Expressed consent Consent that involves some action on the part of a user, such as his or her signature.

False positive A false alarm; for example, if an IDS detects an "intrusion," and that detection is incorrect, that is a false positive.

File integrity checker It is very difficult to compromise a system without altering a system file, so file integrity checkers are important to detect intrusion. A file integrity checker computes a **checksum** for every guarded file and stores the result. At a later time, a checksum is computed again and tested against the stored value to determine if the file had been modified. This capability should be used with commercial host-based intrusion detection systems. The primary checksum method had used a 32-bit CRC (cyclic redundancy check). But attackers have been able to modify a file in ways the CRC checksum could not detect, so stronger checksums, known as *cryptographic hashes,* are recommended. Examples of cryptographic hashes include MD5 and snefru. One challenge in using a file integrity checker is the false positive problem. When files are updated or systems are patched, files change. Creating the initial database of signatures (checksums) is easy, but keeping it up-to-date is much harder. However, even if a checker is run only when a system is first installed, it can be run any time to determine which files have or have not been modified. It is very important that the reference database be stored offline so attackers cannot compromise the system and hide their tracks by modifying the reference database.

File transfer protocol (FTP) A telecommunications protocol used to transmit files. This protocol does error checking to ensure that the entire file was received correctly.

Filter A tool for monitoring and intercepting packets to determine whether they should be allowed or blocked. Filters look at signatures to determine whether to allow or block access. Firewalls use filters. See **Allow** and **Block**.

First-party risks Risks that concern the company itself, such as risks to company information assets.

Firewall A security feature designed to prevent unauthorized access to or from a private network. Firewalls can be implemented in both hardware and software or a combination of both. Firewalls control authentication routines, decide which packet types to admit into the network and which to deny, and can check both incoming and outgoing traffic. Conceptually, these are the functions that firewalls are designed to perform. In practice, firewalls do not always offer security as claimed. The main types of firewall techniques are packet filtering, application gateway, circuit-level gateway, and proxy server.

Fixed IP address An address permanently assigned to a computer or account. Also referred to as a *static* IP address, in contrast to a dynamic IP address that changes every time a new connection to the network is made. When the Internet connection is permanently assigned, every email sent by that Internet user will contain the same IP address. See **ADSL** and **Internet protocol (IP) address.**

Flame wars Highly contentious email exchanges where participants shoot off insults at each other via email.

Gateway A special-purpose network device or software that routes packets.

Gnutella A peer-to-peer (P2P) file-sharing network.

Goner A devastating computer virus that spread at a rate of 100,000 computers per minute. Goner was designated as a level-4 virus—the highest level of destructiveness. It proved that gullible computer users are a serious security risk. Goner arrived as an email with the subject "Hi" and disguised itself as a screensaver. It was written in Visual Basic Script (VBS) but compressed into UPX format, making it hard to detect by AV software. This format also enabled Goner to bypass corporate firewalls, which had no filters in place to protect against it.

Gramm–Leach–Bliley Act (GLB) Regulations pertaining to the financial services industry require board and management involvement in the development and implementation of an information security program. The board must approve an insti-tution's written information security program and then oversee the program's development, implementation, and maintenance.

Gray hat hackers Gray hat hackers have characteristics of black and white hat hackers. Like black hats, they illegally break into systems or servers, but they notify companies about the break-ins and generally don't interfere with business processes.

Hacker A person who is either a computer enthusiast or accesses computer networks to steal, corrupt, extort, etc.

Hacking Unauthorized access to a network or computer system. Hacking is illegal according to Section 2701(a), which states that whoever intentionally accesses without authorization a facility through which an electronic communication service is provided; or intentionally exceeds an authorization to access that facility, and thereby obtains, alters, or prevents authorized access to a wire or electronic communication while it is in electronic storage in such a system shall be punished.

Handshake A sequence of messages that are exchanged between two or more networks to synchronize themselves so that they can transfer data.

Health Insurance Portability and Accountability Act (HIPAA) A regulatory obligation by organizations, imposed by legislation, that specifies the privacy, security, and electronic transaction standards with regard to patient information for all health care providers.

Hidden directory A directory that is deliberately concealed, which makes it difficult to detect. Hackers use these directories for storing files to escalate their attacks.

Hits Requests for service.

Hoaxes An email that contains bogus warnings usually intended to frighten or mislead users. The best course of action is to merely delete these hoax emails.

Honeynet or Honeypot The decoy or tool to learn about hackers or other intruders. A honeynet is a network of systems deliberately designed to be compromised by hackers so that they can be caught or stopped from doing damage to production systems or Websites.

Hop-through A computer that is used as a host in an attack but that is not the target of the attack. Hackers may use hop-through computers in their attacks to disguise their activities.

Host computer A computer system on a network that has full two-way access to other computers on that network.

HTTP (hypertext transport protocol) A protocol to request Websites or html (hypertext markup language) documents from the Web.

Hybrid threats See **Blended threats.**

ICQ An Internet service for finding users and sharing information. ICQ is known to have serious security vulnerabilities.

Identity theft The theft of personal information, including credit cards, Social Security and account numbers, or any other information to gain unlawful access to a person's cash, credit line, or identity. The FBI estimates there are 350,000 to 500,000 incidents of identity theft in the United States each year.

ILoveYou virus A virus that spread rapidly because of its attention-grabbing email subject. It tricked and enticed recipients to open it, mostly at work, and unleashed over a billion dollars of destruction in May 2000. Also known as the LoveBug.

Inbound or Inbound packet A packet that arrives from a remote computer or from outside the network.

Incident This term refers to a harmful or threatening event in an information system or network. Incident implies *harm* or *attempt to harm.*

Incident management Products that support integration and correlation of network events to identify an incident.

Incident response policy A policy that provides guidance on what to do when faced with an attack on the system, which may have legal consequences. It also defines the scope of the powers, authority, and discretion that the team has in responding to the attack and focuses management's attention on security and response issues

Information Sharing and Analysis Center (ISAC) An ISAC comprises a secure database, analytic tools, and information-gathering and distribution facilities designed to allow authorized individuals to submit either anonymous or attributed reports about information security threats, vulnerabilities, incidents, and solutions. ISAC members also have access to information and analysis relating to information provided by other members and obtained from other sources, such as U.S. government and law enforcement agencies, technology providers, and security associations, such as the CERT® Coordination Center.

InfraGard The FBI and local leaders in several U.S. cities have teamed up to create the InfraGard, a cooperative effort to share security expertise and information about threats to the region's critical infrastructure.

Instant messaging (IM) The highly utilized IM programs let people chat in real time over their computers. With the added capability of exchanging file attachments, and due to the constant server connections required, IM allow for greater exposure to bugs and vulnerabilities.

Integrity A functional requirement of hardware and software that the information must be protected from unauthorized, unanticipated, or unintentional modification.

Integrity checker If a company cannot prevent hostile code from being installed or executed, the last defense mechanism is to examine the system for changes using an integrity checker. Integrity testers create a baseline record of files on the system. That baseline is used in later scans for comparisons to determine if there have been any changes in the files. See **File integrity checker.**

Internal intrusions Intrusions that are carried out by employees or insiders.

Internet protocol (IP) The protocol of the Internet for email and file transfers. The IP performs only two functions to deliver a package of bits (a datagram) from a source to a destination over a network. First, it defines a datagram that can be routed through the Internet. Second, it provides a means for breaking up datagrams into packets for transmission and then reassembling those packets back into the original datagrams when they reach their destination. There are no mechanisms for end-to-end data reliability, flow control, sequencing, or other services provided by the IP. The IP relies on the services of networks to provide various types and qualities of service.

Internet protocol (IP) forgery Sending a packet with a fake or incorrect source address.

Intranet An organization's internal network based on the Internet's TCP/IP protocols. Access is usually limited to insiders. Intranet Websites act like Internet Websites but have firewalls to help prevent unauthorized access.

Intrusion detection system (IDS) An IDS refers to a category of defense tools that is used to provide warnings indicating that the system is under attack or intrusion. IDSs must be configured to work correctly and be programmed to look for specific types of network behavior. For example, an IDS sensor can be set to look at all traffic into and out of a network and to block traffic that indicates an internal or external intrusion.

IP address The numeric address of a Website or computer that is attached to the Internet. Every computer on a network has a unique address, called its *IP address*. IP addresses are somewhat comparable to physical addresses or telephone numbers. IP addresses identify a specific computer on a specific network. Technically, an IP address is a logical network address whose parts identify the network that the computer is on and the computer itself. More technically, an IP address is a unique 32-bit identifier for a specific TCP/IP host computer on a network. An example of an IP address is 192.168.1.201

IP addresses consist of four sets of numbers (which are the address fields) separated by decimal points. Since the infrastructure of the Internet consists primarily of a set of gateway computers and packet routers, the routing of packets is based on their IP addresses. The IP address can be static (always the same) or dynamic (as when someone dials into the Internet via

their ISP). When the hookup is permanent, every email sent by that Internet user will contain the same IP address—the static IP address. In contrast, when an Internet user must dial up to access the Internet, the user will have a different IP address for each Internet session—a dynamic IP address. During each such session, every email message sent will share the same IP address, but new sessions mean new IP addresses.

IP address forgery Also called *IP spoofing*. IP forgery is the sending of packets using a fake IP address. The fake IP address is used to hide the sender's true source. For example, it can make the message look as though it is coming from a trusted host.

IP spoofing See **IP address forgery.**

Iptest A tool that is part of the free and publicly available ipfilter security package that automatically forges packets for the purpose of testing configurations or routers and other IP security setups.

Internet service provider (ISP) A company that provides access to the Internet.

ISDN (integrated services digital network) International communications standard for transmitting voice, video, and data over existing telephone lines. ISDN uses digital technology that allows data to be transmitted much faster than it would be over standard phone lines.

ISO 17799 An international standard for *best practices in information security*.

IIS (Internet Information Server) Microsoft's Web server that runs on Windows NT platforms. These servers are particularly vulnerable to buffer overflows.

Java A general-purpose, high-level, object-oriented, cross-platform programming language developed by Sun Microsystems.

KaZaa A peer-to-peer (P2P) file-sharing program on the Gnutella network.

Kerberos A security system used for user authentication in a client–server environment.

Key In encryption, a key is a sequence of data that is combined with the source document to produce output that is unreadable until it has been decrypted. See **Asymmetric cryptography.**

Klez The most prevalent virus throughout January 2003. It was successful because of its ability to send itself to addresses found on infected PCs within address books and documents, such as resumes. In this way, infected messages appeared to their recipients to be coming from a familiar and trusted source.

Knowledge management (KM) The capture and storage of unstructured information.

LAN (local area network) A communications network that connects users within a single location, such as in an office.

Legal action Civil or criminal legal actions, which include civil disputes, criminal cases, class actions, and government investigations.

Liability exposure Risk from an organization's failure to take action, which results in harm.

Lightweight directory access protocol (LDAP) A standard that makes it possible to maintain or remove an employee's set of access privileges in one place and have those settings apply across all systems that are impacted.

Linux worm A worm that probes the Internet looking for vulnerable Linux networks or servers to victimize.

Listen Ports are set to *listen* for incoming requests for a connection and accept them. For example, port 80 listens for requests for connections to the Website to accept the connection. Listening ports are potential access points into a network and need to be secured.

Listserv An external email distribution list that must be subscribed to.

Load The amount of activity on a network server or router.

Local Refers to the organization's or user's computer or network, in contrast to remote ones. See **Remote.**

Log or log file A file or record that lists all access requests or activities on a computer or network so that they can be analyzed for security purposes.

Logic bombs Malicious codes that can be triggered on command to destroy or disrupt a computer network or application.

LoveBug virus See **ILoveYou virus.**

Malware Malicious software. Increasingly, shrewd social engineering methods are being used by malware to dupe victims. For example, a user receives an email appearing to be a warning from a software vendor that claims to detect or protect against a virus; but in reality, the message contains a mechanism to infect the victim with a new virus.

Marginal cost–benefit analysis A tool for evaluating alternative decisions. See **Economic model of marginal cost–benefit analysis.**

Melissa virus The Melissa virus was one of the first major viruses to wreak havoc as a friendly email containing the subject line "Important message from" followed by the name of a familiar person. If an Outlook user opened the attachment, the virus would send itself to the top 50 listings in the user's address book and add that person's name to the subject of the message. Although the virus itself was not considered malicious because it did not delete files, the exponential multiplication of messages caused some systems to come to a grinding halt.

Memory buffer The section of computer memory that stores the destination and transmission data. See **Buffer overflow.**

Meta-data Descriptions or properties of data files or email, examples of which are dates/times an email or file was created or accessed. When these electronic documents or logs are requested or subpoenaed in a legal action, they become e-evidence.

Microsoft SQL Server 2000 These were the servers that were vulnerable to the SQL Slammer worm.

MIME (multipurpose Internet mail extensions) The standard protocol for transmitting nontext multimedia (audio, video, binary) email messages. It is an extension of SMTP (simple mail transport protocol).

National Information Infrastructure Protection Act (NIIPA) The National Information Infrastructure Protection Act of 1995 increased protection for both government and private computers, and the information on those computers, from the growing threat of computer crime.

National Infrastructure Protection Center (NIPC) The NIPC was established by a presidential directive in 1998. The NIPC is a global reporting partnership between the FBI and the private sector. It is the federal government's first line of defense against information warfare—attacks on strategic computer systems by cyber terrorists. The NIPC is directed to detect, prevent, and respond to any physical or cyber threats against the country's critical government installations, public utilities, and private industry. One of the NIPC's missions is to partner with the business community to help executives protect their critical information systems.

Negligent supervision Under the theory of negligent supervision, the employer's duty of care and liability may extend to actions **outside the scope of employment.**

Negligent tort Conduct that creates an unreasonable risk of harm. Failure to exercise a degree of care that a prudent person would exercise under the same circumstances

Network A channel for computer communications, such as the Internet or local area network (LAN).

Network address translation (NAT) An Internet standard that enables an internal network, or LAN, to use two sets of IP addresses. One set of IP addresses is for internal traffic, and the second set is for external traffic. This effectively disguises the home network by assigning a hidden IP address to each protected device.

Network device A hardware device that connects a computer to a network.

Nimda Nimda is by definition a **worm,** but it also has a virus component by which it attaches itself to files to do damage, which makes it a blended threat. It is more virulent than most viruses, such as the Code Red, because of its multifaceted modes of attack. Once Nimda has infected a PC, it will try to do a mass emailing to addresses listed in the user's Microsoft Outlook and potentially infect the PCs of the recipients. PCs can get infected during a visit to a Website that is hosted (stored) on an infected server. The worm can modify files on a Web server to allow anonymous access to it, wherein the server has no protection against destruction, theft, or defacing.

Nonrepudiation A functional requirement of hardware and software that the origin or the receipt of a specific message is verifiable by a third party and cannot be denied.

Nonreproducing malware See **Nonviral malware.**

Nonviral malware Malicious code that does not reproduce or replicate itself. This category of malicious code is largely unstoppable by AV software. Examples of nonviral malware are password crackers, traffic sniffers, keystroke loggers, data scroungers, and remote access Trojans (RATs). These electronic burglar tools are used by attackers (both insiders and outsiders) to capture passwords and spy on network traffic or private communication or for unauthorized stealth communication with remote hosts. Corporate servers can become vulnerable to malware when users download popular software, for example, P2P or remote access programs, because they open up holes in the corporate firewall.

Null password A setting in which no password has yet been specified, so anyone can gain access. A severe security breach.

Operating system (OS) A low-level control program that runs the computer; for example, OS/2, Linux, Windows XP, Unix, Mac OS 10.

Opportunity costs Measurements of missed or lost sales or profits.

Organization for Economic Cooperation and Development (OECD) An international organization whose mission is to protect privacy. The organization has developed a set of guiding principles for the processing, retention, and disclosure of personal data.

Outbound or Outbound packet A packet that is sent from a local computer or from inside the network.

Outside the scope of employment Activities not directly related to work.

P2P (peer-to-peer) A network in which each computer has equivalent capabilities and responsibilities. Many Web-based P2P applications, such as Napster, AIM, or Groove, tunnel through corporate firewalls via HTTP or other open ports. In effect, this allows employees to create their own ad hoc VPNs.

P3P (Privacy Preferences Project) A software standard for browsers and Websites designed to automate the implementation of privacy policies. They can be programmed to interact with a Website in specific ways.

Packet A unit of data for transmission over a network that contains header and control information. This term is often used instead of *datagram*.

Packet filtering A firewall technique that looks at each incoming and outgoing packet and accepts or rejects it according to rules defined by the company or IT staff. It can be effective and transparent to users if it is configured correctly, which is difficult. The limitation of packet filtering is that it is susceptible to IP spoofing.

Packet switching The Internet uses a technology called *packet switching* to carry data. Packet switching works as follows. The computer that sends a document file (sending computer), such as a music file or digital image, cuts the document up into many small portions of information called a *packet*. Each packet contains the *IP address* of the destination Website, a small portion of data from the original document, and an indication of the data's place in the original document. The sending computer then sends all the packets through its local network to an external router. Since packets from the sending computer take entirely different routes over the Internet (i.e., traveling over different routers and cables) to their final destination, they arrive out of their original order. Because each packet has a header section with information that identifies its place in the original document, the destination computer is able to reassemble the original document from the disorganized packets. If the packets were sent using TCP/IP, the destination computer sends a message back to the originating computer either reporting that it received the full message or requesting that the originating computer resend any packets that never arrived. See **Router.**

Password crackers Software that can "crack," or decipher, a password.

Passwords A sequence of characters used for authentication. Weak passwords provide no protection against unauthorized access. The most commonly used passwords are "password," names of the area's major sports team, popular words from Star Trek's Klingon dictionary, or none at all (null password). Passwords typically used to protect financial files and entry to company LANs, intranets, and extranets pose only a minor hacking challenge. As such, computer security problems will increase dramatically as the Internet becomes more prevalent in PDAs, mobile phones, and pagers and migrates to video game devices and TV.

Patch Software provided by the operating system (OS), such as Microsoft or UNIX, or application program vendors to fix a problem or vulnerability.

Payload The mechanism by which a virus causes damage.

PBX (private branch exchange) A private telephone network owned and operated by an organization.

PDA (personal digital assistant) A handheld device that functions in several capacities— as a cell phone, fax sender and personal organizer, among other things. PDAs use a stylus, or pen, rather than a keyboard.

Permission Privileges granted to each user on a network that control what data and applications that user is allowed to access. The system administrator controls permissions.

Personally identifiable health information (PIHI) Health or health care information that can identify an individual. HIPAA regulations protect the privacy of individually identifiable health information.

Ping (Packet Internet Groper) This is a software utility program used to determine whether a specific IP address is real and accessible. The term is often used as a verb; for example, "ping a server."

Port Ports are interfaces, or entry/exit points, to a network. They are numbered and usually associated with a specific process. For example, port 80 is associated with HTTP used for access to Web pages.

Port scanners Tools or techniques for inspecting computers connected to the Internet for accessible open ports. Some of these tools are Foundstone's SuperScan, Fyodor's nmap, NetScanTools Pro 2000 (NSTP2K), Legion Network's port scanner, and X-Scan.

Port scanning The process of connecting to TCP or UDP (user datagram protocol) ports on a target system to identify services that are active, or running, and ports that are listening to traffic.

Pretty good privacy (PGP) PGP is an effective encryption technique commonly used to protect messages sent via the Internet. PGP is based on PKI, which uses a public key and a private key. PGP is available for free from several sources, including the Massachusetts Institute of Technology.

Privacy The state of being left alone and free from surveillance is a fundamental right protected by the U.S. Constitution.

Privileged access Greater access authority than at the end-user level. For example, root access.

Product suite A collection of software products; for example, Microsoft Office.

Propagation The way a virus replicates locally and over a network. Also called *migration*.

Protocol A standard method of communication, such as IP (Internet protocol).

Proxy server A type of firewall designed to hide the identity or IP address of the organization's servers. To prevent packets from revealing any critical IP addresses, a proxy server, or simply proxy, intercepts and relays all inbound/outbound requests.

Prudent man rule A rule that imposes on organizations the duty to protect information assets as a prudent person would.

Public key infrastructure (PKI) A system of digital certificates to identify and authenticate the sender or receiver of an Internet message or transaction. See **Key.**

Qaz Trojan A Trojan horse malware program. The Microsoft trespassers (in October 2000) apparently used the Qaz Trojan, a widely available program, to take control of the computers.

RAT (remote-access Trojan) A program that gives unauthorized computer or network access after it has been installed on a victim's computer. Examples are Back Orifice and NetBus. As is the case with Trojans, it

is disguised as an innocuous program that can be transmitted via email as an executable file, downloaded from a Website, or installed by someone with physical access to the computer.

Reconnaissance probes Refers to the activities, such as port scanning, that are done in preparation for an attack. This is also called *recon*.

Recons Slang for reconnaissance probes.

Regression Regression testing is generally used to certify all updates to key components before application, but this process can be costly and time-consuming. It is often impractical given the frequency with which these patches are released.

Remote Refers to a computer or network that is not local to the company or user. Remote is the opposite of local. See **Local.**

Remote and local exploit tools Tools used to gain high-level privileged access (root access to all other files and directories) to a company's network and systems. See **Root access.**

Respondeat superior With respect to cyber security, *respondeat superior* is a liability risk a company may face for not diligently monitoring the cyber activities of its employees.

Return on investment (ROI) The ratio of the net gain from a proposed investment divided by its total costs.

Right A legal claim that others not interfere with a protected interest, such as the right to privacy. Personal rights are those rights that one possesses solely by virtue of being a person and a citizen. See **Duty.**

Risk analysis The purpose of risk analysis is to fully identify and assess risk factors, then to balance the expected costs (damages) of incidents with the cost of defenses needed to avoid incidents.

Roles An effective way to manage permissions and access rights is to divide users into roles, or access-level categories.

Root access This is the greatest (most intrusive) degree of access into a system—basically it means getting "access to the root." This access level gives a user (or a hacker) access to, and control of, all files on a network or PC.

Rootkit Tools used by hackers to collect passwords. They are available freely on the Internet.

Router A device that transfers packets between two or more networks. A router contains continuously updated directories of Internet addresses called *routing tables*. The router takes each packet from the original document and sends it to the next available router in the direction of the destination Website. Because each router is connected to many other routers, and because the connection between any two given routers may be congested with traffic at a given moment, packets from the same document are typically sent to different routers. Each of these routers, in turn, repeats this process, forwarding each packet it receives to the next available router in the direction of the destination Website. Collectively, this process is called *dynamic routing*. See **Packet switching.**

Sapphire See **SQL Slammer.**

SarbanesOxley Act An investor protection bill passed by Congress in 2002 after financial scandals at Enron, WorldCom, and other companies. The Sarbanes–Oxley Act orders the SEC to issue rules requiring disclosure of financial transactions.

Scope of employment See *Respondeat superior*.

Script Computer code (language) that can be executed directly by a program that understands the language the script was written in. Scripts can be executed without first being compiled. Examples of script languages are Visual Basic script (VBScript) and Java script.

Script kiddie A novice hacker who uses existing hacker tools and virus-building code. Script Kiddies may not know enough to develop new viruses, but they can be just as disruptive and destructive as expert hackers.

Secure sockets layer (SSL) A widely used encryption security mechanism on the Internet. The 128-bit secure socket layer encryption is used to protect Internet transactions; for example, financial transactions. Hackers have tried tackling this 128-bit encryption by marshaling enough computers together to crack SSL.

Security Security is defined as the policies, practices, and technology that must be in place for an organization to transact business electronically via networks with a reasonable assurance of safety. This assurance applies to all online activities, transmissions, and storage. It also applies to business partners, customers, regulators, insurers, or others who might be at risk in the event of a breach of that company's security.

Security audits Reviews of all aspects of the security program, including technology, procedures, documentation, training, and personnel in some cases. They work best when they are conducted both internally and certified by a recognized third-party expert.

Server Servers are computers that store files and documents and make them available over the Internet through TCP/IP (transmission control protocol/Internet protocol). Every Website is made up of document files, which have a unique URL (universal resource locator) that identifies its physical location on a server in the Internet's infrastructure. Users access documents by sending request messages to the servers that store the documents.

Service pack A service pack is an up-to-date software patch to fix a vulnerability.

Signature IP traffic patterns are defined or described by their signature. A signature is the identifier by which a virus is detected by AV software. Viral signatures are the patterns used to identify a virus within a file.

SirCam worm An email virus that sends itself, along with local files from the infected PC, to all users found in the Windows address book.

Slammer A computer virus that attacked computer server systems and shut down ATM operations at some of the nation's largest financial institutions in late January 2003. Slammer shut down server systems by attacking and overloading computer networks that use Microsoft Corp.'s SQL Server 2000 servers.

Slow sweep Scanning probes that are deliberately intermittent to avoid detection.

SMTP (simple mail transfer protocol) Protocol for sending email messages between servers. Most email systems that send mail over the Internet use SMTP to send messages from one server to another.

Smoking gun A term used by the legal or litigation community to describe a physical or electronic document that constitutes strong evidence in favor of the claim being made.

Sniffer An eavesdropping program or device that can monitor and steal data traveling over a network. Sniffers are a common weapon of hackers. They can be used for legitimate network management functions or to steal information from a network. Unauthorized sniffers are a network security risk because they are almost impossible to detect.

Social engineering This is the method that Kevin Mitnick used to gain access to servers and networks. It's the ability of a hacker to break into a system simply by fooling an employee into revealing access codes, passwords, or other confidential information. *Social engineering* is an elaborate term for using fraud to obtain passwords. A common hacker trick for obtaining a user's password is to pretend in a phone call to be a member of the firm's IS staff.

Spam Spam is junk email. Officially, it is called *unsolicited commercial email* (UCE) or *unsolicited advertising.*

Spammer Anyone who sends junk email.

Spamming The sending of junk email, or spam.

Spam relay An offensive attack wherein a company's domain mail system is used as the host to deliver, or relay, spam. This can result in a DOS because while the (host) company's email server is occupied by the processing of spam mail, it cannot handle legitimate inbound and outbound email.

Spamware Software that automatically searches the Web to collect what it recognizes as email addresses.

Spoliation Spoliation means "destruction of evidence." It involves the destruction of evidence having potential evidentiary value. It may be viewed as a criminal obstruction of justice. Under federal law, spoliation is the destruction or significant alteration of evidence or the failure to preserve evidence for pending or reasonably foreseeable litigation. Thus, spoliation involves two elements: a duty to preserve evidence and the intentional destruction of that evidence.

Spoof To trick, disguise, or deceive. For example, a spoofed Website is one wherein a correct Web address is replaced with a phony one. Identities of email senders can also be spoofed to disguise the true identity of the sender or to pretend to be someone else.

Spoofing system or Website A system or Website that looks exactly like a legitimate one and that presents the same login interface.

Spyware Software that covertly gathers information about a user through the user's Internet connection. The information is collected without the person's knowledge and disclosed without the person's consent. Spyware has the ability to monitor keystrokes, scan hard drive files, and snoop other applications, including word processing and spreadsheets.

SQL slammer (also called Sapphire) A worm that caused chaos around the world by sending out a flood of messages that jammed networks. This global traffic jam substantially slowed down the Internet in January 2003.

Standard of reasonableness The duty of care imposed by law that is measured against the conduct of a reasonable, prudent person.

Stateful inspection A type of firewall that compares the fields in the inbound IP packet to fields in the outbound messages that had preceded it. This information is used to build a database of characteristics of legitimate traffic.

Static IP address See **Fixed IP address.**

Statute A written rule or law.

Subnet (subnetwork) A network that is segmented into smaller networks.

SubSeven A Trojan horse that was rampant in P2P networks and could open company networks to script kiddies' backdoor attacks.

Symmetrical DSL Bandwidths to and from a user's PC that are at the same speed; for example, 384K. Downloading and uploading speeds are the same. See **DSL** and **ADSL.**

SYN flood attack An attack on a network that prevents a TCP/IP server from servicing other users.

T-1 A leased telephone line connection with a transmission speed of 1.544 Mbps. A single T-1 line can handle 24 voice or data channels at 64 Kbps. Capacity sold at less than full T-1 rates is known as fractional T-1.

Taxonomy of threats and vulnerabilities (TTV) A classification of intruders and intrusions that organizations and users are exposed to.

TCP/IP (transmission control protocol/ Internet protocol) TCP/IP makes it possible for all types of computers to communicate with each other. It is a set of operating and transmission protocols that enables the Web to operate.

TCP/IP ports Every IP address is broken down into small components called TCP/IP ports. To ensure that packets get delivered to their intended application, TCP/IP port numbers are assigned to each application on a network.

Telnet A program that lets users connect to other computers on the Internet.

Third-party risks Risks that are threats to the company's customers, suppliers, business partners, or competitors, who may seek legal redress by lawsuit.

Token A physical device, analogous to an ID card, designed to be used by only one person to prove his/her identity. Tokens are better than ordinary passwords, which are effective only as long as they are secret. A token, which a user must physically possess, in conjunction with a password offers far better authentication.

Torts Legally, any civil wrong that may be grounds for a lawsuit. Two categories of torts are negligent torts and strict liability torts. Intentional torts are any wrongs that the defendant knew, or should have known, would occur through his actions or inactions. Negligent torts occur when the defendant's actions were unreasonably unsafe.

Total Quality Management (TQM) A popular business strategy for improving quality and reducing cost.

Trade secret Any information protected by a business because it provides the business with a particular economic advantage.

Trigger The action that activates a virus.

Trojan program (Trojan) Harmless-looking software programs or executable code that can damage computers or steal information from them. Often the user is unaware of the transmission and installation of a Trojan on his or her PC. Trojans can be sent as email attachments. When the recipient highlights or opens the infected email message, the Trojan can invisibly install itself on the PC. Trojans can give the sender complete access to the PC that it has infected. Afterwards, that PC could be commanded to send unauthorized email (see **IP address forgery)** or launch attacks on other PCs, causing a DOS. See **Worm.**

Tunnel Tunneling is the enclosing of one protocol or data stream within another. For example, a VPN (virtual private network) tunnels data by encrypting it for transfer via the Internet.

Unicode A 16-bit code used to represent alphanumeric characters in binary form.

Unicode bug The so-called Unicode bug was used by the Dutch hacker Dimitri to gain unauthorized access to Microsoft's systems in October 2000. Microsoft had first patched this security hole on August 10, 2000 and issued a security bulletin on October 17, 2000 pointing customers to the same software patch. On its TechNet Website, Microsoft refers to the bug as the "Web Server Folder Traversal" vulnerability.

Unicode hole A vulnerability or "security hole" that lets hackers get deeper into a Website and control it.

Uniform Electronic Transaction Act (UETA) UETA is a uniform law approved in July 1999 by the National Conference of Commissioners on Uniform State Laws. If adopted by state legislatures, UETA will elevate electronic records and signatures to the same legal status accorded paper records and handwritten signatures.

USA PATRIOT Act The USA PATRIOT Act broadly expands law enforcement's surveillance and investigative powers. In particular, the law raises complicated questions with respect to what constitutes a business record and the law's broad definition of computer trespassers. The law also creates a new relationship between domestic criminal investigations related to foreign intelligence.

Virtual hacking A type of Internet attack referred to as a blended threat. This type of hack attack can be conducted using worms to exploit vulnerabilities in Microsoft's Internet Information Services (IIS). Nimda had infected hundreds of thousands of networks by moving through email, Web browsing, and files shared across networks In effect, blended (or hybrid) threats create virtual hackers by automating the ways hackers break into systems.

Virtual private network (VPN) A VPN uses the public Internet for private communication, which is accomplished though encryption.

Virtual workplace Any place where company business is being conducted using company-provided equipment.

Virus A virus is a malicious computer program. Viruses infect computers by attaching themselves to programs and data files, replicating on a hard drive, and then doing damage, such as deleting files. A virus consists of two parts: the propagation (replication) mechanism and the payload, which does the damage. See **Worm.** Many viruses attempt to hide themselves. They may insert themselves into unused space within a program so as not to change the size or other characteristics of those files, though they would affect a checksum.

Visual Basic Script (VBS) Visual Basic Script is a language developed by Microsoft and supported by Microsoft's Internet Explorer Web browser. VBScript enables Web authors to include interactive controls, such as buttons and scrollbars, on their Web pages.

Voice over IP (VoIP) Voice transmission over the Internet rather than phone lines. The quality is generally not as good as phone transmission, but it's much cheaper.

VPN (virtual private network) A VPN is a private connection, or network, that is created

by tunneling within the Internet. The connection can be between (1) remote users and the company network or (2) two or more remote LANs. VPNs use encryption to provide the security of private networks, which are not always secure. See **Tunnel.**

Vulnerability An exposure to risk or threat. Users can minimize their vulnerability by constantly updating antivirus and firewall software; turning off always-on broadband connections when not using them; staying out of chat rooms, usenet news groups, and instant messaging; deleting email with attachments or from strangers; and by not forwarding email or opening forwarded email.

WAN (wide area network) A communications network that connects widely separate locations. Think of WANs as the interstate highways and LANs as the secondary roads connecting them.

WAP (Web application protocol) The telecommunications protocol used on personal digital assistants (PDAs) and mobile phones.

Warez (pronounced *wares*) Commercial software that has been pirated and made publicly available via electronic bulletin boards or Websites.

Warez site (plural: Warez sitez) A hacker site for obtaining or downloading freeware tools or commercial software, including password crackers and keystroke loggers.

Web bugs Web bugs are links to small images that are often 1 pixel in size and thus not visible. They are placed within host Web pages specifically to eavesdrop an visitors without their knowledge.

White-collar crime (WCC) Any nonviolent crime committed in a commercial context. Examples of WCC are embezzlement, bribery, and fraud.

White hat hackers Hackers whose hobbies or job it is to find security weaknesses in computer systems or business applications and help correct them.

Whois database An online database of domain names that can be queried by anyone to find out information or identities of the owners of those domain names. The database reveals information such as company domains, network, and hosts; the name, address, telephone, fax, and email address of the administrator of the domain name. The data revealed by Whois is used for social engineering or to gain access to the system administrator's network account. The data provided when registering a domain name is a serious security leak that can be avoided by using generic email (e.g., info@companyname.com) and other indirect contact information.

World Wide Web (WWW) The WWW is often mistakenly referred to as the Internet. The Internet is the physical infrastructure consisting of hardware, software, and telecom devices—servers, computers, network, cables, and routers. The Web is the data, documents, and multimedia files that are accessed via the Internet.

Worm A type of software attack that infects one computer and then attempts to infect other computers that are attached to the same network. These programs can reproduce themselves and overload networks. An automated worm can randomly probe the Internet looking for vulnerable networks to victimize. The speed with which worms can spread across the Internet makes them ideal delivery mechanisms for setting up a network of clients that can be later exploited to launch DDOS or other types of attacks. In the future, worms can be expected to become stealthier or more lethal to computer systems. See also **Nimda.**

XML (extensible markup language) A Web programming language that can be used instead of HTML. It is used for Websites and database applications that need to share data between applications and organizations. There is no agreed-upon industry standard for XML.

Zombie A computer program used to infect a computer and then to remotely activate the infected computer to launch a DDOS. Zombies can be used to send an enormous number of bogus requests to a targeted Website or server to which the server cannot respond so that the Website becomes unreachable. This is a serious threat to electronic commerce. Hackers seek out millions of vulnerable PCs to take control over—like zombies. Zombies, also called *denial-of-service programs*, can be simultaneously installed on several host computers through automated attack scripts (e.g., Trojans or viruses) that exploit vulnerabilities in a computer network. Thus, zombies are used to orchestrate DDOS attacks. Many corporate Websites have been attacked by zombies that resided on other corporate host computers. These host computers are effectively secondary victims (targets) that are coordinated to attack one or more primary victims or targets. "Secondary victim" companies whose servers are used to launch DOS attacks on primary victims may be held liable for, in effect, aiding the DDOS attack.

ABBREVIATIONS AND ACRONYMS

NUMBERS AND SYMBOLS

802.11 Wireless protocol. Also referred to as WiFi.

// (double forward slashes) Double forward slashes at the beginning of filenames mean that the files exist on a remote server (computer). The // is common to the Internet and Websites.

§ Section or subsection.

ACFE Association of Certified Fraud Examiners

ACL Access-control list

ACLU American Civil Liberties Union

ADSL Asymmetric digital subscriber line

AIM America Online Instant Messenger

AMA American Management Association

ARIN American Registry for Internet Numbers

ASP Application service provider

ATM Asynchronous transfer mode

AUP Acceptable-use policy

AV Antivirus

BCC Blind carbon copy

bps Bits per second

BS British standard

C-SPAN Cable-Satellite Public Affairs Network

CA Certification authority

CCIPS Computer Crime and Intellectual Property Section of the Criminal Division of the DOJ

CD Compact disc

CDA Communications Decency Act

CDT Center for Democracy and Technology

CEO Chief executive officer

CERT® Computer Emergency Response Team

CFAA Computer Fraud and Abuse Act

CFE Certified fraud examiner

CFO Chief financial officer

CGI Common gateway interface

CGI-Bin Common gateway interface binaries (programs)

CIA Central Intelligence Agency

CIRT Computer incident response team

CISO Chief information security officer

CNN Cable News Network

COPPA Children's Online Privacy Protection Act

CPPA Child Pornography Prevention Act

CPU Central processing unit

CRC Cyclic redundancy check

CRM Customer relationship management

CSI Computer Security Institute, Inc.

CTO Chief technology officer

DCA Distributed coordinated attacks

DDOS Distributed denial of service

dig sig Digital signature

DLM Digital liability management

DMS Defense message system

DMV Department of Motor Vehicles

DMZ Demilitarized zone

DNS Domain name server

DOS Denial of service

DOJ Department of Justice

DOT Department of Transportation

DPH Digital Pearl Harbor

DRM Digital rights management

DSL Digital subscriber line

Ecommerce Electronic commerce

ECPA Electronic Communications Privacy Act

EFF Electronic Frontier Foundation

email Electronic mail

EPIC Electronic Privacy Information Center

ERM Electronic records management

ESIGN Electronic Signatures in Global and National Commerce Act

ESSENCE Electronic Surveillance System for the Early Notification of Community-based Epidemics

EU European Union

Fax Facsimile

FBI Federal Bureau of Investigation

FedCIRC Federal Computer Incident Response Center

FinCEN Financial Crimes Enforcement Network

FISMA Federal Information Security Management Act

FTC Federal Trade Commission

FTP File transfer protocol

G-8 Group of Eight
GAAP Generally Accepted Accounting Principles
GAO General Accounting Office
GB Gigabyte (1024 megabytes)
GIF Graphic interchange format
GLB Gramm–Leach–Bliley Act of 1999
GPS Global Positioning System
HAZMAT Hazardous materials
HIPAA Health Insurance Portability and Accountability Act
HR Human Resources
HTML Hypertext markup language
HTTP Hypertext transfer protocol
HTTPS Hypertext transfer protocol secure
ICANN Internet Corporation for Assigned Names and Numbers
ICMP Internet control message protocol
ICQ "I-seek-you"
IDS Intrusion detection system
IFIA Internet False Identification Prevention Act of 2000
IIS Internet Information Services (Microsoft)
IM Instant message
IP Internet protocol
ISACs Information Sharing and Analysis Centers
ISDN Integrated services digital network
ISO International organization for standardization
ISP Internet service provider
ISS Internet security systems
IT Information technology
JS JavaScript
KBps Kilobytes per second
KM Knowledge management
LAN Local area network
LDAP Lightweight directory access protocol
LLC Limited liability corporation
MBps Megabytes per second
MD Message digest
MIME Multipurpose Internet mail extensions
MP3 Moving Picture Experts Group Layer-3 Audio
NASA National Aeronautics & Space Administration
NAT Network address translation
NIIPA National Information Infrastructure Protection Act of 1996
NIPC National Infrastructure Protection Center
NIST National Institute of Standards and Technology

NLRB National Labor Relations Board
OCC Office of the Comptroller of the Currency
OEM Original equipment manufacturer
OECD Organization for Economic Cooperation and Development
OS Operating system
OWASP Open Web Application Security Project
P2P Peer-to-peer
P3P Privacy Preferences Project
PBX Private branch exchange
PC Personal computer
PDA Personal digital assistant
PGP Pretty good privacy
PIHI Personally identifiable health information
Ping Packet Internet groper
PKI Public key infrastructure
R&D Research and development
RAT Remote-access Trojan
RF Radio frequency
ROI Return on investment
SAINT Security administrator integrated network tool
SAN Storage area network
SANS System Administration, Auditing, Networking, and Security Institute
SATAN Security administrator tool for analyzing networks
SEC Securities and Exchange Commission
SET Secure electronic transmission
SIPRNET Secret Internet protocol router network
SMTP Simple mail transport protocol
SSL Secure sockets layer
SSO Single sign-on
SQL Structured query language
TCO Total cost of ownership
TCP Transfer control protocol
TCP/IP Transmission control protocol/Internet protocol
TFN Tribe Flood Net
TFN2K Tribal Flood Net 2000
TTV Taxonomy of threats and vulnerabilities
TQM Total quality management
TXT Text
UCE Unsolicited commercial email
UDP User datagram protocol
UETA Uniform Electronic Transaction Act of 1999
UPX Ultimate packer for executables
URL Uniform resource locator

USA PATRIOT Uniting and Strengthening America by Providing Appropriate Tools Required to Intercept and Obstruct Terrorism
USC United States Code
USCG United States Coast Guard
VB Visual Basic
VBS Visual Basic Script

VoIP Voice over Internet protocol
VPN Virtual private network
WAN Wide area network
WAP Web application protocol
WCC White-collar crime
WWW World Wide Web
XML Extensible markup language

REFERENCES

Adams, Lee S., and Martz, David J. "Survey: Developments in CyberBanking." *The Business Lawyer.* (57 Bus. Law. 1257). May 2002.

Albrecht, W. Steve, and Conan C. Albrecht, "Root Out Financial Deception: Detect and Eliminate Fraud or Suffer the Consequences." *Journal of Accountancy.* Vol. 193, No. 4. April 1, 2002. P. 30.

"Allfirst Bank Trader Pleads Guilty To $691 Million Derivatives Fraud." *White-Collar Crime Reporter.* Vol. 17, No. 1. December 2002. P. 25.

Anderson Peter J., and Alana Rae Black, "Accountants' Liability After Enron." *S&P's The Review of Securities & Commodities Regulation.* Vol. 35, No. 18; October 23, 2002. P. 227.

Andress, Mandy. "An Overview of Security Policies." http://searchsecurity. techtarget.com/originalContent/ 0,289142,sid14_gci822681,00.html

Arkfeld, Michael R. "Policing Your Firm's Technology: Address Missteps before They Occur." *Arizona Attorney.* (37 AZ Attorney 10). June 2001.

Arkin, Stanley. "Analysts' Conflict of Interest: Where's the Crime?" *New York Law Journal.* February 14, 2002. P. 3.

Armstrong, Illena. "Computer Forensics." *SC Magazine.* April 2001. http://www. scmagazine.com/scmagazine/2001_04/ cover/cover.html

Arthur, Charles. "Web Designer who Created Computer Virus is Jailed." *The Independent (London).* January 22, 2003. P. 7.

Bachman, Justin. "Scandals Made It Easy to Spot the Losers This Year." (AP) *The Buffalo News.* December 30, 2002.

Barbaro, Michael. "Internet Attacks On Companies Up 28 Percent, Report Says." *The Washington Post.* July 8, 2002. P. E5.

Behr, Mary E. "Vacation To-Do List: Relax, Check E-Mail." *PC Week.* July 2001. http://www.pcmag.com/article2/ 0,4149,391797,00.asp

Bloom, Jennifer Kingson. "The Tech Scene: Quality Counts As Banks Jump into Dig-Sigs." *American Banker.* July 19, 2000. P. 1.

Bowman, Frank O., III. Statement of Frank O. Bowman, Associate Professor of Law Indiana University School of Law, *Committee on Senate Judiciary Subcommittee on Crime and Drugs.* "Penalties for White Collar Offense: Are We Really Getting Tough on Crime?" June 19, 2002.

Bray, Hiawatha. "Net Security Chief Leaves Too Many Questions Unanswered." *The Boston Globe.* October 14, 2002. P. D4.

Bridis, Ted. "Al-Jazeera Web site is Sabotaged by Hackers." *Associated Press.* March 28, 2003.

Brown, Ken, Gregg Hitt, Steve Liesman, and Jonathan Weil. "Andersen Fires Partner It Says Led Shredding of Documents." *The Wall Street Journal.* January 16, 2002.

Brunker, Mike. "Cyberspace Evidence Seizure Upheld." *Cybercrime-Alerts.* June 3, 2001. http://www.mail-archive.com/ cybercrime-alerts@topica.com/msg00439.html

Burke, Patrick J. "Learning from Wall Street's E-Mail Nightmare: Discovery and Admissibility of E-Mail." *The Metropolitan Corporate Counsel.* September 2002. P. 48.

Burkitt, Mike. "Security Strategy Must Go Beyond Technology." *Computing.* March 28, 2002. P. 35.

"Business IT Strategy—Calculating Risks." *Accountancy.* December 27, 2001. P. 56.

Cavallini, Silvia. "The E-Mail Read 'Round the World'." *The Industry Standard.* May 22, 2001.

Chidi, George A. "Patriot Act Opens ISPs to Monitoring." *PCWorld.com.* November 2001. http://www.pcworld.com/news/article/ 0,aid,69662,00.asp

Cohen, Fred. "Collaborative Defense." March 2000. http://www.all.net/journal/netsec/2000-03.html

Comey, James B., Jr. *Statement of James B. Comey, Jr. United States Attorney Southern District of New York, Committee on Senate Judiciary Subcommittee on Crime and Drugs.* "Penalties for White Collar Offense: Are We Really Getting Tough on Crime?" June 19, 2002.

Conry-Murray, Andrew. "Deciphering the Cost of a Computer Crime." *Network Magazine.* April 1, 2002. P. 44.

Convention on Cybercrime, November 23, 2001, http://conventions.coe.int/Treaty/en/treaties/html/185.htm

Costello, Sam. "Goner Worm Spreads, Tries to Delete Firewalls." *InfoWorld.* December 4, 2001. http://www.infoworld.com/articles/hn/xml/01/12/04/011204hngoner.xml

Costello, Sam. "'Nimda,' 'Code Red' Still Alive and Crawling." *CNN.com.* May 8, 2002. http://www.cnn.com/2002/TECH/internet/05/08/nimda.code.red.idg/index.html

"Cyber Security: Hackers Replace Arab Web Site With Patriotic Messages." *National Journal's Technology Daily.* March 28, 2003.

Daniels and Ballou v Worldcom Corporation, et al., U.S. District, Lexis 2335 (ND Texas 1998).

Darby, Christopher. "The Dollars And Cents Of Security—Make the Case for Security Investments with Facts, Figures, and Sound Economics." *Optimize.* October 1, 2002. P. 28.

Dasgupta, Partha. "Cyber Terrorism." *The Statesman* (India). May 24, 2002.

Davis, Erin M. "The Doctrine of *Respondeat Superior:* An Application to Employer Liability for the Computer or Internet Crimes Committed by their Employees." *Albany Law Journal of Science & Technology* (12 Alb. L.J. Sci. & Tech. 683). 2002.

Delio, Michelle. "Yahoo's Opt-out Angers Users." *Wired News.* April 2002. http://www.wired.com/news/privacy/0,1848,51461,00.html

DeMaria, Michael J. "Gone in 6.0 Seconds." *Network Computing.* September 30, 2002. P. 77.

Dennis, Warren L., and Susan Brinkerhoff. "Document Management Policies In the Post-Enron Environment." *Aviation Litigation Reporter.* Vol. 20, No. 25. February 18, 2003. P. 12.

Doerner, Saunders, and James C. Milton "Document Retention after Enron: When Should I Press 'Delete'?" *Oklahoma Employment Law Letter.* Vol. 10, Issue 6. May 2002.

Dratch, Dana. "Protect Your PDA." Special to the *Fulton County Daily Report.* May 20, 2002.

Ernst & Young *2001 Information Security Survey.* http://www.ey.com

Ernst & Young *P3P Dashboard Report.* January 2003. http://www.ey.com

Editor interview of Michael Prounis. "Plan For Electronic Discovery Now—And Avoid 'Bet The Company' Mistakes." *The Metropolitan Corporate Counsel.* August 2002. P. 24.

Epstein, Richard A. *Cases and Materials on Torts,* 6th ed. Boston: Little, Brown & Co., 1995, P. 218.

Etzioni, Amitai. "Implications of Select New Technologies for Individual Rights and Public Safety." *Harvard Journal of Law & Technology.* (15 Harv. J. Law & Tec 257) Spring 2002.

Evers, Joris. "'Kournikova' Virus Writer Appeals Sentence." May 6, 2002. http://europe.cnn.com/2002/TECH/internet/05/06/kournikova.sentence.idg/index.html

"'Explosive' E-Mails Allowed into Evidence in Enron Loan Trial." *Digital Discovery and e-Evidence.* Vol. 3, No. 1. January 2003. P. 14.

Federal Rule of Civil Procedures 34(b).

Fein. David B., and Mark W. Heaphy. "Options When A System Has Been Hacked: Fear of Bad Publicity Elicits Corporate Fight or Flight." *Connecticut Law Tribune.* Vol. 27, No. 51. December 17, 2001.

Fisher, Dennis. "Cyber Attacks Decline; Vulnerabilities Surge" *eWeek.* February 3, 2003. http://www.eweek.com/article2/0,3959,857004,00.asp

Fisher, Dennis. "How Sharing Thwarts Hacks." *eWeek.* January 13, 2003. http://www.eweek.com/article2/0,3959,825430,00.asp

"Former Computer Network Administrator at New Jersey High-Tech Firm Sentenced to 41

Months for Unleashing $10 Million Computer 'Time Bomb.'" *U.S. Department of Justice, United States Attorney, District of New Jersey.* February 26, 2002. http://www.cybercrime.gov/lloydSent.htm

Fonseca, Brian. "IT Security Under the Gun." *ITWorld.* March 12, 2001. http://www.itworld.com/Sec/3832/itwnws010312security/

Fraley, David, and Ron Cowles. "Could Terrorists Bring Down the Public Switched Telephone Network?" *Gartner Group.* September 3, 2002. http://www.gartnerg2.com/site/FileDownload.asp?file=qa-1002-0104-109349.pdf

"Fraud: *United States v Rusnak:* Allfirst Bank Trader Pleads Guilty to $691 Million Derivatives Fraud." *Bank & Lender Liability Litigation Reporter.* Vol. 8, No. 12. November 14, 2002. P. 8.

FTC Press Release, "COPPA Civil Penalties to Date in Settlements with Mrs. Fields Cookies and Hershey Foods." February 27, 2003. http://www.ftc.gov/opa/2003/02/hersheyfield.htm

Fundamentals of Computer Fraud. No. 99-5403. ACFE. 1999. PP. 35–36.

Gainer, Glen B., III. *Statement of Glen B. Gainer, III, State Auditor of West Virginia Chairman, Committee on Senate Judiciary Subcommittee on Crime and Drugs.* "Penalties for White Collar Offense: Are We Really Getting Tough on Crime?" June 19, 2002.

Gartner Report. "Dealing with Cyberterrorism: A Primer for Financial Services." Reference Number: qa-1002-0104. Oct. 2, 2002. https://www.gartnerg2.com/qa/qa-1002-0104.asp

Gasparino, Charles. "State Inquiry to Follow Close on Heels of Departing Merrill Lynch Analyst." *Wall Street Journal.* Dec. 10, 2001.

Gelles, Jeff. "Email Headed for a Spam Jam." *The Philadelphia Inquirer.* September 7, 2002.

Gellman, Barton. "Cyber-Attacks by Al Qaeda Feared." *The Washington Post.* June 27, 2002. P. A1.

Gibbons Paul, Lauren. "How to Tame the Email Beast." *CNN.com.* October 2001. http://www.cnn.com/2001/TECH/internet/10/18/email.beast.idg/index.html

Gleim, Invin N., and Jordan B. Ray, with Eugene P. O'Connor. *Business Law/Legal Studies.* Gainsville, FL: Gleim Publications, Inc., 1992.

Goodman, Marc D., and Susan W. Brenner. "The Emerging Consensus on Criminal Conduct in Cyberspace." *UCLA Journal of Law and Technology*, Vol. 3. 2002.

Gordon, Marcy. "WorldCom Stock Drops to 6 Cents." *AP Wire Story.* July 1, 2002. 12:58 P.M.

Government Computer News, January 13, 2003. http://www.gcn.com/vol1_no1/daily-updates/20862-1.html

Guider, Ian. "Computer Conmen." *Business and Finance.* November 21, 2002. P. 22.

Hafner, Katie, and John Briggs. "In Net Attacks, Defining the Right to Know." *The New York Times.* January 30, 2003. (G) P. 1.

Harrington, Mark. "Computer Experts to Root Out Missing Files." *Newsday.* February 5, 2002. http://www.newsday.com/business/local/newyork/ny-bzenro052576192feb05.story

Harley, David. "The Future of Malicious Code." *Information Security.* May 2002. P. 36.

Hearing of the Senate Governmental Affairs Committee. Senator Joseph Lieberman, Chair. "Securing our Infrastructure: Private/Public Information Sharing." Washington, D.C. *Federal News Service.* May 8, 2002.

Henry-Stocker, Sandra. "Analysis: Understanding Viruses." *CNN.* January 2001. http://www.cnn.com/2001/TECH/computing/01/30/understanding.viruses.idg/index.html

Hicks, Matt. "Scaling toward the Petabyte." *Eweek.* June 2002. http://www.eweek.com/article2/0,3959,1670,00.asp

Hu, Jim. "Intel Scores in Email Suit." *CNET News.com.* December 1998. http://news.com.com/2100-1023-218747.html?legacy=cnet

Huffman, Lisa, and James Hamilton. "Employee Revenge." June 4, 2002. http://www.techtv.com/cybercrime/features/story/0,23008,3386967,00.html.

Hulme, George V. "Guarded Optimism—Even as Companies Plug More Holes, the Threats Grow More Sophisticated." *InformationWeek.* July 8, 2002. P. 36.

Hulme, George V. "In Lockstep On Security." *InformationWeek*. March 18, 2002. http://www.informationweek.com/story/IWK20020315S0008

Hulme, George V. "Intrusion-Prevention Tools Prove Themselves by Stopping Worms Like Slammer in their Tracks." *InformationWeek*. February 3, 2003. http://www.informationweek.com/story/IWK20030202S0002

Hulme, George V. "Networks Without a Safety Net: Wireless LANs Present Security Challenges for Businesses." *InformationWeek*. June 21, 2002. http://www.informationweek.com/story/IWK20020621S0001

Hulme, George V. "One Step Ahead. Security Managers Are Trying to Be Prepared for the Next Blended Threat Attack." *InformationWeek*. May 20, 2002.

In re Logue Mechanical Contracting Corp., 106 B.R. 436, 439 (Bankr. W.D. Pa. 1989).

Iqbal, Anwar. "FBI Investigates Al-Jazeera Hacking." *United Press International*. March 28, 2003.

Iwata, Edward. "Enron Case could be Largest Corporate Investigation." *USA Today*. February 18, 2002. http://www.usatoday.com/life/cyber/tech/2002/02/19/detectives.htm

Iwata, Edward. "Hackers Scope Out New Prey: Wireless Users." *USA Today*. July 16, 2001. http://www.newsbytes.com/news/01/167981.html

J.P. Morgan Chase Bank v Liberty Mutual Insurance Co., 01 Civ. 11523 (http://www.law.com).

Jacobson, Heather, and Rebecca Green. "Computer Crimes." 39 *American Criminal Law Review,* 273. Spring 2002.

Jainschigg, John. "Securing your Switch; Your Phone System and its Peripherals May Be an Achilles Heel." *Communications Convergence*. Vol. 10, No. 4. April 1, 2002. P. 55.

Kercheval, Nancy. "What Led to the Allfirst Trading Scandal?" *The Daily Record* (Baltimore, MD). January 11, 2003.

Klein, Melissa. "Accounting Firms Mine Growing Niche in Forensics." *Accounting Today*. Vol. 15, No. 10, June 4, 2001. P. 1.

Knight, Will. "Staff Oblivious to Computer Security Threats." May 2, 2001. http://news.nwfusion.com/newsletters/fileshare/2001/00768553.html

Knox, Noelle. "5 More Wall Street Firms Subpoenaed." *USA Today*. April 11, 2002. P. B1.

Koniak, Susan P. "Accountability Issues: Lessons Learned from Enron's Fall." Prepared Testimony before the Senate Judiciary Committee. *Federal News Service*. February 6, 2002.

Konrad, Rachel. "Duped by Worm Hoax, Victims Seek File Fix." *CNET news.com* May 31, 2001.

Lawrence, Patti. "Acceptable Use: Whose Responsibility Is It?" *SANS Institute*. http://www.sans.org/rr/acceptable/responsibility.php

Lebihan, Rachel. "Business Braced for Worm Onslaught." *Australian Financial Review*. January 28, 2003. P. 29.

Lee, Chris. "US Approves Tougher Cybercrime Penalties." May 9, 2002. http://www.vnunet.com/News/1131635.

Leibowitz, Wendy. "As I was Saying: Imposing Order on E-Chaos." *Law Practice Management*. November/December 2002. Vol. 28, No. 8. P. 8.

Leyden, John. "Germany, Austria Take Stand Against EU ISP Data Retention Laws." *The Register*. Nov. 2002. http://www.theregister.co.uk/content/6/28228.html

Lohse, Deborah. "Illegal Snooping Costs Allstate Access to Online DMV Records." *San Jose Mercury News*. January 16, 2003. http://www.siliconvalley.com/mld/siliconvalley/4965810.htm

Loomis, Tamara. "Electronic Mail: A Smoking Gun for Litigators." *New York Law Journal*. Vol. 227. May 16, 2002. P. 5.

Loney, Matt. "Your Worst Security Threat: Employees?" *ZDNet (UK)*. April 23, 2002. http://zdnet.com.com/2100-1105-889542.html

"Looking Forward: What Will 2002 Hold for Internet and Cyberspace Lawyers?" Interviews by the editors. *Cyberspace Lawyer*. Vol. 6, No. 11. February 2002.

Los Angeles Times. February 4, 2001. http://www.rtmark.com/more/articles/latimes20010204.html

Marron, Michael. "Discoverability of 'Deleted' E-Mail: Time for a Closer Examination." *Seattle University Law Review (25 Seattle Univ. L. R. 895).* Spring 2002.

Martin, Mark. "DMV Cuts Off Allstate Access to Digital Records." *The San Francisco Chronicle.* January 17, 2003. P. B2.

McAuliffe, Wendy. "2001: The Year of the Virus." *ZDNet (UK).* http://news.zdnet.co.uk/story/0,,t269-s2101493,00.html

McCafferty, Joseph. "The Phantom Menace." *CFO.* Vol. 15, No. 6. June 1, 1999. P. 89.

McClure, Stuart, Joel Scambray, and George Kurtz. *Hacking Exposed,* 3rd ed. New York: Osborne/McGraw-Hill, 2001, P. 38.

McCullagh, Declan. "Axed Intel Man Loses E-Mail Case." *Wired.com.* December 2001.

McHugh, John, Alan Christie, and Julia Allen. "Defending Yourself: The Role of Intrusion Detection Systems." *IEEE Software.* September/October 2000. P. 42.

Melnitzer, Julius. "Keeping Track of the Invisible Paper Trail: What Legal Departments Can Learn From Boeing's Experience." *Corporate Legal Times.* February 2003. P. 15.

Middleton, James. "Xbox Web Hoax Installs Trojan Horse." May 10, 2002. http://www.vnunet.com/

Mimoso, Michael S. "SQL Worm Slows Internet: Some Root DNS Servers Down." *SearchSecurity.com.* January 2003.

Myers, George, Jr. "Keeping Eye on Workers: Monitoring Software Used to Help Restrain Growth of Internet Abuse at Office." *The Columbus Dispatch.* January 21, 2003. P. 01C.

Nagel, Scott. "Develop an Electronic Document Retention Policy." *Law Practice Management.* September 2002, Vol. 28., No. 6. P. 40.

National Infrastructure Protection Center at http://www.nipc.gov/ or the InfraGard at http://www.infragard.met/

National Institute of Justice, U.S. Department of Justice. *Computer Crime: Criminal Justice Resource Manual* 2. 1989.

NCR Corporation Press Release. *Teradata Takes Data Mining Beyond Beer and Diapers.* July 31, 2002. http://www.ncr.com/media_information/2002/jul/pr073102b.htm

New York State Press Release. August 28, 2002. http://www.oag.state.ny.us/press/2002/aug/aug28a_02.html

Nimsger, Kristin M., and Michele C. S. Lange "Computer Forensics Experts Play Crucial Role." *The Lawyers Weekly.* Vol. 2., No. 2. May 10, 2002.

Nimsger, Kristin M. "Same Game, New Rule: E-discovery Adds Complexity to Protecting Clients and Disadvantaging Opponents." *Legal Times.* March 11, 2002. P. 28.

NIPC (Infragard_unsecured) Daily Report. August 15, 2002. Daily Report.

Northcutt, Stephen. *Network Intrusion Detection: An Analyst's Handbook.* Indianapolis, IN: New Riders Publishing, 1999, P. 195.

"Northwest Air Probes Union Computer Files." *The Wall Street Journal.* February 10, 2000.

"Now More than Ever, Cybersecurity Audits are Key." *National Law Journal.* Section: News. Vol. 24, No. 27. March 11, 2002. P. C8.

OECD Guidelines on the Protection of Privacy and Transborder Flows of Personal Data. September 23. 1980. Part Two. http://www.oecd.org/oecd/pages/home/displaygeneral/0,3380,EN-document-43-1-no-no-10255-0,00.html

O'Harrow, Robert, Jr., and Ariana Eunjung Cha. "Internet Worm Unearths New Holes; Attack Reveals Flaws in How Critical Systems Are Connected." *The Washington Post.* January 29, 2003. P. A01.

Oram, Andy. "Cyber Hygience, Not Cyber Fortress Protects our Networks." June 2, 1998. American Reporter. http://www.oreilly.com/~andyo/ar/cyber_hygiene.html

Pappas, James L., and Eugene F. Brigham "Risk Analysis." *Managerial Economics,* 3rd ed., Boston, MA: Course Technology/Dryden Press, 1979. PP. 73–82.

Power, Richard. "2002 CSI/FBI Computer Crime and Security Survey." *Computer Security Journal.* Vol. XVIII, No. 2. Spring 2002.

President George W. Bush's *The National Strategy to Secure Cyberpace.* February 2003. http://www.whitehouse.gov/

"Protesters For and Against War Target Web Sites." *Newsday.* March 29, 2003.

Prounis, Michael. "The Impact of the Sarbanes–Oxley Act: If You Can't Teach That Old Dog New Tricks, You May Have To Visit Him at the Pound." *The Metropolitan Corporate Counsel.* September 2002. P. 53.

Public Law 104491, Health Insurance Portability and Accountability Act of 1996, August 21, 1996. http://www.hcfa.gov/medicaid/hipaa/content/more.asp

"Putting it All Together." *The Economist.* U.S. Edition. October 26, 2002.

Rasin, Gregory I., and Joseph P. Moan. "Fitting a Square Peg into a Round Hole: The Application of Traditional Rules of Law to Modern Technological Advancements in the Workplace." *Missouri Law Review* (66 Mo. L. Rev. 793). Fall 2001.

Raysman, Richard, and Peter Brown. "Computer Security Breaches—Who May Be Held Responsible?" *New York Law Journal.* Vol. 227. May 14, 2002.

Reason, Tim. "Reporting: See-Through Finance?" *CFO Magazine.* October 2002.

Reich, Kenneth. "Allstate Loses Access to DMV Computer Data." *Los Angeles Times.* January 17, 2003. Part 2. P. 8.

Reuters. "'Viruses costing world billions' says Bush advisor." October 15, 2002. http://www.zdnet.com.au/newstech/security/story/0,2000024985,20269076,00.htm

Richardson, Robert. "Keeping Your Data Smart." *Alert.* October 2002. P. 1, 8.

Rodgers, T. J. "No Excuses Management." *Harvard Business Review.* July/August 1990. Vol. 68, Issue 4. P. 84.

Rogers, Paul. "Enemies of a CEO?" *Chief Executive.* November 1, 2002. P. 32.

Rothke, Ben. "Put it in Writing." *Access Control and Security Systems Integration.* May 2001.

Rowan, David. "Tech Salvos." *The Times* (London). March 25, 2003. P. 2, 16.

Rozenberg, Gabriel. "Computer 'Nerd' Jailed for Global Virus Attack." *The Times (London).* January 22, 2003. P. 9.

Salgado, Richard P. "Forensics and Incident Response." *Framework and Best Practices: Managerial and Legal Issues.* (8.5) SANS Institute. March 2003.

SANS Institute. "Resources on acceptable use and employee awareness programs." http://www.sans.org/rr/aware/

"Say It Again, Uncle Sam." *CIO Magazine.* November 1, 2001. http://www.cio.com/archive/110101/court_content.html

Scalet, Sarah D. "Fear Factor." *CIO Magazine.* October 15, 2002.

Scalet, Sarah D. "'See You In Court,' Prepared for Cyber-Terrorism? Security Experts Say Attacks on Corporate Networks May Already be Under Way." *CFO Magazine.* December 1, 2001. http://www.cfo.com/article/1,5309,5988,00.html

Scheindlin, Shira A., and Jeffrey Rabkin. "Outside Counsel Retaining, Destroying and Producing E-Data: Part 2." *New York Law Journal.* Vol. 227. May 9, 2002. P. 1.

Schultz, David H., and J. Robert Keena. "Discovery Perils in E-information Age." *New Jersey Lawyer.* April 22, 2002. P. 7.

Shein, Esther. "Are Companies Prepared for Cyber-Terrorism? Security Experts Say Attacks on Corporate Networks May Already be Under Way." CFO Magazine. Dec. 1, 2001. http://www.cfo.com/article/1,5309,5988,00.html

Shepherd, Ritchenya A. "Firms May Be Liable When Hackers 'Hijack' Computers." *New York Law Journal.* March 2, 2000. P. 5.

Shinder, Debra Littlejohn. *Computer Networking Essentials.* Indianapolis, IN: Cisco Press, 2001.

Shipley, Greg. "Secure to the Core." *Network Computing.* January 23, 2003. P. 34.

Silicon.com. Jan. 29, 2003. http://zdnet.com.com/2100-1105-982554.html

Skolnik, Bradley. Statement of Bradley Skolnik, Securities Commissioner of Indiana Chairman, Enforcement Division North American Securities Administrators Association. *Committee on Senate Judiciary Subcommittee on Crime and Drugs.* "Penalties for White Collar Offense: Are We Really Getting Tough on Crime?" June 19, 2002.

"Slammer Worm Cripples Some Computers in Buffalo Area." *The Buffalo News.* January 28, 2003. P. B-6.

Statement for the Record of Louis J. Freeh, Director FBI, on *Cybercrime* before the Senate Committee on Judiciary Subcommittee for the Technology, Terrorism, and Government Information. Washington, D.C. March 28, 2000. http://www.fbi.gov

Stover, Dawn. "Viruses, Worms, Trojans, and Bombs." *Popular Science.* Vol. 235, No. 3. September 1989. P. 59.

Swanson, Marianne. "Security Self-Assessment Guide for Information Technology Systems." *National Institute of Standards and Technology Report,* August 2001.

Tahmincioglu, Eve. "Management: Vigilance In the Face of Layoff Rage; Employer Miscues Can Breed Retaliation." *The New York Times,* August 1, 2001. Section C; P. 1.

Tambe, Jayant W., and Jonathan M. Redgrave. "Electronic Discovery Emerges as Key Corporate Compliance Issue." *The Metropolitan Corporate Counsel.* October 2002. P. 6.

"Technology; Group Test; Intrusion Detection Systems." *Network News.* March 27, 2002. P.19.

"The Stakes are Huge." *Government Computer News/Washington Technology.* March 2003.

The U.K. Dept. of Trade & Industry— PricewaterhouseCoopers Information Security Breaches Survey, 2002. P. 17.

United States v Carroll Towing Company, 159 F. 2d 169, 173 (2d Cir. 1947).

United States v Morris, 928 F. 2d 504 (2d Cir. 1991).

United States v Rusnak, No. 02-CR-280, guilty plea entered (D. Md. Oct. 24, 2002).

U.S. Department of Justice, United States Attorney, District of New Jersey. "Former Computer Network Administrator at New Jersey High-Tech Firm Sentenced to 41 Months for Unleashing $10 Million Computer 'Time Bomb.'" February 26, 2002. http://www.cybercrime.gov/lloydSent.htm

U.S. Department of the Treasury. January 17, 2003. http://www.occ.treas.gov/moneylaundering2002.pdf

U.S. Government Press Release. http://www.cybercrime.gov/eitelbergArrest.htm

Vamosi, Robert. "Instant Messaging: The Next Hacker Target." *Anchor Desk.com.* May 29, 2002.

Varchaver, Nicholas. "The Perils of E-Mail." *Fortune.* February 3, 2003.

Veta, D. Jean, Paul W. Schmidt, and Rochelle E. Rubin. "Is Your Company Protected? Developing a Comprehensive Cyber-Security Plan to Mitigate Legal Exposure From Cyber-Crime." *Cyberspace Lawyer,* Vol. 7, No. 5. July/August 2002.

Vise, David A., and Daniel Eggen. "FBI Warns of Cyber-Attack Threat: U.S. 'Very Concerned' About Vulnerability of Infrastructure." *The Washington Post.* March 21, 2001. P. A16.

Vispoli, Tracey. "Security for Financial Institutions in a Wired World: A Holistic Approach to Risk Management." *Electronic Banking Law & Commerce Report.* Vol. 6, No. 9. March 2002. P. 1–9.

Valdmanis, Thor. "Fired Analyst Turns Up Heat on Morgan Stanley Discrimination Lawsuit, Requests $1.78B in Damages." *USA Today.* June 25, 1999. P. 1B.

Waite, Beverly. "Malicious Code Attacks Had $13.2 Billion Economic Impact in 2001." *Computer Economics.* January 4, 2002. http://www.computereconomics.com/article.cfm?id&=133

Ward, Mark. "Employees Seen as Computer Saboteurs." *BBC News Online.* April 29, 2002.

Wasow, Omar. "Dangers of Cyber-Terrorism Now that the War with Iraq has Begun." *National Public Radio.* March 20, 2003.

Woodward, Victor. "It's the email, stupid!" December 1998. http://www.dominopower.com/issuesprint/issue199812/legal.html

Zuckerman, Michael J. "A Letter from Washington, *DC3.*" In *Alert. Computer Security Institute (CSI) Newsletter.* September 2002.

Zwillinger, Marc J. "Cybercrime Developing a Computer Policy Framework: What Every General Counsel Should Know." *The Internet Newsletter including Legal. Online.* Vol. 6, No. 3. June 2001.

ONLINE REFERENCES

SECURITY ALERTS

Bugtraq http://bugtraq@securityfocus.com/
CERT http://www.cert.org
Computer Security Institute
http://www.gocsi.com
FBI http://www.fbi.gov
Foundstone http://www.foundstone.com/
Internet Security Systems http://www.iss.net
Internet Storm Center http://www.incidents.org/
SANS Institute http://www.sans.com
Federal Office of Critical Infrastructure and Emergency Preparedness (Canada)
http://www.ocipep.gc.ca/

FILE INTEGRITY CHECKER TOOLS AND INTRUSION DETECTION SYSTEMS (IDS)

Tripwire http://www.tripwiresecurity.com
SamSpade http://www.samspade.org
Sniffer Technologies (InfiniStream)
http://www.sniffer.com/
Funk Software (Proxy v4.05)
http://www.funk.com

DESCRIPTION OF TOOLS FOR SECURING SYSTEMS AND DETERRING INTRUSIONS

CERT http://www.cert.org/tech_tips/
security_tools.html
Foundstone http://www.foundstone.com/
rdlabs/proddesc/ntlast.html
Practically Networked http://www.
practicallynetworked.com/

HIPAA

Cerner Corporation http://www.cerner.com
eClickMD http://www.eclickmd.com/

CYBERTERRORISM AND INFOWARFARE

Information Warfare Research Center of the Terrorism Research Center
http://www.terrorism.com/infowar/
index.shtml
ExtremeTech Security http://www.nyq.
extremetech.com/

MALWARE DETECTORS AND TROJAN-TERMINATING UTILITIES

Anti-keylogger http://www.anti-keylogger.com/
Anti-malware comparison chart http://www.
pestpatrol.com/Whitepapers/Comparison/
Features.asp
LockDown Millennium Pro http://www.
lockdowncorp.com/
Security for P2P applications http://www.
infosecuritymag.com/articles/february01/
cover.shtml
TDS-3 http://www.diamondcs.com.au/
Technical comparison of Trojan detectors
http://www.staff.uiuc.edu/~ehowes/
trojans/tr-tests.htm#Intro
Tripwire http://www.tripwire.com/

MONITORING TOOLS AND UTILITIES

John the Ripper http://www.openwall.com/john/
PC Activity Monitor http://www.keyloggers.com/

SIGNATURE SCANNERS

Mailsweeper by Clearswift http://www.
clearswift.com/
PestPatrol http://www.pestpatrol.com/
SVC http://www.checkpoint.com/

LEGISLATION

Computer Fraud and Abuse Act (18 U.S.C. 1030) http://www.cybercrime.gov/
1030_new.html
USA PATRIOT Act http://www.cybercrime.gov/
PatriotAct.html

Health Insurance Portability and
Accountability Act of 1996 (HIPAA)
http://www.hcfa.gov/medicaid/hipaa/
content/more.asp
National Infrastructure Protection Center
(NIPC) http://www.nipc.gov/

IDENTITY THEFT AND PRIVACY RESOURCES (.GOV AND .ORG WEBSITES)

Federal Trade Commission (FTC) http://www.
consumer.gov/idtheft/
Social Security Administration (SSA) http://
www.ssa.gov/pubs/idtheft.htm
AARP—Identity Theft http://www.aarp.org/
confacts/money/identity.html
Identity Theft Resource Center http://www.
idtheftcenter.org/
Identity Theft http://www.identitytheft.
org/index.htm
Privacy Rights Clearinghouse http://www.
privacyrights.org/

IDENTITY THEFT AND PRIVACY RESOURCES (.COM AND .NET WEBSITES)

American Express http://www.
americanexpress.com
CheckPoint Software Technologies Ltd.
http://www.checkpoint.com
Gartner Group http://www4.gartner.com/Init
KPMG http://www.kpmg.com
Pretty Good Privacy program http://
www.pgpi.com/

INVESTIGATION OF COMPUTER INCIDENTS

http://www.cert.org/tech_tips/
FBI_investigates_crime.html
http://www.cert.org/tech_tips/
incident_ reporting.html
http://www.nipc.gov/incident/incident.htm

CYBER SECURITY SOFTWARE AND DEVICES

8e6 Technologies: http://www.8e6.com
AET http://www.AET.com
Akonix http://www.akonix.com
Aspelle http://www.aspelle.com
Authenex http://www.authenex.com

Blockade Systems Corp. http://www.
blockade.com
Canaudit http://www.canaudit.com
Check Point http://www.checkpoint.com
Citadel http://www.citadel.com
Computer Associates http://www.ca.com
Configuresoft http://www.configuresoft.com
CryptoCard http://www.cryptocard.com
CyberGuard http://www.cyberguard.com
Eagle Software http://www.eaglesoft.com
Entercept Security Technologies http://www.
entercept.com
FireVue http://www.firevue.com
ForeScout Technologies http://
www.forescout.com
Fortinet http://www.fortinet.com
Guidance Software http://www.
guidancesoftware.com
High Tower Software http://www.
hightowersecurity.com
IDNet http://www.idnetinc.com
Internet Security Systems http://www.iss.net
Intrusion http://www.intrusion.com
IntruVert Networks http://www.intruvert.com
Microsoft http://www.microsoft.com/isas
NetIQ http://www.netiq.com
NetScreen Tecnologies http://www.
netscreen.com
NFR Security http://www.nfrsecurity.com
Nokia http://www.nokia.com
NwTech, Inc. http://www.nwtechusa.com
Okena, Inc. http://www.okena.com
Open Service http://www.open.com
Packeteer, Inc. http://www.packeteer.com
Patchlink http://www.patchlink.com
Permeo: http://www.permeo.com
Peterbuilt Technologies http://www.
peterbuilt.com
Preventsys, Inc. http://www.preventsys.com
Qualys http://www.qualys.com
Radware, Inc. http://www.radware.com
Rainfinity http://www.rainfinity.com
S4 Software http://www.s4software.com
Sanctum, Inc. http://www.sanctuminc.com
Secure Content Solutions (SCS) http://
www.scs-ca.com
SolSoft http://www.solsoft.com
Sophos http://www.sophos.com
Sourcefire http://www.sourcefire.com
SPI Dynamics http://www.spidynamics.com
St. Bernard Software http://www.stbernard.com

Stonesoft http://www.stonesoft.com
SurfControl http://www.surfcontrol.com
Sygate http://www.sygate.com
Symantec http://www.symantec.com
Symark http://www. symark.com
Symmetricom http://www.sync-server.com

Teros, Inc. http://www.teros.com
Top Layer http://www.toplayer.com
Tripwire, Inc. http://www.tripwire.com
Websense http://www.websense.com
Zone Labs, Inc. http://www.zonelabs.com

INDEX

Note: Page numbers with *f* indicate figure; *t* indicates table, *n* indicates note.